FREE THE CHILDREN!

Conflict Education for Strong, Peaceful Minds

FREE THE CHILDREN!

Conflict Education for Strong, Peaceful Minds

Susan Gingras Fitzell

NEW SOCIETY PUBLISHERS

Cataloguing in Publication Data records for this title are available from the Library of Congress and the National Library of Canada

Cover design by Warren Clarke
Graphics by Kathy Strissel

Printed in the United States of America on partially recycled paper using soy-based inks by Capital City Press, Montpelier, Vermont.

Inquiries regarding requests to reprint all or part of *Free The Children!* should be addressed to New Society Publishers at the address below.

Paperback   ISBN: 0-86571-361-8
Hardback   ISBN: 0-86571-360-X

To order directly from the publishers, please add $3.00 to the price of the first copy, and $1.00 for each additional copy (plus GST in Canada). Send check or money order to:

New Society Publishers,
P.O. Box 189, Gabriola Island, BC V0R 1X0, Canada.

New Society Publishers aims to publish books for fundamental social change through nonviolent action. We focus especially on sustainable living, progressive leadership, and educational and parenting resources. Our full list of books can be browsed on the world wide web at http://www.newsociety.com

NEW SOCIETY PUBLISHERS
Gabriola Island, BC, Canada, and Stony Creek, CT, U.S.A.

Dedication

This book is dedicated to my husband Michael and to my children Shivahn and Ian. Their patience, encouragement, and support (and housekeeping) while I spent hours at the computer were gifts of love that I will hold in my heart forever.

It is also dedicated to David Sobel. He challenged my thinking, encouraged my writing, and provided valuable critique and support. Without David, this book would never have been.

TABLE OF CONTENTS

Acknowledgments

I would like to thank my mentor and friend Dr. Terrence Webster-Doyle for providing me with opportunities to expand my awareness and free my thinking. He encouraged me to go beyond my self-imposed limits.

I would like to express my sincere appreciation to Joe Forseze, Debbie Idzelis, Kathy Archer, and Judy Buckley for welcoming me into their school and classrooms to test my theories and curriculum. Without their assistance, this book would have been a work done 'in the clouds'.

I cannot thank Ed Baechtold and Peter Laquerre enough for saving my book from the corrupted files monster that lived in my computer.

I give special thanks to John O., my first workshop partner and cheerleader.

And, Arlene Iverson, your love and warm support through the writing of this book meant more to me than you can imagine. My heart fills with warm fuzzies when I think of you. Thank you.

Special thanks are due to David Sobel, Dr. David Nazro, Meg Bienick, Mark Marandette, Marilyn Marshall, Naomi Wakan, and Chris Plant, who painstakingly took the time to read my manuscript and provide valuable suggestions. Sincere thanks, too, to Kathy Strissel for the icon graphics that she prepared specially for the book.

Some of the activity boxes and hand-outs in this book have been adapted from other sources:

Eggbert the Slightly Cracked Egg lesson plan and *Mental Self Defense Techniques* were adapted from Atrium Society Publications' *Why Is Everybody Picking On Me* Curriculum. *Safety Plan* for relationship violence was adapted from *Domestic Violence: The Facts — A handbook to stop violence* from Peace at Home (Boston).

To the following teachers, friends, and supporters, I offer my sincere appreciation for their help: Tom Martinson, Sr. Yvette, Sr. Theresa, Paula Jones, Pat Lee, Carrie Hilliker, Allison Rowe, Carolyn Wicker-Field, Steve Fitzell, Kathy Wicker, Peter Murphy, Linda Murphy, Lori Casey, and all the children and teens who helped with their honest comments, poems, and written contributions.

Foreword

Terrence Webster-Doyle

Free the Children!: Conflict Education for Strong, Peaceful Minds. So many titles of books are vague generalizations, promising to enlighten the reader in ways that are questionable. But this book is different because it focuses on the real causes of conflict.

Educating children to understand the causes and symptoms of conflict, that which prevents peace, is no longer an option. It's an urgent necessity for their survival. This is not a doomsday statement, a negative or fatalistic point of view, but rather a positive realization. Teaching children to understand what prevents right relationship is the only intelligent thing we can do. Academic excellence is a given, or it should be. But the right foundation for the proper use of intellectual skills is right relationship, for this is the basis of living. By not understanding human behavior, we have, as history has shown us, used our intellectual skills in terribly destructive ways.

Educating young people to understand relationship is not a moral issue, for the process of conventional morality creates conflict by conditioning children to believe in an established, fixed point of view. What is necessary is to educate children to be intelligent, to question, to inquire into what prevents peace with open and free minds. This open and free inquiry is the essence of democratic thinking. And this is, in my estimation of *Free the Children!*, what the author is trying to accomplish: to give children the insights and resources to free their minds from the rigid conformity of established conditioned thinking so that they can intelligently perceive the chains that bind us to the old patterns of behavior that create conflict and prevent peace. This freedom is the essential quality in all learning, that is, starting from a fresh observation of the facts and not from already established conclusions, especially in the field of learning about human behavior which in itself is ever changing and alive. We cannot expect young people to understand these established conditioned patterns of behavior through imposing upon them the very limitations that have held us in the past. We need to help them be free of the past and to look at the present condition with new, unclouded eyes. And in order to do this, the teachers of these children have to be also questioning, inquiring into the conditioned patterns of behavior that create such tremendous violence in human relationship.

What we need to do, and what we haven't done, although many have intended to do so, is to create a comprehensive educational program that is truly peacemaking, where children can be engaged in activities that will enlighten them and help them understand the whole structure of conflict, and thus the nature of human relationship. What has prevented us from doing this is our own conditioned thinking which makes us unquestioningly accept that conditioning is what we should be doing to our children, for after all it was done to us and though in actuality it has created tremendous conflict, in our conditioned view of life it seemed to create a semblance of security within our ethnocentric tribal belief systems. What is needed now is to see our conditioning and the fact that it really no longer provides security, that what is necessary is to go beyond these isolating, divisive established boundaries in order to think and act globally, to be free to act as a member of the human race. In my view, this book starts the process of educating the educators to be free and inquiring, so that they in turn can impart these insights and free the children.

Introduction

Who should read this book?

This book was written for both parents and teachers. Many teachers are parents. Parents are their child's first teachers. Therefore, you will see references to both the classroom and the family throughout this text. On a more general level, the book is intended to be a resource for anyone who works with children and wants to pursue conflict education.

How this book is organized

Free the Children! has been carefully designed so that the reader either can read the book from cover to cover or, as is typical with this type of book, can pinpoint a specific age group and topic. It is recommended that everyone should read Part One to understand the basic underlying philosophy proposed in the book. In Part Two, chapters are not particularly dependent upon those that precede them. Where a chapter mentions a topic covered elsewhere, the reader will be directed to the section that covers the information in greater detail.

There are more than 20 pages that have been designed to be reproducible for classroom or home use; these are specially formatted, and listed in Appendix F. All books mentioned in the text can be found in the Bibliography.

***

My initial work in the area of conflict education was based on the work of Terrence Webster-Doyle, author of the Education for Peace Series.[1] I prefer Terrence Webster-Doyle's approach to conflict education over that of most other sources; it is direct, visual, clear, concise, and powerful. Other materials are wonderful supplements.

Most curricula seem to deal with conflict resolution on the world peace or community peace level, without really looking at the root of conflict within and amongst ourselves. Many of them seem superficial.

I remember being very frustrated one evening after speaking with a colleague about conflict education curricula. He wanted a curriculum that was broken into neat 15-minute chunks so a teacher could rush in, grab the lesson, and teach it without prepwork or planning. He didn't want to have to think about it. This attitude is prevalent in our culture. It frustrates me. Violence is a major issue in our society, and people want a quick fix, a band-aid that they can apply without having to give any thought as to how to fix the problem. Well, that will *not* work. This attitude needs to change.

When I confront my own fears and try to determine what scares me about the path I am on, I find it is this quick-fix attitude that frightens me. Somehow, I have to find a way to deal with this attitude, to encourage insight, and to continue my "mission" without becoming exhausted and discouraged. Hopefully, my personal experience with conflict has prepared me for the road ahead. It would obviously be so much easier to resign myself to the state of the world and to go on as I had been.

But I have always wanted to help kids. I have considered law school and advocacy work. It has occurred to me that what I am doing is just that: helping kids before they are abused or in crisis. I am simply doing it through a different vehicle. I am educating. Rather than fighting the battle for one child as a lawyer or case-worker or advocate, I am paving the way for many children to be able to stick up for themselves, to recognize abuse, and to do something about it.

Teaching and using conflict resolution skills, in conjunction with encouraging personal growth through an understanding of oneself and of others, is a very rewarding path. There is hope for our future. Violence need not prevail as the norm. We need to start with ourselves, and then teach our children a better way.

Part One

CONFLICT EDUCATION: THE PROCESS

Chapter 1

THE FIVE ESSENTIAL COMPONENTS OF A CONFLICT EDUCATION PROGRAM

In this book, when I refer to 'conflict,' I am referring to 'interpersonal conflict between two or more people.' I call what I teach 'conflict education' rather than 'conflict resolution' because I believe it is necessary to educate *before* there is a conflict. Much of the material available for teaching conflict resolution skills is simply what it says it is: activities that teach skills to deal with issues *after* there is already a conflict. Much of it is geared toward wide age ranges. encouraging a pick-and-choose approach that does not lend itself to a comprehensive, developmentally appropriate process. I say 'process' rather than 'program' because teaching character and conflict education is not something that can be done in a set of isolated lessons in a curriculum program.

Through my research and experience, I have determined that five areas need to be addressed on a continuous basis to achieve long-term results from a character and conflict education process. These five components are

- Modeling: role-modeling for children
- Relationship: the connections between people
- Conditioning: the effects of culture on our children
- Empowerment: making decisions, taking responsibilities
- Skills: relationship, conflict resolution, and mediation

These five components are critical to an effective character and conflict education curriculum. They apply to all developmental levels. Without all five aspects in the curriculum on a consistent basis, long-term results cannot be achieved. Let's look at these five components in fuller detail.

4

Modeling

Modeling appropriate behavior is a vital and necessary component
of an effective conflict education curriculum.

BELIEFS AND ATTITUDES OF THE ROLE-MODEL

Who we are, what we think, and what we believe is revealed
through our words and behavior. If we buy into the adage that "boys will be
boys," our words and behavior will reflect it. If we have prejudices, they will be
apparent. If we say that "our good country" should just go over and blow up "that
bad country," our children will hear it. Everything we say and do provides the
foundation for children's belief systems and attitudes. Sometimes, we are not
even conscious of what we do believe. Often, until we find ourselves reacting to a
situation we feel strongly about, we don't really know that we have bought into a
stereotype, a prejudice, or an attitude that limits us. Only when we become self-
aware can we change our attitudes and beliefs to reflect the image we want our
children to model. We can use all the curricula, books, sing-along peace tapes,
and words we want to teach children how to live peacefully, but if our words and
behavior send a different message, children will be confused. They are more likely
to do what we *do*, rather than what we *say*.

THE ROLE-MODEL AND DISCIPLINE

Sometimes as teachers and parents, we don't realize the way we speak to children. Our tone of voice and choice of words, especially when we're disciplining,
may be reinforcing negative patterns of behavior with children. This has become
glaringly obvious to me as I listen to my seven-year-old when she is angry with
me. I often hear my words and my tone and see my facial expressions coming
from her little body.

A small child does not categorize behavior.
He/she does not say, "Oh, this is the tone I can
use when I am a parent (or a teacher) reprimanding my child." Rather, the behavior is
interpreted as "This is the tone I use when I am
angry." For example, "If you don't listen to me
right now, I'm going to spank you!" translates to
"If you don't give me that toy right now, I'm
going to hit you!" Often, children will go directly
to the hitting and forget the warning.

Traditionally, authoritarian discipline has been
used in schools and homes to manage children's
behavior. An authoritarian approach, where directives and punishments are determined by the adult
without enlisting the child in the formation of
rules and consequences, produces children who

> **The parents who are
> most effective, the
> research indicates,
> are "authoritative" —
> requiring obedience
> from their children but
> providing clear reasons
> for their expectations, so
> that children eventually
> internalize the moral
> rationale and act
> responsibly on their own.
> — Thomas Lickona,
> Educating for Character**

obey when with that adult. The downside to authoritarian discipline is that children do not learn to self-discipline. And they learn to get what they want by using directives and meting out 'punishments.'

While I don't believe in authoritarian discipline, I also don't advocate permissiveness; rather, I recommend an *authoritative* approach to discipline. An authoritative model involves children in the rule-making process. Consequences are established and firm limits on behavior are kept. A teacher or parent who uses an authoritative model of discipline is teaching children skills critical to sound character and conflict management.

When children are involved in developing rules and consequences, they learn to use words to solve problems, to govern themselves, and to feel empowered. When rules deemed necessary by the teacher are explained and consequences are logical, children learn to be fair and trusting. When children who break the rules are involved in determining ways to "solve their own problem," they learn to control their own behavior. When children are taught to see situations from another child's point of view and are required to make restitution to the hurt party, they learn empathy, forgiveness, and caring.

TREAT CHILDREN WITH RESPECT

Lack of respect from our youth is a common complaint heard from adults today. I am often astounded, however, by the lack of respect adults show towards youth. They are often treated as lesser beings. Children are ordered around without a "please" or a "thank you." Because they are defenseless, they are often the scapegoats of misplaced anger. Their needs are often disregarded. I have witnessed parents and teachers ridicule children for their failures and poke fun at their shortcomings.

All of us may be guilty of disrespecting our children's rights sometimes when we are tired, frustrated, or angry. It must be the exception, not the rule. When we do treat our children in a disrespectful way, the most empowering thing we can do for ourselves and our children is to admit we made a mistake. When we admit our errors to our children, we teach them that it is OK to make mistakes. Mistakes are for learning. We are modeling a willingness to be honest, to own our behavior, and to learn from it. This is a powerful example to set for our children. It is the same behavior we want from them when they make a mistake. Should we expect less of ourselves?

MODELING — PRACTICAL SUGGESTIONS

- Model appropriate behavior.
- Use authoritative discipline.
- Treat children always with respect, even when you are angry, tired, and/or frustrated.
- If you 'lose it' because of anger, fatigue, or frustration, admit your mistake. Talk about it. Set the example.
- Take an interest in stopping violence and bullying.

Discipline vs. Punishment:

What is the Difference?[1]

PUNISHMENT	DISCIPLINE
• Punishment is unexpected. It is usually based on personal authority and arbitrary power.	• Discipline is expected. It is based on logical or natural consequences.
• Punishment is too severe.	• Discipline is fair and reasonable.
• Punishment reinforces failure. The individual has no options.	• Discipline reinforces success. Options are kept open as the individual is willing to take some responsibility.
• Punishment focuses on guilt, shame, blame, and fault.	• Discipline focuses on restitution and learning a better way.
• Punishment is meted out in the spirit of anger.	• Discipline is nurturing and caring.
• Any one of these can make a situation punishment-oriented rather than discipline-oriented.	

[1] Based on work done by Diane Gossen, Perry Good, Barnes Boffey and William Glasser.

'HOW TO' RESOURCES TO GET YOU STARTED

- *Discipline with Dignity* by Richard Curwin and Allen Mendler
- *Discipline Without Shouting or Spanking: Practical Solutions to the Most Common Preschool Behavior Problems* by Barbara Wyckoff, and Unell
- *Discipline: 101 Alternatives to Nagging, Yelling, and Spanking* by Alvin Price and Jay Parry
- *Educating for Character* by Thomas Lickona
- *Get Out Of My Life but first could you drive me and Cheryl to the Mall?: A Parents' Guide to the New Teenager* by Anthony E. Wolf
- *How to Get Your Kids To Clean Their Rooms and Other Impossible Tasks* by The Parenting Resource Group
- *How to Talk so Kids Will Listen and Listen so Kids Will Talk* by Adele Faber and Elaine Mazlish
- *In Pursuit of Happiness: Knowing what you want, getting what you need* by E. Perry Good
- *Positive Discipline A to Z: 1001 Solutions to Everyday Parenting Problems* by Jane Nelson, Lynn Lott, and Stephen Glenn
- *Raising a Daughter* by Don and Jeanne Elium
- *Raising a Son* by Don and Jeanne Elium
- *Raising Good Children* by Thomas Lickona
- *STEP: The Parents' Handbook* by Don Dinkmeyer and Gary D. McKay
- *Teaching Children to Care: Management in the Responsive Classroom* by Ruth Sidney Charney
- *Time Out: Abuses and Effective Uses* by Jane Nelson and Stephen Glenn

Relationship

THROW OUT PATTERNS OF THINKING THAT ACCEPT OR EXCUSE BULLYING

We have reached a point in our society where it can no longer be acceptable to sit back and watch children engage in name-calling, taunting, pushing, and grabbing, as if resigned to the inevitability of this kind of bullying. Also, in regards to gender stereotypes, the adage that "boys will be boys" is a dinosaur. If we want children to be of good character and able to handle conflict peacefully, we need to cast out patterns in our thinking that say, "This behavior is normal. It's been going on forever. There is nothing I can do about it." There IS something you can do! Children need to have their natural sense of empathy fostered and encouraged. They need to be taught to see other people's points of view. It is important that the consequences of their actions are explained to them in terms that drive the point home.

REACT WITH 'MORAL FEELING'

Thomas Lickona in *Educating For Character* (1992) states, "Recent childrearing research finds that children who are the most empathic and altruistic have parents who react strongly to their children's offenses." For example, you might say, "You hurt Amy. Pulling hair hurts! Don't ever pull hair!" rather than "How do you think it feels when you pull Amy's hair?" or "Do you think it's a good idea to pull Amy's hair?" It's the combination of the parents' moral reasoning and moral feeling that appears to motivate children to take seriously what they have done and to become sensitive to the feelings of others. I personally have found this to be true with my children. If emphatic moral feeling is attached to the reprimand and reasoning, children pay attention. By simply saying, "Don't pull Amy's hair. It's not nice." — with or without punishment — we will not teach the child to relate his/her behavior to another's hurt.

REDUCE AND MONITOR TELEVISION VIEWING

It is also important to note that learning relationship skills is taking a back seat to watching TV and videos and playing video games. Children are not interacting with each other to build necessary social skills. Children bring their computer games to school, which further decreases interactive games and activities. Preschool and primary school teachers repeatedly tell me that children are coming to school without basic social skills. These teachers believe that the media play a large role in this situation. The TV is a wonderful baby-sitter! The price we pay for that "baby-sitter" is costing our children the ability to develop socially.

TEACH SOCIAL SKILLS AND EXPECT COURTESY

We need to teach relationship skills in our classrooms and homes. We get so many mixed messages from society and our culture that it is sometimes difficult to know which relationship skills we are missing. Courtesy has gone by the wayside. We often don't even notice when our children don't say "please," "thank you," or "excuse me." Language has become littered with vulgarity. Vulgar language seems so commonplace now that it is the accepted norm in many families. "Put-downs" are a form of accepted humor. This is reinforced by countless "sit-coms" where we are entertained by family members and friends insulting each other all in the name of humor.

RELATIONSHIP — PRACTICAL SUGGESTIONS

- Teach social skills.
- Teach and reinforce courtesy.
- React with 'Moral Feeling'.
- Throw out patterns of thinking that accept or excuse bullying:
  "Boys will be boys!"
  "Hazing is a tradition!"
  "Name-calling is normal!"
- Reduce and monitor television viewing. Encourage interactive play with other children.

'HOW TO' RESOURCES TO GET YOU STARTED

Preschool through Grade Three:

- *Feeling Good About Others: Activities to Encourage Positive Interaction* and *Manners Matter: Activities to Teach Young People Social Skills* by Debbie Pincus
- *How I Learned To Be Considerate Of Others* by Lawrence Shapiro
- *Keeping the Peace: Practicing Cooperation and Conflict Resolution with Preschoolers* by Susanne Wichert
- *Teaching Young Children in Violent Times: Building a Peaceable Classroom* by Diane E. Levin
- *The Peaceful Classroom: 162 Easy Activities to Teach Preschoolers Compassion and Cooperation* by Charles Smith

Elementary School:

- *Teaching Children to Care: Management in the Responsive Classroom* by Ruth Sidney Charney
- *The Friendly Classroom for a Small Planet: A Handbook on Creative Approaches to Living and Problem Solving for Children* by P. Prutzman, L. Stern, M. Burger, and G. Bodenhamer
- *You Can't Say You Can't Play* by Vivian Gussin Paley

Junior High & High School:

- *Flirting or Hurting?: A Teacher's Guide on Student-to-Student Sexual Harassment in Schools* by Nan Stein and Lisa Sjostrom
- *Get Out Of My Life but first could you drive me and Cheryl to the Mall?: A Parents' Guide to the New Teenager* by Anthony E. Wolf
- *Sexual Harassment and Teens* by Susan Strauss
- *The Relationship Workbook for Teens* by Judy Zerafa

General Resources:

- *Educating for Character* by Thomas Lickona
- *How to Talk so Kids Will Listen and Listen so Kids Will Talk* by Adele Faber and Elaine Mazlish
- *Just Family Nights: 60 Activities to Keep Your Family Together In a World Falling Apart* by Faithquest
- *Raising Good Children* by Thomas Lickona
- *Raising Peaceful Children in a Violent World* by Nancy Lee Cecil
- *Teaching Peace: How to Raise Children to Live in Harmony — Without Fear, Without Prejudice, Without Violence* by Jan Arnow
- *The Dance of Anger: A Woman's Guide To Changing Patterns of Intimate Relationships* by Harriet Goldhor Lerner

Conditioning

THE EFFECTS OF THE ENVIRONMENT
ON OUR CHILDREN

It was 1987. She was a foster child, unwanted by her natural parents, at odds with her foster mother. The deck was stacked against her. I wanted to take her shopping to buy her decent clothes. If she had a decent haircut and learned to apply a little makeup, maybe she wouldn't draw such negative attention to herself. But then, she'd still open her mouth. Out from her mouth came all the words that screamed, "I AM A VICTIM!" Her manner, style, and body language reinforced this image. Kennie was a scapegoat, a target for all other insecure people to taunt and use to get spare change, petty favors, and a good laugh.

One day, I watched as an older, larger aggressive girl verbally took Kennie apart and left her in pieces on the classroom floor. My directives for the verbal attack to end went unheeded. The audience was thrilled with the display the two presented. Kennie ran away. She ran out of the classroom, out of the building, and out into the street. The bell rang. Chaos ensued. I cornered her attacker. I was enraged, furious that one human being could be so cruel to another. I wanted to lay her out flat. She was twice my size. I spoke, choosing the mildest words I could manage, given how I felt. I told her that sometimes she acted like a complete asshole! I didn't care whether what I said was appropriate. I was angry and fed up with the abuse Kennie suffered day after day. I was at a loss as to how to help her. What I saw, however, triggered in me tremendous emotional pain, pain buried deep in my psyche, pain I could not forget.

It was 1972. Patched bell bottoms were the uniform. Boys' sneakers, army jackets, and skin-tight tops were the rage. The social dress code forbade white socks. My mother, like most mothers, had set ideas on how a girl should dress. My teenage self believed that her ideas were far from fashionable. My wardrobe did not include the grungy, tie-dyed, patched clothing of the times. Some well-meaning aunts would give me bags of outdated clothes they had tired of or outgrown. Consequently, my dress was quite out of style.

One day, I was walking to the store in my fifties' style hot pink stretch pants, white socks, and girls' sneakers. Then I saw them up ahead. Immediately, fear penetrated my soul. Pride kept me from running. They had been taunting me for weeks. There were five of them. There was an obvious ringleader. She was huge and appeared to be a few years older than I. "Hey, fag! Hey, fag with the white socks!" The next thing I remember, I was surrounded. She was screaming something at me. She wanted to fight. I wouldn't. I didn't know how. There was no escape. I was outnumbered. The slap across my face stung. Angry and humiliated, I swore at her. There was no thought, just reaction. At that moment, the

> **Peace cannot be achieved through violence, it can only be attained through understanding.**
> **— Ralph Waldo Emerson**

crowed parted. A friend and neighbor from across the street saw what was happening and summoned her older brother to help. They provided for my escape. The girls never bothered me again. I would be eternally grateful for this act of kindness.

That memory of cruelty and abuse, compounded by many, many others witnessed in the classroom over the years, compelled me to search for a deeper understanding of who I am, what I believe in, and how I could act on those beliefs. Thus emerged my philosophy. Children are born with a wisdom waiting to unfold and manifest itself in personality. That personality, however, is directed by the environment in which the child lives. I believe that whether personality traits, strengths, and weaknesses take a positive or negative path, whether children reach their potential or not, depends on the children's environment. Once children have internalized the education provided by their environment, their behavior becomes set in patterns of reaction and response to that environment. This is why self-knowledge with an understanding of the origins of our attitudes, beliefs, and prejudices is necessary before we can change what isn't working for us in relationships and consciously keep what does work. Only when the Kennies of the world can look at themselves, their behavior, their body language, and their appearance with insight and awareness, can they begin to understand what they need to do to change from being a victim to being an empowered self.

> **Where ignorance is our master, there is no possibility for real peace.**
> **— Dalai Lama**

When people are empowered, they free themselves from the victim role. They are no longer victims or oppressors. They are clear, focused, and centered in the strength of who they are.

We, as teachers of our children and our students, need an awareness of how our environment (media, culture, family values) shapes the way we think and feel. Once we have that awareness, it is our responsibility to educate our children. The alternative is to act blindly on impulses, feelings, and belief systems that have no known source or purpose.

Our culture, the media, and our individual family values have an impact on how we think.

Before they are two years old, children are aware of racial differences. By the age of three, they may attach value judgments to those differences. Between the ages of four and six, they show gender-stereotyped behaviours, and may reject children who differ from themselves in terms of race or physical disability.

How do stereotypes come about at such an early age? The first influences are the attitudes of immediate family members, often acquired unconsciously. Later, children absorb stereotypical messages from books, television, movies, magazines and newspapers.

— Susan Fountain, Education for Development

Scientific evidence presents a convincing argument that heredity and genetics play a major role in who we are. Studies also indicate, however, that our environment has an impact on how we develop. In the section on "Child Warriors" (Chapter Two), I discuss in greater detail the impact of the media on our children. This is a form of conditioning. It is only when we are aware of this "conditioning" that we can act to change it.

Children are perceptive beings. If adults engage them in discussion of the conditions in their environment which affect the way they think and feel, children can learn to *act* rather than to react. We adults are very aware and lament the negative influence that environmental factors such as the media and the commercial market are having on our children. It is important that we pass this awareness on to our children. We should point out those things in the environment that condition children to accept stereotypes and bigotry, that desensitize them to violence and vulgarity, and that create in them reactive, inappropriate, emotional responses. Awareness and knowledge give them the power to make proactive decisions.

CONDITIONING — PRACTICAL SUGGESTIONS

Point out the factors in children's environments that condition them to
- accept stereotypes and bigotry
- become desensitized to violence and vulgarity
- react emotionally or physically to conflict situations

'HOW TO' RESOURCES TO GET YOU STARTED

- *Boys Will Be Boys* by Myriam Miedzian
- *Brave New Child: Education for the 21st Century* by Terrence Webster-Doyle
- *Bullying At School: What We Know and What We Can Do* by Dan Olweus
- *Control Theory: A New Explanation of How We Control Our Lives* by William Glasser
- *Endangered Minds: Why Children Don't Think and What We Can Do About it* by Jane Healy
- *Facing History and Ourselves* by Facing History and Ourselves National Foundation
- *Raising Peaceful Children in a Violent World* by Nancy Lee Cecil
- *Reviving Ophelia: Saving the Selves of Adolescent Girls* by Mary Pipher
- *Teaching Peace: How to Raise Children to Live in Harmony — Without Fear, Without Prejudice, Without Violence* by Jan Arnow
- *War: What is it Good For?* by Terrence Webster-Doyle
- *Who's Calling the Shots?: How to Respond Effectively to Children's Fascination with War Play and War Toys* by Nancy Carlsson-Paige and Diane Levin
- *Why is Everybody Always Picking On Me* by Terrence Webster-Doyle

Empowerment

Empowerment is believing that you can do something and having the skills and resources to do it. Empowerment is having the ability, power, and authority to act on your own behalf. Empowerment is believing that you are in charge of yourself, your choices, and your decisions. Children become empowered when they are allowed to make decisions and take responsibility for those decisions. Everything we do is a choice. Even indecision is a choice: we decide *not* to decide. When we realize that we have choices and own the outcome of those choices, we are empowered. When we are affirmed because of our choices and the learning derived from them, we are empowered.

> If we could raise one generation with unconditional love, there would be no Hitlers. We need to teach the next generation of children from Day One that they are responsible for their lives. Mankind's greatest gift, also its greatest curse, is that we have free choice. We can make our choices built from love or from fear.
> — Dr. Elizabeth Kubler-Ross

When children feel powerless, they cannot act on their own behalf. Children who do not feel empowered will not be able to stand up for themselves against a bully or against peer pressure and drugs. Empowerment and self-esteem go hand in hand. One truly cannot exist without the other.

A SPECIAL NOTE...

Affirming children is one way to encourage a sense of empowerment. I've always believed in the power of suggestion. So, every night before I retire, I check on my sleeping children. I kiss them good-night and say two things to them: "I love you" and "You are very special." Sometimes, in their sleep, they smile and agree with me. I've done this since they were infants. I've read about people learning from tapes while they are sleeping. I figure it's worth a try.

EMPOWERMENT — PRACTICAL SUGGESTIONS

- Use authoritative discipline.
- Create opportunities for decision making, problem solving, and leadership.
- Teach the 'bully' to get what he/she needs without bullying.
- Teach the 'victim' how NOT to be a victim.
- Teach children WHY people do what they do. Understanding reduces fear. Fear is the greatest obstacle to empowerment and self-esteem.
- Teach skills that help children to feel empowered.

'HOW TO' RESOURCES TO GET YOU STARTED

Preschool through Grade Three:

- *Keeping the Peace: Practicing Cooperation and Conflict Resolution with Preschoolers* by Susanne Wichert
- *Don't Feed the Monster on Tuesdays!* by Adolph Moser
- *How to Be a Super-Hero* by Lawrence E. Shapiro

Elementary School:

- *Teaching Children to Care: Management in the Responsive Classroom* by Ruth Sidney Charney
- *The Friendly Classroom for a Small Planet: A Handbook on Creative Approaches to Living and Problem Solving for Children* by P. Prutzman, L. Stern, M. Burger, and G. Bodenhamer
- *Why Is Everybody Always Picking On Me?* by Terrence Webster-Doyle

Junior High & High School:

- *Go For It!* by Judy Zerafa
- *Stick Up For Yourself: Every Kid's Guide to Personal Power and Positive Self-Esteem* by Gershen Kaufman and Lev Raphael
- *The How To Book Of Teen Self Discovery: Helping Teens Find Balance, Security and Esteem* by Doc Lew Childre
- *Why is Everybody Always Picking On Me?* by Terrence Webster-Doyle

General Resources:

- *Educating for Character* by Tom Lickona
- *Personal Empowerment Programs:* http://www.empowerme.com/index.html
- *Raising Kids Who Can: Using Family Meetings to Nurture Responsible, Cooperative, Caring, and Happy Children* by Betty Lou Bettner
- *Raising Self-Reliant Children in a Self-Indulgent World* by H. Stephen Glenn
- *That's Me! That's You! That's Us! Selected Current Multicultural Books for Children and Young Adults Presenting Positive, Empowering Images* (Third Edition) by Francenia L. Emery
- *The Quality School* by William Glasser

Skills

RELATIONSHIP, CONFLICT RESOLUTION, AND MEDIATION

Without the skills to handle relationships and conflicts, all the reasoning and understanding we impart to our children is of little value. It is fine to tell a child, "Just say no!" or "Don't fight!" or "Walk away." However, if we don't teach kids how to do these things — what they can say in different situations, what tone of voice they should use, how their body language is interpreted and allow them to *practice* these skills *often*, we are not giving them the tools they need to be successful. Instead, they struggle with what they were told they should do, and what they think they can do without losing face.

Just as you would not expect a first grader to learn to read with one 45-minute lesson a week, you cannot expect character and conflict resolution skills to be internalized in that short amount of time. I cannot emphasize enough the importance of using conflict situations — in the classroom itself, in the literature being studied, or in the issues being debated in social studies classes — to provide discussions that will suggest alternative solutions to violence, bigotry, taunting, and negative relationships. It is crucial to point out, praise, encourage, and role-play non-violence, acceptance of diversity, empathy, respect, and responsibility.

It is, therefore, critical to teach manners and courtesy. Expect them! They are very valuable skills. "Please," "thank you", and "excuse me" are simple words with incredible power. As parents and teachers, we need to use these words consistently with students and adults (even our friends, spouses, and children). We have become desensitized to the fact that so few people use these words. Many fights, misperceptions, and hurts could be alleviated with the use of these words. Conflict often arises because an accident happens, someone gets bumped, or an innocent comment is taken as an insult. If people choose to sincerely say, "Excuse me," "Please," "Thank you," "Are you all right?", or "I'm sorry, I didn't mean to hurt you," much conflict would be diffused and avoided before it begins. We cannot place too much importance on the significance of common courtesy. Using courteous words increases self-respect and effectiveness, and instills good feelings in others. This kind of language needs to become "cool" again, even with teens and adults.

> Remember and help America remember that the fellowship of human beings is more important than the fellowship of race and class and gender in a democratic society. Be decent and fair and insist that others be so in your presence.
> Don't tell, laugh at, or in any way acquiesce to racial, ethnic, religious, or gender jokes or to any practices intended to demean rather than enhance another human being.
> — Marian Wright Edelman, The Measure Of Our Success

SKILLS — PRACTICAL SUGGESTIONS

- Role-play and role-play some more.
- Teach rules for fighting fair.
- Teach manners and courtesy.
- Teach 'I-statements.'
- Teach listening skills.
- Teach mediation and negotiation skills.
- Teach 'body language'— how to interpret it — and how to use it.
- PRACTICE DAILY!!

'HOW TO' RESOURCES TO GET YOU STARTED

Preschool through Grade Three:

- *Keeping the Peace: Practicing Cooperation and Conflict Resolution with Preschoolers* by Susanne Wichert
- *Peacemaking Skills for Little Kids* by Grace Contrino Abrams Peace Education Foundation
- *Teaching Young Children in Violent Times: Building a Peaceable Classroom* by Diane E. Levin
- *The Peaceful Classroom: 162 Easy Activities to Teach Preschoolers Compassion and Cooperation* by Charles Smith

Elementary:

- *Education for Development: A Teacher's Resource for Global Learning* by Susan Fountain
- *Getting Along!: A Social Skills Curriculum* by Charlotte Danielson and Priscilla Snow Algava
- *Mediation for Kids: Kids in Dispute Settlement* by Fran Schmidt, Alice Friedman, and Jean Marvel
- *The Friendly Classroom for a Small Planet: A Handbook on Creative Approaches to Living and Problem Solving for Children* by P. Prutzman, L. Stern, M. Burger, and G. Bodenhamer

Junior High & High School:

- *Education for Development: A Teacher's Resource for Global Learning* by Susan Fountain
- *Helping Teens Stop Violence: A Practical Guide for Counselors, Educators and Parents* by Allen Creighton. (*Battered Women's Alternatives*) with Paul Kivel, (Oakland Men's Project)
- *Mediation Games: Teenage Conflicts* by David W. Felder
- *Violence Prevention Curriculum for Adolescents* by Deborah Prothrow-Stith
- *Violence Prevention: General Packet* (Second Edition) Compiled by NAME
- *Why is Everybody Always Picking On Me* by Terrence Webster-Doyle

General Resources:

- *Active Parenting: Teaching Cooperation, Courage, and Responsibility* by Michael Popkin
- *Black Communication: Breaking Down The Barriers* by Evelyn B. Dandy
- *Control Theory* by William Glasser
- *Educating for Character* by Thomas Lickona
- *Getting to Yes: Negotiating Agreement Without Giving In* by Roger Fisher and William Uri
- *Raising Peaceful Children in a Violent World* by Nancy Lee Cecil

- *Teaching Peace: How to Raise Children to Live in Harmony — Without Fear, Without Prejudice, Without Violence* by Jan Arnow
- *The Anger Workbook* by Les Carter and Frank Minirth

Part Two

CONFLICT EDUCATION FOR DIFFERENT AGES

Chapter 2

THE PRESCHOOL/KINDERGARTEN CHILD

'Different' Children

Recently, I was speaking with Claire, the mother of one of my son's friends. Claire and I have common views on parenting. Claire has two sons; I have a daughter and a son. Our children are about the same ages. While sharing beliefs and concerns about parenting in today's world, we acknowledged a common fear. In raising our children in an environment free of media violence and typical stereotypes (as free as we are able, given our humanness and society's influence), were we creating children who were 'different?' How would being 'different' affect our children? More specifically, how would it affect our sons?

It was reassuring to me to see Claire's boys and to speak with her about common concerns. I had begun to have a few doubts and felt that maybe I was doing my son an injustice by rearing him with an awareness of stereotypes and a minimum of media violence. I noticed a common 'difference' between our children and others. Our children were gentle. In a culture that holds up aggressive, macho males as the masculine ideal, could the 'gentle' man survive with self-esteem intact? I thought that my son's love of beauty and aesthetics in his surroundings and nature were nurtured and encouraged because he had an older sister. There were no sex-stereotyped boundaries drawn in his dress-up play. He was not physically aggressive. I'd see him with other little boys and notice an obvious difference. I didn't worry until the time when he was playing with a male friend and was reduced to tears because he chose to play with a toy that his friend disdainfully called "girlish." The scene broke my heart. Was I doing the right thing? I started to talk to my son about American culture.

There was little difference between the gentleness in Claire's boys and the gentleness of my own children. Her five-year-old had an older brother. My theory that my son was gentle and a lover of aesthetics because he had an older sister went out the window. Claire had the same concerns as I. She knew she was raising children who were 'different'. We discussed the ramifications of our choice to raise peaceful children. We considered the price our children would pay because of our beliefs. We decided that the cost of allowing them to be raised with acceptance of media violence and sexual stereotypes would be greater. She was considering karate lessons for her older son so that he would have the confidence 'not to fight,' but also the skill to defend himself if he absolutely needed to. My children both take karate for the same reasons. This choice was reinforced in one of my workshops when a mother described how her son, whom she had brought up to be peaceful, was being bullied by other boys who did not have the same value system. Confused and distraught, she questioned her choice because she felt it set her son up as a victim.

I remember a conversation with another mother of a five-year-old boy. Sharon recalled a time when she had not yet heard of Power Rangers. She had managed to protect her child from Ninja Turtles and felt good about that accomplishment. At her son's fifth birthday party, however, Power Ranger products were the gift of choice. Not knowing anything about the show, she started to watch it with her son. It didn't seem quite so bad. After all, it had a moral at the end of every story. It eventually became an acceptable pastime in their home. She was torn between her personal beliefs, the popular attitude that "it can't really hurt them," and a key comment her son had made. He shared with her that he was happy he had Power Rangers. Now he wouldn't feel left out. She was struck by the fact that her five-year-old had already experienced the exclusion felt by kids who are 'different'. She was in conflict. She did not want her son to feel excluded or 'different.' I could see her dilemma. As she spoke with me, I could sense her mixed feelings: her need to defend her choice to allow Power Rangers in her home and her guilt at doing so at the risk of some vague possibility that it could have a harmful effect on her child. What does a parent do?

My husband and I did not buy my children Power Ranger toys. They have not watched the show in our home. We did not, however, forbid them to watch the show when at friends' homes. When they received Power Ranger toys with a fast food kids' meal, we allowed them to keep them. We walk a tight line between allowing them to do things other kids do and keeping with our values. We don't want the backlash that comes with forbidden fruit. Instead, we talked to our children about how Power Rangers solve their problems. We used language they could understand to discuss how commercials sell toys and how toy companies try to make a lot of money regardless of the cost to children's development. We spoke to them about what really happens when people are kicked or punched. We talked to them about how the families of the 'bad guys' might feel when their children or siblings are killed. We conceded and bought Bat Man toys without guns. We also found a video of the original movie: the one we watched as kids. (Yes, that movie is hokey and unsophisticated; however, my kids enjoyed it. Children don't need the sophistication and violence present in today's shows.) Hopefully, we can find a balance in a world that presents thousands of violent images to children each week.

As you read the rest of this chapter, understand that I am empathetic to the plight of parents in our culture. There is so little support for parents attempting to buffer their children from the violence in our world. On the contrary, there is tremendous pressure to give in and conform. Much of this pressure is subtle. It comes in the form of facial expressions, body language, and comments that tell us we are silly to be so concerned about the toys our children play with and the shows our children watch. After all, we watched Bugs Bunny and played with guns when we were kids! Parents who believe media violence won't hurt their children may feel judged and defensive when confronted with arguments against media violence and stereotypes. Another obstacle to overcome in our busy, fast-paced world is the lack of time to reflect on our own attitudes and conditioning. Society sends out so many mixed messages affecting how we think that we may not be sure about what we believe. Until we know who we are and where we stand on these issues, we cannot give clear messages to our children about conflict, violence, or gender stereotypes. Once we know where we stand on these issues, we can begin to educate our children. If they are 'different' because they are peaceful, we can feel confident that we did our best to stand by what we believe is right.

Cognitive and Moral Development

EMOTIONAL DEVELOPMENT

Preschoolers, especially the four-year-olds, are extreme in their emotions. Their feelings are intense. They love things or they hate things. They see things as all good or all bad, all right or all wrong. Potent emotions and black and white thinking pave the way for frequent conflicts and aggression.

POINT OF VIEW

If you are considering teaching peaceful classroom or conflict resolution skills to preschoolers, the most important developmental aspect to keep in mind is that they are unable to see another person's point of view. They are very egocentric. They have, however, a natural developmental capacity for empathy that needs to be allowed to flourish. Have you had the experience of sharing stories in circle time with preschoolers and one child had a sad story to tell? Maybe his dog died and he started to cry. The next thing you know, several children are crying inconsolably. What happened? Empathy happened. Preschoolers have the emotional ability to pick up on the feelings of other children and to match them to their own. If, in a given situation, they cannot do this, it is often because they do not have the vocabulary for the emotion. They cannot identify with the feeling if they cannot label it. Therefore an excellent tool to use with preschoolers is one of those posters with all the labeled 'emotion' faces. Children can spot how they're feeling on the poster. You can give them the name for the emotion. As they develop a vocabulary for their emotions, they are able to empathize with that emotion.

DISCIPLINE

I found it frustrating when, after I had used all the 'right' words in disciplining my preschool children, one of them would say, "I was bad." Often they needed a hug afterwards to reassure them that they were still loved. I remember a school of thought that preached, "If you hug children after they have been disciplined, it undoes the discipline. You'll spoil them." I disagree! A hug can be accompanied with, "I still love you. I just don't like what you did." It is best to specifically describe the unacceptable behavior. Many times, my children's understanding of what they did wrong was totally different from mine.

RULES

Children of this age are conscious of rules and see them as sacred and untouchable, although they may not always follow them. They obey rules out of a fear of punishment or a fear of losing someone's love and support. When they disobey, it is often because they are in the moment, following their impulses and curiosities. They do not have the cognitive ability to analyze consequences of their behavior ahead of time. Preschool children have difficulty seeing cause and effect. It is hard for them to understand how their behavior affects other people. They often cannot predict what impact their

> Moral (obligatory) values can be further broken down into two categories: universal and non-universal. Universal moral values — such as treating all people justly and respecting their lives, liberty, and equality — bind all persons everywhere because they affirm our fundamental human worth and dignity.
> — Thomas Lickona, Educating for Character

actions might have on someone and, once they have acted, may be unable to look back and connect the behavior to the consequence. They also have extreme difficulty explaining why they did something. They truly don't know. It is better not to ask. Asking "Why?" is an exercise in futility.

When a rule is broken, it is the size of the consequence, not the intention of the rule breaker that is important to preschool children. They are very literal and concrete. If someone steps on a child's toy and breaks it, it is the broken toy that is focused on, not the intent of the person who stepped on it. Whether the toy got broken accidentally or intentionally, the toy's owner will react the same. Conceptually, "He did it on purpose" or "It was an accident" are not clear statements to the preschooler. The vocabulary in itself is problematic for preschoolers. My son would do something accidentally and tell me he did it on purpose. The concepts of 'deliberation' and 'accidentality' were too abstract for him.

SELF-ESTEEM

Preschool children want to be accepted, liked, and loved. Consequently, teachers and parents often hear (or see) from the child as a reaction to discipline, "You hate me!" Because children's primary goal is to be loved, their reaction to disapproval of their behavior is to fear that love has been withdrawn. For this reason, it is very important that children not be labeled 'bad.' "You are a bad girl" means to the preschooler, "You are not accepted" or "You are not loved". *Children aren't bad; behavior is bad, and as such unacceptable.* I cannot emphasize this distinction enough. Even if you are diligent about speaking to children about their behavior, reassuring them that they are OK and loved but that their behavior is not OK, children of this age will still have difficulty separating the two.

> **During the Reagan era, the FCC moved to deregulate the broadcasting industry. In 1984, it eliminated the advertising time restrictions. It also ruled that product-based shows were legal. These rule changes made the "program-length commercial," the marketing of toys as part of the programs, legal for the first time.**
> **— Nancy Carlsson-Paige and Diane E. Levin, Who's Calling the Shots?**

SUPERHERO WORSHIP

Preschoolers are very much involved in "superhero worship" and violence. This is a normal developmental phase based on the child's fears and feelings of vulnerability. Pretending to be a superhero, ready and able to defeat the "bad guy," gives the child a sense of power. The difficulty here is the inundation of violent media heroes in children's television viewing, games, toys, clothing, lunch boxes, etc. Combine the excessive influence of these violent characters with the real violence prevalent in our society and with the preschool child's difficulty of distinguishing between what really exists and his/her dreams, wishes, imaginings, or lies, and the potential exists for children hurting and getting hurt.

Practical Approaches And Techniques

CURRICULUM

Some curriculum materials that teach 'peace' to preschool children focus on world concepts. While it is 'nice' to introduce global awareness to young children, they cannot relate to it yet. To effectively teach 'peace' to preschoolers, begin with their world, their everyday conflicts, and their personal emotions.

Provide opportunities in the classroom to learn about emotions

For a group activity, ask children: "What does feeling happy feel like? Look like? What color is it? What animal is a happy animal? What does feeling angry feel like? Look like? What color is it? What animal is an angry animal? How do we act when we are happy? When we are angry? How do we treat other people?" Act these feelings and actions out in role-play, and role-play alternative responses.

One teacher of four-year-olds was having trouble with arguments and fighting in her class. She felt that she had to address the problem directly with the entire group, as well as individually, if she was to see consistent results. She writes this about her experience:

This year in the Pre-K class we began by identifying feelings. We talked about how various situations make us feel. Our goal is to encourage the children to use words to express feelings and thus to avoid some confrontations and conflicts.

One activity to encourage talking about feelings was the following: Each child made stick puppets whose faces reflected basic emotions (happy, sad, mad). We discussed various situations (when a friend hurts you, when you have pizza for lunch, when a parent is sick, when you spend time with a grandparent...) and the children used the puppets to display how they would feel.

As a follow-up to this, we now have the children express their feelings, following a conflict, come up with a solution, shake hands to show they agree with it, and plan how to implement the solution. For example, following a physical argument between two children, they talked about why they were pushing and what they could do to make each other feel better. The solution was to listen when one person was asking the other something. The children made up with a hug and a handshake.

— Allison, Pre-K teacher

Give children a vocabulary for their emotions

Give children a vocabulary for their emotions so that they can name their feelings. An excellent tool for helping children to identify their emotions is the Emotions Poster available through Childswork/Childsplay(see Additional Resources). It features photos of real kids expressing 28 different feelings. Children may not have the word for what they are feeling, but they may recognize the emotion in the expression on a child's face. Ask children to point to the face that best expresses their own feeling. Give them the label for that feeling, using it as a springboard for discussion.

Use music to teach concepts of peace, cooperation, and sharing

Use music to teach concepts of peace, cooperation, and sharing. Make music a part of every day. Preschoolers love music. It is amazing how much they can learn from the music that they listen to. When my daughter was 18 months old, I discovered Brite Music (see Additional Resources). Brite Music has a tape called *Safety Kids* that teaches children safety rules, including their telephone number and what to do if they are lost in a store. By the age of 2 1/2, my daughter could sing her phone number. When we'd go to the mall, I would ask her what she should do if she got lost. She could tell me. She learned through the music. Consider how children learn their ABC's. Look at the power of music and jingles in commercials. Music makes an impression that is remembered. I highly recommend Brite Music. My favorite Brite Music tape is *Someone Special You.* This tape not only has a message for children, it has

> **Chapter Four and Additional Resources list ways to help you find songs and music for social action.**

a message for all of us. Songs like "I Made A Mistake" (mistakes are for learning), "Think, Feel, Do Polka," and "I Can Choose The Things I Think" are empowering and uplifting. Another excellent tape is *Teaching Peace* by Red Grammer. Although this tape is a bit worldly for this age group, some of the songs relate to children and their feelings. Others relate to world concepts. It is positive music that introduces concepts of peace and world 'oneness.' Developmentally, it's a little above preschoolers, but I think it still has value.

> Stories, read or told, have always been among the favorite teaching instruments of the world's great moral educators. Stories teach by attraction rather than compulsion; they invite rather than impose
> — Thomas Lickona, Educating for Character

Use children's literature as a tool for exploring emotions

Small children love to have books read to them. Stories are an age-appropriate and effective teaching tool for small children. Choose a story with a moral. (A list of excellent picture books with themes of conflict resolution, peace, and kindness can be found at the end of this book under "Additional Resources".) Read the book to the children, noting facial expressions, emotions, conflicts, actions, and reactions to the characters and outcomes. Give the children a vocabulary for the characters' emotions. Children might even act out facial expressions of the characters and role-play the scripts or alternatives to the action in the story.

Put on puppet shows

Use puppets to act out conflict situations. Engage the children in a discussion of how the puppets can resolve their problems peacefully. This can be done spontaneously, or as a planned activity.

Spontaneous activity:

If a conflict is occurring in the classroom, choose puppets to act out the conflict. The teacher may play one of the characters, using words the children would use in the conflict. One of the children could control the other puppet. The puppets 'act out' the conflict. The teacher could use the puppets to act out two or three different ways of handling the conflict. Ask the children to suggest what the child puppet might say in response.

Planned activity:

The teacher and the children could make up several skits using the puppets. They should be kept very short for this age group. Have the skits demonstrate a peaceful way to resolve a typical conflict. (Choose conflicts that occur within the classroom.) Demonstrate a 'fighting' way to resolve a conflict and an 'avoiding' way to handle conflict. After the puppet shows, talk about the puppets' behavior.

Using puppets to act out real conflicts for the children puts the situation at a safe distance from their emotional reality. This enables the children to be more objective and comfortable with the activity.

AT SCHOOL AND AT HOME

The media's impact on our culture

Take the time to discuss with children, at a level they can understand, the effect TV shows have on them

I think that my five-year-old believes that if he watches too much TV, he will have brains that look like oatmeal. That's the only visual image he has for "mush." Yes, I sometimes answer in exasperation to the many "Why?"s I get when I enforce our TV watching rules, "...because TV turns your brains to mush!" Actually, that's not far from the figurative truth (I address what physically happens to the brain in the section "Child Warriors"). Four -, five -, or six-year-old children developmentally are not able to understand that their brain is being conditioned by media messages. At some level they can begin to understand that TV *teaches* them something. I say to my children, "When you watch Mr. Roger's, you learn about people and the jobs they do. What else do you learn?" or "TV teaches you about... (fill in with something positive that is very concrete to them, such as ABC's, counting, etc.). When you watch Power Rangers, or VR Troupers, you are learning also. How do Power Rangers solve their problems? (Most children will answer: "Fighting or they beat up the bad guys.") This show is teaching you to solve problems by fighting." This is an important conversation to have. Variations of this conversation need to happen regularly.

Help children to understand that on TV a person can get kicked ten times and can then get up, but in real life getting kicked hurts

Sometimes people are hurt badly enough that they don't get up: "A 5-year-old girl was murdered Saturday, in Norway, by three boys — two 6-year-olds and a 5-year-old. The boys reportedly kicked and stoned her and then left her to freeze in the snow. All three supposedly were fans of the cartoon *Teenage Mutant Ninja Turtles* and other U.S. children's shows, although officials there have not officially linked the girl's death to any particular program".[1] Of course, this is an extreme scenario. The average child will not commit such deadly, violent acts in his/her play. I personally know of many daycare centers, however, that have banned Power Ranger play, toys, and costumes in an effort to stop the increasing incidents of karate-type aggression displayed by the children. Children were getting hurt.

Discuss with children ways that superheroes can solve problems without violence

Living in a society saturated by violent images, parents have a difficult road to follow if they are going to take a stand against media violence. Somehow, a balance needs to be achieved. If we completely

> In 1950, when TV was in its infancy, in the entire United States only 170 persons under the age of fifteen were arrested for serious crimes such as murder, rape, robbery, and aggravated assault. By 1979 the rate of serious crime committed by children under fifteen had increased by 11,000 percent.
>
> — Myriam Miedzian, Boys Will be Boys

deprive our children of all media violence, we worry that they will eventually rebel against our standards, making violence a steady diet, or will feel that they don't fit in with their friends. A moderate path would be to carefully choose the shows that your child is allowed to watch. Monitor the amount of time your child watches those shows. Watch with your child. Discuss their values, lessons, and methods of problem-solving. Discuss what is real and what isn't. Discuss the real life consequences of behavior modeled on the television show. In the classroom, teachers can take an interest in their students' favorite shows. Discuss the shows with the students to help them to understand what is real and what isn't. Help them to employ alternatives to violence in their own play.

Encourage and reinforce empathy

This is the single most important thing that you can do for preschoolers in the area of 'character and conflict education.' Preschoolers cannot see another person's point of view. To require three- through five-year-olds to see someone else's point of view is developmentally inappropriate. Preschoolers can feel empathy. Empathy needs encouragement to flourish. Here are some examples of how to encourage empathy.

Allow children to talk about their emotions

Empathy is reinforced when we acknowledge a child's feelings and give the child a vocabulary for those feelings. For example, when children are angry because they are not getting their way, say, "I can see that you are feeling angry right now." If they are embarrassed, say, " You seem to be feeling embarrassed because...". If a child has hurt another child, point out how that child feels and make the child look at the hurt child's face, see the emotion in that child's face, and attach the vocabulary for that emotion to that facial expression.

Children need opportunities and encouragement to talk about their feelings. A child's temperament and language skills will affect how well a child can do this. Help children to 'label' their emotions so they have words for what they are feeling. Model dialogue for them so that they will learn the communication skills necessary to resolve conflict and to express their feelings.

Notice a child sharing or showing concern for others

When you notice a child caring for another child by helping, comforting, or welcoming that other child into a game, let the child know you 'noticed'. You could say for example: "Jane, I noticed how you helped Matt tie his shoe this morning. That was a very caring thing to do" or "Jake, I noticed that you invited Sam to play with you and Jeff. Sam was feeling very lonely. He was happy to have a friend." I use the phrase "I noticed" rather than "That was great" or other forms of praise. Praise is OK in moderation, but 'noticing' without superfluous praise helps a child to internalize the positive feelings rather than to look for them externally.

Hold class/family meetings

Preschoolers may initially have some difficulty with the 'discussion' and 'question and answer' process involved in a meeting. However, when they get accustomed to the routine, flow, and expectations of the meeting, they begin to share and think ahead about what they want to say, and begin to assert themselves.

My husband and I have been having family meetings since our son was three and our daughter six. My son initially had difficulty participating appropriately in the meetings. But we felt strongly that he should participate. We had attended a workshop where an approach to family meetings and rituals was outlined and highlighted as a major plus to family value and connection. We were motivated to start and did not want to wait until our son could 'communicate better.' So we allowed him the time and encouragement he needed. The workshop presenter had stated that "saying nothing" shouldn't be allowed as an answer. That sounded good to my husband and me, so we adopted it as one of our rules. When my son said nothing, we'd wait. We'd encourage him. We'd share with him our ideas for the question at hand until he came up with something. Whatever he came up with was OK.

The point is that he was participating in a family meeting. His words and feelings were valuable. We wanted to hear from him. Now, we have trouble getting him to stop talking. But the important thing is that he contributes to the family meeting. His words are written down. He counts. Because his first-born older sister usually out-talks him, his participation in the family meeting is a significant boost to his self-esteem. It takes a tremendous amount of patience and conviction to get through a family meeting with a preschooler, but I think it is worth it.

Have an agenda

For this age group, consistency is important. Children will look forward to the meetings and as they get used to the format, they will begin to think ahead. In *Raising Good Children*, Thomas Lickona gives a thorough explanation of how to conduct a family meeting. *Raising Good Children* is a beneficial resource for every parent and is especially helpful in guiding parents to use a fairness approach with children (see the next page for a sample Family Meeting Agenda).

Family meetings should be held consistently once a week

Have a special ritual to go with the family meeting. We do it after a candlelight dinner. Allow NOTHING to interfere with this meeting, with only unavoidable exceptions. Don't answer the phone; put the answering machine on. This lets the child know that you believe communication with the family is important.

Class meetings can be held for 15 minutes every day

For the preschool child, class meetings take the form of circle time or sharing time. The format is informal. The primary purpose of these meetings is for children to practice expressive communication and listening skills, to participate in group decision making, and to share responsibility for the workings of the classroom. It is also an excellent opportunity for children to learn a vocabulary for their emotions. Labeling emotions is an important part of reinforcing empathy.

Thomas Lickona (1992) and Diane Levin provide a wealth of information on how to set up these meetings and a thorough discussion of benefits to be gained by them (see Annotated Bibliography).

See Chapter Three for more information on how to set up class meetings.

EMOTIONS, DISCIPLINE, AND THE GROWTH OF EMPATHY

React with 'moral feeling'

When a child hurts another child intentionally, react with "moral feeling" (Lickona, 1992). Explain how the behavior hurts the other child and point out the expressions and feelings of the hurt child. For example, if John hits Jane on the head with a block, say with moral feeling, "You hit Jane on the head. That hurt Jane. Look at her face. Look at how sad she is. It hurts to get hit on the head! We don't hit people because it hurts! How would you feel if Jane hit you on the head?" You may not get the answer to this question that you want, but the answer you do get will tell you something about the child's frame of mind and what needs to be worked on. If it seems appropriate, I might also add, "What can you do to help Jane feel better?" Sometimes it is better to wait until both children calm

> **One of the ways teachers can foster caring about what's right is to show how deeply they care. They can do that by the way they react to violations of moral values.**
> **— Thomas Lickona,**
> **Educating for Character**

FAMILY MEETING AGENDA

(Adjust this agenda to meet your specific family values
and preferences.)

Each family member addresses the following items:

- Call Family Meeting to order.

- Tell one thing learned this week.

- Do you have an issue, problem, or concern to talk about?

- What has gone right in your life this week?

    - What is the best news of the day or week?

    - Tell something good, funny, or surprising that happened
    to you this week.

- Discuss chores/chore schedule (negotiate).

- Make weekend plans. Kids help select.

- _____

- _____

- _____

- _____

- _____

- _____

- Say something kind, a thank-you or a compliment to someone in
the room (you may also say something nice about yourself!).

- Adjourn

down before you ask this question. A consequence, such as time-out, may also be in order. Each situation is individual. You have to use your judgment. The most important part of the dialogue is reacting with 'moral feeling' and encouraging children to feel empathy for the child that was hurt.

Require restitution

When a child hurts another accidentally or intentionally, assist the child who did the hurting to figure out a way to comfort or help the hurt child. It is important that the child who caused the hurt is part of the decision and the other child is comfortable with it. Do not force apologies. Instead, encourage care: holding the ice pack, helping to wipe the spill, rebuilding the knocked-down building, etc.

Separate the children from their behavior

Even when you tell small children that it is their *behavior* that you don't like but that you like/love *them*, they still might need the concrete physical reassurance of a hug. (Note, however, that in Canada and perhaps elsewhere, teachers are by law not allowed to hug students.) Also, avoid saying "Good girl/boy", "Bad girl/boy" to convey your pleasure over or disapproval of a child's behavior. If we tell a child "Good girl!" for what we feel she has done right, then the next time she doesn't repeat that behavior, she will deduce that she is bad.

Provide the consistency necessary for children to feel secure in their environment

- Have a set schedule and routine.
- Involve children in establishing meaningful rules and consequences with consistent follow-through.
- Establish rituals or traditions, especially those that build a feeling of togetherness in the classroom, the community, or the family.
- Foster caring.
- Discourage warplay centered on media superheroes (Power Rangers, Ninja Turtles).

Corporal punishment

When we consider the parent or teacher as the role model for the behavior we want children to internalize, we have to reflect seriously on what corporal punishment teaches. Corporal punishment is a form of violence. If we use violence as a means to control our children, are we not being hypocritical when we tell our children to solve problems with words and not fists? Also, research studies indicate that the negative effects of corporal punishment far outweigh any perceived positive effect. Corporal punishment is a model for violent behavior. As Cecil shows, it breeds resentment, mistrust of authority, and fear. It actually retards moral growth. Emphasizing rule compliance out of fear of physical punishment, it is counterproductive. According to Duska and Whelan, "Setting rule compliance as a moral goal actually hinders moral development because such an approach reinforces and prolongs the period of moral realism, where the child is not subjecting rules to the critical examination necessary to gain autonomy". Thus, if we use corporal punishment as a standard form of discipline, we are defeating our goal of parenting peaceful, self-confident, empowered, and moral children.

> **See Appendix B for more facts and information on corporal punishment.**

SUMMARY

Curriculum

- Provide opportunities in the classroom to learn about emotions.
- Give children a vocabulary for their emotions.
- Use music to teach concepts of peace, cooperation, and sharing.
- Use children's literature as a tool for exploring emotions.
- Put on puppet shows to act out conflict situations.

At School and at Home

- Take the time to discuss with children, at a level they can understand, the effect TV shows have on them.
- Help children to understand that on TV a person can get kicked ten times and can then get up, but in real life getting kicked hurts.
- Discuss with children ways that superheroes can solve problems without violence.

Emotions, Discipline, And The Growth of Empathy

- Encourage and reinforce empathy.
- Allow children to talk about their emotions .
- Notice a child sharing or showing concern for others .
- Hold class/family meetings.
- Use authoritative discipline.
- When a child hurts another child intentionally, react with 'moral feeling'.
- When a child hurts another accidentally or intentionally, assist the child who did the hurting to figure out a way to comfort or help the hurt child.
- Separate the children from their behavior.
- Provide the consistency necessary for children to feel secure in their environment.

Child Warriors: Are We Priming Our Children's Brains for Violence?

Are we, by allowing our children to be exposed to violence on TV, setting up an environment that physically changes the brain by making it 'good at' thinking violently? In doing so, are we also increasing the possibility that the next generation of children will inherit a brain adapted physically to warlike thinking? Carlson-Paige and Levin write that "at no other time in history have children had daily exposure to so many images removed from direct experience, many of which focus on violence." How might this exposure to violence affect the physical structure of the brain?

According to Jane Healy (1990), neuroscientists understand that "...what children do every day, the ways in which they think and respond to the world, what they learn, and the stimuli to which they decide to pay attention ... shape their brains. Not only does it change the ways in which the brain is used (functional change), but it also causes physical alterations (structural change) in neural wiring systems." Healy refers to the work of E. James Potchen, who has studied 18,000 brains: "Dr. Potchen tells of both animal and human brains that have restructured themselves significantly on the basis of learning experiences." If the average child spends approximately 24 hours a week watching TV and Power Ranger-type videos, it would follow that this activity becomes a significant part of his/her learning experience.

Says Marian Diamond, professor of neuroanatomy at the University of California, Berkeley: "There is absolutely no doubt in my mind that children's brains are changing. Whatever they're learning, as those nerve cells are getting input, they are sending out dendritic branches. As long as stimuli come in to a certain area, you get more branching; if you lose the stimuli, they stop branching," (Healy). This contention is backed up by Michael D. Chafetz in his book *Smart for Life*: "Whenever brain cells are activated by seeing, speaking, or solving problems, they begin to change. They take in more chemical energy and remodel nerve endings and receptors. They form new connections."[2]

New scientific studies and advanced technology have taken our understanding of how the environment affects us beyond the psychological foundations of conditioning: "People, including children, tend to develop a taste for what they are conditioned to. There is no indication that in the 1950's boys enjoyed TV less because it was less violent.... It is an acquired taste that the media have played an important role in developing." The National Institute of Mental Health published a report in 1982 which confirms that "children who watch a lot of violence on television may come to accept violence as normal behavior" (Miedzian, 1991).

If one takes these concepts to a logical conclusion, one might deduce that not only are children who have violent media input as part of their learning experience being psychologically conditioned to think in violent ways, but their brains are developing the neural connections and dendritic branching for violent thinking. Psychological conditioning physically changes the brain. Violence in the media is creating a psychological and physical predisposition for violence in our children.

As parents or educators, what can we do? According to Terrence Webster-Doyle (1989), "being conscious of the influence of advertising and of programming that is unhealthy is of utmost importance since media has such a tremendous effect on the brain." We need to stop denying the impact the media are having on our children and to be aware of the effects. Scientific evidence indicates that television viewing creates passive learners unable to think: "If our society wants citizens who can reflect as well as respond, who can come up with solutions to the problems of a complex world, it must teach its children to stop, listen, and think as well as react" (Healy). Violence is a pervasive problem in our complex world! In order for our children to be able to deal effectively with conflict and violence, they need to be able to stop, think, talk through problems, plan ahead, and act rather than react impulsively.

Some suggestions for parents and teachers:

- Place firm limits on television and video viewing. Address what children should watch and how long they should watch.
- Participate with children whenever possible. Talk with them about television content, methods of audience manipulation, point of view, etc.
- Give substitute caregivers strict guidelines regarding TV and video use.

Violence in the media is a problem with devastating consequences. Not only are our children being conditioned to think in terms of combat, to think of it as entertainment, and to accept it as normal, but there is also strong evidence indicating that it physically alters the brain. However, we are not without hope. As parents and educators, we must take action. It's up to us to make a difference.

Chapter 3

THE LOWER ELEMENTARY SCHOOL CHILD

What is Peace to a Second Grader?

 I did a 'peaceable classroom' lesson with a group of 27 second graders. Prior to the lesson, I spent nearly six hours poring through various well-respected books on conflict resolution trying to find lessons that would hit home with these kids, that would hold their attention and allow for continuity and progression of a theme, point, or focus. I found the task quite frustrating. I think these authors put out wonderful activity books that create an awareness in children of what peace is and of how to negotiate, mediate, and incorporate a win-win philosophy. The goal of these lessons is to teach children to create peaceable classrooms. Nevertheless, except for a few disconnected activities (10 to 20 out of hundreds), the activities are skill-oriented or focused outward. They deal primarily with concepts of global peace and awareness that are wonderful for kids to begin to understand, but are so separate from their everyday lives that they cannot relate to them. I agree that peace, global awareness, and negotiation skills are critical to our children's educational experience, but kids have difficulty relating to peace because they don't 'live in' world peace. The focus is off themselves. The second grader is still somewhat egocentric and developmentally just beginning to see other people's points of view.

The second graders I worked with during that first lesson could not relate to the abstraction of peace, nor could they relate personal (emotional and physical) safety to a peaceable classroom. According to Diane Levin in *Teaching Young Children in Violent Times*, "young children usually focus on the concrete aspects of concepts and the visible aspects of experience, not the abstract meanings or internal, less visible features or motivations. A concept like 'war' can be easier for young children to understand than 'peace' because of all the powerful and salient aspects of war they see." My experience with the second grade class concurred with Levin's point.

The second graders could give me very few examples of peace.
When I asked them "What is peace?", I got the following responses:

Peace is...
- quiet
- nice
- not fighting
- being a good listener

But the second graders were very good at telling me what was *not* peaceful. They understood war at some level—much better than they could understand peace.
I got these responses:

War is:
- noisy
- punching, kicking, and pushing
- using a sub-machine gun to kill people
- calling names
- being angry

They could give me these responses, but I could see that they really didn't understand, couldn't relate much of it to themselves, and consequently became very, very wiggly very fast. When I tried to relate the idea of peace to their safety and the necessity of a peaceable classroom to their ability to feel good expressing themselves, they could not begin to understand. These were questions and objectives from activities in highly acclaimed resource books recommended for primary grades or all grades. What the children wanted to talk about was the last time they got picked on, their friend who got picked on, their world as they knew and understood it.

Activities that don't relate to the children's everyday life don't teach children how to *see* their feelings or how to *understand* where they come from. Nor do they show how to *change* the way they think so that the next time a similar situation occurs, it doesn't trigger a fight or flight response.

The ultimate goal of a complete peace, empowerment, and conflict resolution program is to teach kids

- to become aware of their fight or flight reactions in a conflict
- to understand the impact of their environment on their thinking and emotions (conditioning)
- to understand relationships and to develop empathy
- to be empowered
- to have conflict resolution skills.

With developmentally appropriate education they can, rather than react, begin to learn to stop, think, and choose which conflict resolution skill will work best for them in a tense situation. As Jane Healy says in *Endangered Minds*, "...adults must be involved in showing children how to ask the right questions, talk through problems, plan ahead, and generally insert language (and some associated thought) between impulse and behavior".

According to *The Piaget Primer*, children between the ages of 7 and 11 are becoming aware of others' viewpoints: "The child searches to justify his own viewpoint and to coordinate the views of others."[1] Children at this developmental stage are very concrete and literal. Consequently, 'peace education' needs to be made concrete and literal and must relate to their developmental ability to perceive others' viewpoints. Adults in the children's life need to model the behavior desired from the kids. They can be taught conflict resolution skills and a mediation corner can be set up in the room, but if that is all that is being done, it won't yield long-term results.

So I decided to change my approach with the second graders. I used as a foundation Terrence Webster-Doyle's *Why is Everybody Always Picking on Me: A Special Curriculum For Young People To Help Them Cope With Bullying* (1994). His methods are concrete: they are based on kids' real feelings, experiences, and attitudes. His format is sequential and cumulative. His books are geared toward the ten- to fourteen-year-old child, so I substituted his reading material with material in children's books and children's tapes geared for the second-grade level. Two of the lessons I adapted from *Eggbert, the Slightly Cracked Egg* and *Don't Feed The Monster On Tuesday* are highlighted in this chapter. (See "Additional Resources" for additional children's book suggestions.) Music, puppetry, activities involving material in their environment such as coloring books, sale fliers, advertisements, toys, and role-plays are tools necessary in a second-grade curriculum. The revised lesson with the second graders incorporated concepts of empathy: we talked about why people do what they do and how their environment affects them. The children's response was enthusiastic. They understood the basic concepts and related to the approach. They began to develop an understanding that victims and bullies have the same feelings. Both need conflict resolution skills and the ability to feel good about themselves. The lesson worked

Cognitive and Moral Development

POINT OF VIEW

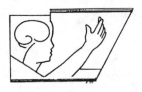

Lower elementary school children are beginning to see others' points of view. They are still quite egocentric at the younger end of this stage; however, they are beginning to consider others' feelings. Children of this age search to justify their own view points and try to coordinate their views with the views of others. When the 'Golden Rule' is explained to them and used as an example for behavior, they can relate to its meaning. As a result, children of this age are able to feel true empathy. It is not unusual for a child of this age to read or hear a sad story and to start to cry. The story or event may come up in conversation for days as the child tries to process the information into something he/she can handle.

I live near an airport that is expanding. Consequently, the flight path has stretched over neighborhoods and woods in our area. One day we were driving to the neighborhood post office and discovered that all the trees in the area had been cut down. Neighborhood houses that had been purchased by the airport stood bare. The sight was devastating. Even the postoffice had lost all but three birch trees. They stood alone, the last remnant of what was once a lovely landscaping. My eight-year-old daughter was visibly upset. She expressed concern over all the animals and birds that would no longer have homes or food to eat. She grieved for the lost beauty of the trees and flowers. Every time we drove down that road for weeks, she announced her displeasure and her concern for the animals, birds, and plants. Finally, I suggested that she do something about it. She had a voice. She could write. She wrote a letter to the head of the airport. She waited impatiently for an answer. It came. She was told that the devastation to the wildlife was necessary to install an Instrument Landing System for the safety of the neighborhood. She was assured that the trees would be replaced with slower growing trees such as dogwoods and red maples. Barren land would be seeded with wildflowers. All this had to wait until the days got cooler. My daughter could process this information and reconcile it with her feelings. She felt better. She could understand the 'point of view' of the airport staff as well as the animals and birds. My five-year-old son was still too young to relate to such a situation.

WORLD VIEW

Children of this age are also beginning to relate world events to their understanding of themselves and their lives. They are just barely starting to see themselves as members of a society and culture. They become very interested in their heritage. Because they are still very literal and their logical thinking is limited to physical reality, they have tremendous difficulty separating what is happening in other parts of the world from the reality of their world. Consequently, they worry! For example, if a seven-year-old sees pictures of starving, hurting children from a Third World country on television, it is as real to him cognitively and emotionally as if the children were living next door. I know a child who saw Medusa turn people to stone on TV and agonized over the picture it left in her mind for months.

The Oklahoma City bombing was difficult for children of this age to deal with because they could not comprehend how it related or didn't relate to their lives. I heard more than one parent express outrage at the vivid images on the front pages of newspapers and on the news. Parents were hiding newspapers and issues of news magazines so their primary-school children would not see them. Many of these children would read anything they could get their hands on without the ability to fully comprehend the meaning. Their parents were well aware of their children's capacity for empathy and their difficulty in separating the incidents from their own lives. It was the stuff of nightmares!

THE AGE OF JUSTICE

Lower elementary-age children are at the age of justice! Because they feel empathy and are beginning to see other people's point of view, they will also take up others' battles. They often seem to take on the role of public defender. Comments such as, "That's not fair!", "He has more than me!", "She didn't follow the rules!", or "He's being mean to my friend!" emerge with incredible consistency and emphasis. Justice to the six- to eight-year-old child, however, is very black and white. In conflict situations, "getting even" is a common reaction. Children don't often understand the accidental nature of some offenses. If during a game, one child accidentally runs into another child, knocking him down, the offense may be seen as deliberate. The hurt child may want to push the offender to even the score. Teaching children to say "I'm sorry, I didn't mean to hurt you. Are you OK?" is an important lesson at this age (as at all ages, actually). Teach children to help those they hurt.

RULES

Six- to eight-year-olds see the necessity of rules to regulate games and activities. Cheating becomes a major offense and an often-heard accusation. When playing games with younger siblings and friends, they can't differentiate between a smaller child's inability to understand rules and the deliberate breaking of rules. Parents and day care providers who often work with mixed age groups are forever explaining to the older child that the younger child simply doesn't understand cheating. Younger children simply like to make up and follow their own rules. The older child doesn't remember being that way and has difficulty believing it.

WHAT IS A LIE?

For the seven- to ten-year-old child, a lie is something that is not true. It does not matter if it is a mistake or an exaggeration. In his book *Why Kids Lie*, Paul Ekman argues that this may be the case because parents do not clearly explain to small children what a lie is.[2] Recent studies on children's understanding of intent have dispelled earlier developmental theories that children between the ages of four and seven do not understand intent. When children were read stories about a child lying to avoid punishment as opposed to a child lying to protect someone from being hurt, five- to nine-year-old children always saw the child lying to avoid punishment as more wrong. Ekman's conclusion is that even young children understand intent, whereas they may not understand lying.

MORAL CHOICES

Lower elementary school children make choices based on their need to be good in their own eyes as well as in those of others. They want to fit into society's norms for good behavior. Their internal goal is to be loved and accepted, which is why they may still take criticism and reprimands as rejection. They fear that if they are not 'good enough,' they will lose the love and support of significant adults in their lives.

Even though children in this age group respect rules and want approval, they do not have adequate understanding or motivation to be consistent in following the rules.

Practical Approaches and Techniques

CURRICULUM

As I stated in Chapter Two, there are curriculum materials available to teach 'peace' to children of this age that focus on world concepts. As with the preschool child, it may seem appropriate to introduce global awareness to young children. However the reality is that  they cannot relate to it. To effectively teach 'peace' to first through third graders, begin with their world. Base your curriculum on their everyday conflicts, their personal reality, culture, and emotions.

Use music to teach concepts of peace, cooperation, sharing

Make music a part of every day. I have found music to be such a valuable tool for learning. As I mentioned earlier, TV commercial jingles, radio jingles, or the ABC song stick in your mind for years later. I'll bet many of us can still remember the Oscar Myer wiener jingle of the sixties. Music helps us to remember. Advertisers use it—and so can we. There is wonderful music available to teach many different concepts. Some of the best music for teaching and reinforcing such concepts as character, friendship,

> **Chapter Four and Additional Resources help you find songs and music for social action.**

safety, or positive thinking is put out by Brite Music (See "Additional Resources" for their address). I have used this music with children from birth through fifth grade very successfully. Second graders I worked with repeatedly asked me to play Brite Music's Think, Feel, Do Polka. They would dance and sing with the music. By second grade, when they can read, it helps to give them a large print copy of the words. (Be sure to check copyright laws before doing this.) They love being able to follow along.

Role-play

Children of this age love to dramatize. Keep the role-plays simple and take them from actual scenarios that occur in the class. Be careful that the script is changed often enough so no child is singled out.

I would instruct the kids to sit down in a circle on the floor. Because all the children wanted to role-play all at the same time, I passed a decorated stick around the circle to determine whose turn it was. The person holding the stick could role-play or pass. If he/she decided to role-play, the stick would pass to the next person. When we had two children to role-play, they stood in the center of the circle. They would then decide who would be the victim and who would be the bully. The bully would choose the way he/she would bully the victim. If the bully had trouble thinking of something, help would be solicited from the group. Ideas would be tossed out for the bully to choose from. Then the role-play began. The victim would have to think of a way to handle the situation. If the victim was stumped, the outer circle was called upon again to offer suggestions until the victim succeeded.

The children loved doing this activity. As the year progressed, they got better and better at thinking on their feet. Initially, some children were shy about role-playing. In the end, all the children participated. The most timid children were given an opportunity to role-play in pairs with the teacher without observers. I was amazed at their ability to use the skills they had been learning all year.

At the end of the year, the second graders asked if they could role-play with fifth or sixth graders. They expressed that role-playing with children their own age didn't always seem real. They said in their neighborhoods, it was often the older children who picked on them. I got two volunteers from the fifth grade to role-play with the second graders. They were given the option to role-play with someone their own age or a fifth grader. It was very effective. Occasionally, I would check with the children to see if the bullying situations were realistic. They unanimously said yes.

> **Aggression is often learned at an early age. In fact, according to Reason to Hope, the 1994 report by the APA Commission on Violence and Youth, it is possible to predict from an eight-year-old's aggressive behavior in school how aggressive that child will be in adolescence and adulthood — including whether he or she will exhibit criminal and antisocial behavior. This is why prevention programs that start early in childhood and continue throughout adolescence have the best chance for success.**
> **— American Psychological Association**

They wanted to continue. I will never forget one little girl who wanted to role-play with one of the fifth-grade boys. I could see real fear in her eyes. She had no knowledge of what the "bully" would choose to do. She held her head high, stood up to the bully, and talked her way out of the situation. She was so proud of herself that she beamed. I have no doubt in my mind that this little girl will be one step ahead the next time someone tries to bully her.

If a conflict occurs in the class, when possible, role-play alternatives

Have the class as a group come up with alternatives. All brainstormed alternatives are possible options. It is important that student responses are received without judgment. Talk about the potential positive and negative consequences of an action.

Children's literature as a tool for exploring emotions

Use children's books to teach and discuss handling emotions, behavior, and conflict. Be sure to point out the similarities between the book and the children's personal

The Conflict Tool Box[1]

The purpose of this tool box is to have concrete representations of concepts or skills children need to help them resolve conflicts.

The physical/tangible items will help them remember how the assigned concept is to be used.

- Assign a 'tool' to each conflict resolution skill that best represents that skill.

- Place that tangible item in a Conflict Tool Box that remains in the classroom.

- Depending on the conflict resolution technique you are teaching, more items are placed into the box. If you are teaching one technique a week, one tool per week would be placed in the tool box.

- Review all the tools on a weekly basis.

- As conflicts arise, students may use the tool box to help resolve or negotiate the situation.

- It is also possible to make construction paper copies of the tools so that each child can carry a set when the class tool box is not available.

Suggested items include

1. A jar of patience

2. The letter 'I' for 'I statements'

3. Ears for listening

4. A ruler for measuring the rules

5. A texture block with six different expressions on faces (how do you feel?)

6. A detective glass for finding the real issues/interests

[1] Contributed by Justin McClellan.

INCORPORATING THE WRITING PROCESS: AN EXAMPLE

A second-grade teacher had incorporated conflict education lessons into her curriculum. She did this by introducing a specific lesson each week from Why Is Everybody Always Picking On Me? (Webster-Doyle, 1991). She then followed the lesson by carrying the concepts through the regular curriculum during the week. The children also made correlations between the weekly lessons and their social studies, literature, and Whole Language activities. Children also wrote and published their own books as part of the Whole Language process, sometimes using themes from the conflict education lessons. I've included one of these stories. What is more appropriate, developmentally, than to use the work of a second grader with other second graders? This is a story written from a second grader's point of view, using second-grade words.

The Bully On My Street

by Brianna Laderbush[1]

Once upon a time there lived a bully on my street. He was no ordinary bully. He was the meanest and most atrocious bully in all of Manchester, NH! My mom says he is a very nice boy, but she is not in our class.

One day my friends and I were walking down the street when the bully ran out of his house. He was screaming and yelling at us, "Hey, you guys, what do you think you're doing?" "Me to know and for you to find out," yelled my friend Alex. "Yea," I said. "You be quiet," the bully yelled at me. "Now I'm going to get you back for saying that to me," he said. Just then his mother came out of the house. "Kevin, it's time to do your homework," she said. "Run Alex," I yelled. "Let's get away from here while we can!"

When we got to my house, I told my mother what the bully said to us. "Mom, that bully attacked us again!" We shouted together. "How many times have I told you not to call Kevin a bully," my mom said. "But Mom," I said. "Please don't 'but mom' me," said my mother. "Everybody, including Kevin, has something nice to offer," my mom went on.
The next day ...

My friends and I decided that my mother needed a reality check. So we left her alone to talk to herself about how nice Kevin is and we tiptoed up to my room. "Erin, have you heard about the new movie in town?" asked Alex. "I sure would like to go," I said. "Let's go downstairs and ask my mother." My friends and I tiptoed down the stairs to make sure that my mother was not still talking to herself about Kevin. She wasn't.

"Mom, can I go to the new movie in town with Alex and Erin?" I asked.
"OK, dear, but be home by seven o'clock," she said.
"I will," I yelled running out the door.

"Oh, no," I said as we were walking down the street.

"What?" asked Alex.

"Look, the bully!" I said.

"Oh, no," said Alex.

"Hey, where do you think you're going," said the bully. The movie was starting so I whispered, "Let's go," and we ran for the door.

"Hey," yelled the bully, running after us.

"Run!" I screamed.

"I'm running as fast as I can," yelled Alex.

"Please, don't run," said one of the managers at the door.

"It's an emergency," said Alex.

"Well now, what's the emergency?" the manager asked.

"We're being chased by a bully," I said.

"OK," said the manager. "I will let you in and stop the bully."

My friends and I went into the movies. It was a good movie, but I kept thinking about the bully.

"Alex and Erin," I said as we came out of the movies, "we have been babies about this bully."

"We have?" asked Alex.

"Yes," I said, "and I have a plan."

"What?" both of my friends asked.

My friends and I met up with Kevin on the way home.

"Let's go," I said.

"Go where?" they asked.

"To talk to Kevin," I said.

I was scared, but I went up to Kevin anyway.

"Kevin, do you, um, do you want some of my popcorn?" I asked.

"Did you put poison in it?" he asked.

My friends were looking at me like I was crazy.

"No, Kevin, I did not," I said.

"Then why do you want to give some to me?" asked Kevin.

"Because everyone, even you, Kevin, probably likes popcorn," I said.

Kevin took a big handful of popcorn and ate it. Then he smiled at me.

"Hey," said Kevin. "Do you guys want me to walk you home so somebody doesn't pick on you?" asked Kevin.

"Sure!" we all said.

We all ate popcorn and talked on the way home.

When we got to Kevin's house, he asked us if we would like to come over sometime.

We all smiled at the nice, new bully.

[1]Contributed by Brianna Laderbush and printed with permission. Brianna wrote this story as part of a Whole Language program in her second grade class. Her teacher was actively incorporating conflict education concepts into the curriculum.

Eggbert, the Slightly Cracked Egg

Author
Tom Ross

Illustrator
Rex Barron

Publisher
G.P. Putnam
& Sons, 1994

Pages
32

Reading Level
Grade 2

Interest Level
Grades PK-2

INTRODUCTION

Synopsis

Eggbert's pictures are the hit of the fridge. The vegetables, fellow eggs, and hot dogs all derive great joy from Eggbert's paintings until one day it is discovered that he is 'slightly cracked.' Consequently, Eggbert is banished from the fridge. Dejected, Eggbert leaves to find a new home. During his search, he continually paints himself to hide his crack and to blend in with his surroundings. He learns, however, that he cannot hide who he is. He is always "found out and kicked out." One day, Eggbert realizes that the world is filled with many beautiful cracks. He decides that it's not so bad being slightly cracked and accepts himself as he is. As he learns to accept himself, others accept him. Back in the fridge, his friends realize that they miss Eggbert and his pictures.

Objectives[1]

To gain understanding and awareness about:
- why people bully
- bullying behavior
- empathy from reading facial expressions
- the roles people play
- ways we can accept ourselves
- ways we can stop bullying

Read the book to the class.
Discussion for understanding and awareness:

> Note with children how everyone in the fridge likes Eggbert UNTIL they notice he is slightly cracked.

Understanding Why People Bully
- Why did it make a difference that Eggbert was cracked?
- Are we ever uncomfortable around people who are different? Are we ever afraid?
- Point out to the children the faces and body language of the vegetables in the crisper.
- Point out the look on Eggbert's face when he is rejected.
- Who are the other bullies that Eggbert meets? Why do they bully him?

[1] Objectives adapted from Atrium Society Publications, Middlebury, VT 05753,
Why Is Everybody Always Picking On Me: Curriculum

Awareness of Bullying Behavior – Words and Body Language

- Point out to the children the faces and body language of the vegetables in the crisper

Empathy from Reading Facial Expressions

- Point out the look on Eggbert's face when he is rejected.

Understanding the Roles People Play

- Why does Eggbert paint himself to match the scenery?
- Does it help him to feel better? Why or why not?
- Is Eggbert afraid? What is he afraid of? Is Eggbert acting like a victim?
- Does Eggbert feel good about himself?

Changing Our Thinking to Accept Ourselves

- What happens to Eggbert's thinking when he sees the crack in the clouds after the rainstorm?
- What does he think of the crack in the clouds and all the world's wonderful cracks?
- When does Eggbert stop being a victim?
- When Eggbert decides that it isn't such a bad thing to be slightly cracked, what does he do? Does he continue to paint himself to match the scenery?
- How do others start to feel about him? Does he make new friends?
- When he sends his friends back home in the fridge beautiful postcards, how do they feel? Do you think they feel good about having bullied him?

Is It Possible to Stop Bullying?

- Does Eggbert get even with the characters that threw him out of the fridge?
- What does he do? Do you think he feels good about his choices? Why?
- How do you think he would feel if he went back and got even with those people who hurt him?
- Which is the better way? Which way makes people feel happier? Why?

Don't Feed The Monster on Tuesday

Author
Adolph Moser

Illustrator
David Melton

Publisher
Landmark
Editions, Inc.
1991

Pages
55

Reading Level
Grade 2

Interest Level
Grades K-2

Synopsis

"It happens every day. Some people look in their mirrors and scream — OH NO! 'My nose is too long!', 'My ears are too big!'" and on and on. The self-esteem defeating whispers of the green monster inside of us take their toll on our self-image. These negative thoughts make us feel bad about ourselves. And if we listen to these awful things, the green monster feeds on what we hear and gets bigger and bigger until we stop liking ourselves. People who like themselves have strong self-esteem. They don't feed that green monster inside of them. So, to keep the green monster from getting the best of you, choose one day out of the week, like Tuesday, and don't feed the green monster on that day. Instead, say nice things to yourself and to other people. The green monster will go down in size and your self-esteem will go up. Soon it will be easy for you to think positive thoughts every day of the week.

Objectives

To gain understanding and awareness about
▪ the roles people play   ▪ our self-acceptance

Read the book to the class

Discussion

Discuss the roles the characters play in the book and the reasons why they might play those roles. You might even point these out and relate them to real life behaviors observed in the classroom as you are reading. The book is long. I involved the students by leaving out key words toward the middle of the book and letting the group chime in with the word.

Follow-up: Take examples from the book.
Allow the children to choose one and to draw illustrations to hang up in the room. These serve as an ongoing reminder of the day's lesson. Also, look for opportunities (during class discussion, when reading a story etc.) to establish connections to the lessons. Take advantage of the opportunity to integrate the concepts into all you do during the week.
Practice helps them to internalize the concepts.

lives. This correlation will need to be made for them. (See "Additional Resources" for some excellent children's books.) Some books lend themselves well to themes or phrases that can be carried through to other situations over the year. We read one book called *Don't Feed the Monster on Tuesdays*, by Adolph Moser. The monster became the central focus of a bulletin board. The children would tell each other "Don't feed the monster!" when they were using "put-downs" or negative thinking. It became part of their vocabulary, so when they heard the phrase, they remembered the story, smiled, and changed their thinking.

Put on puppet shows

Use puppets to act out conflict situations. Engage the children in a discussion of how the puppets can resolve their problems peacefully. (See preschool kindergarten curriculum for more detail.

AT SCHOOL AND AT HOME

> **See Chapter Two for suggestions on how to incorporate puppet shows into the curriculum and for more information regarding the media and the curriculum.**

The media's impact on our culture

Take the time to discuss with children, on a level they can understand, the effect TV shows and commercials have on them. I engage children in a conversation about their favorite TV shows. We discuss the characters. What 'color' are they? Are they dark or light? Which characters are dark? Which characters are light? What might this be teaching us to think about people who are dark-skinned or light-skinned? Are they male or female? What are the males like? What are the females like? What are these characters teaching us about how boys should act? How girls should act? Are characters peaceful? Violent? Kind? Cooperative, etc.? How do the characters in the shows solve their problems? Are there other ways to solve problems? Discuss with children ways that superheroes can solve problems without violence. Help them to understand that on TV a person can get kicked ten times and can then get up, but that in real life, getting kicked hurts, and sometimes people are hurt badly enough that they don't get up. Discourage warplay centered on media superheroes such as Power Rangers and Ninja Turtles.

Help children to see alternatives to violence in their own play. If they are using media superheroes in their play, help them to create alternative means of handling 'the bad guy.' Encourage them to question if the violence they see in the show is the only way to defeat the villain.

Encourage and reinforce empathy

Children are born with a natural capacity for empathy. If you have a nursery full of babies and one baby starts to cry, soon many of the babies will be crying. At preschool during circle time, if a little boy starts to cry while sharing that his dog died, many of the other children will also cry. This is empathy. Young children cannot see someone else's point of view until somewhere around the eighth year, but they can feel empathy. If this capacity for empathy is not nurtured, it will be repressed, forgotten, and undeveloped. I saw the results of this while watching televised interviews of teenagers who have committed murder. They had no empathy for the people they killed or their families. It is a chilling commentary on what can happen when empathy is not nurtured.

> **See Chapter Two for specific examples of 'what to say' to your child.**

Three Ways That We Can Encourage Empathy

As a parent or teacher, we can encourage empathy in at least three ways. First, when a child hurts another child intentionally, react with 'moral feeling' (Lickona, 1992). Explain how the behavior hurts the other child and point out the expressions and feelings of the hurt child. Second, praise a child for sharing or showing concern for others. Third, give children a vocabulary for their emotions so that they can name their feelings. As I mentioned, a good way to do this is to get a poster with all the faces on it and the emotions below the faces. It's an excellent tool for people of all ages to figure out the 'word' for what they are feeling. (They are available through Free Spirit Press and other sources. See "Additional Resources" for details.)

Allow and encourage children to talk about their emotions

Don't pass judgment on emotions. All emotions are OK. It's how we act on those emotions that creates consequences.

A special note on boys

Boys of this age are already getting the message loud and clear that some emotions are not OK. I had one child whose mother ridiculed him and called him female names if he cried. Other little boys already presented the 'nobody can hurt me' facade. It was OK to admit anger, but it was not OK to admit fear or deep sadness. There were varying degrees of this socialization apparent in the boys. These boys need a safe place to talk about and be in touch with their feelings. They need to know that these feelings are natural, normal, and all right. They need to know that our culture says they aren't OK, but that our culture is wrong. I'll never forget walking into a foreign language class in the high school where I teach and seeing the covers of France's ELLE magazine papering the walls. Many of the issues had covers depicting men crying or looking sad and emotional. I had never seen anything like it. I don't ever remember seeing such pictures of men on the cover of a North American magazine. What price are North American boys paying physically and emotionally because of our culture? How can we encourage empathy when at the same time we teach our boys to deny their emotions? Emotions become a threat to be destroyed. So our boys – through social pressure, 'put-downs', and ridicule – separate themselves from certain emotions. If they can't feel them, they can't empathize with them.

Hold class/family meetings

As I stated in Chapter Two, family meetings in the home and class meetings as part of the school day are a valuable investment in time. They are an excellent way to foster the democratic process and to instill a fairness approach in children. The meetings give children the opportunity to gain a sense of justice and empowerment in the family and school. The aim of the meetings is to value everyone's viewpoint, to plan activities together, to decide chores by consensus, and to solve problems together.

Another wonderful benefit of family meetings is the time capsule they come to represent. My husband and I started family meetings when my son was three and my daughter was six. We take minutes every meeting. We now have years' worth of memories, children's comments, joys, values, etc. to look back on. This document in itself is invaluable. It's become a family tradition and ritual. If we go through a period of time where because of emergencies or vacations we miss a couple of meetings, the children complain. The meetings provide a sense of continuity and commitment. They provide a forum where problems can be solved in a non-threatening environment and positive feedback is expected and looked forward to.

Note: Don't fall into the trap of using the meeting as an opportunity to lecture children about their errant ways. The parent tapes in grownups' heads can easily start to play at these meetings. How often do we get such a captive audience? These tapes, however, are a sure kiss of death to the benefits of the meetings.

> **See Chapter Two for a sample family meeting agenda, guidelines, and resources.**

EMOTIONS, DISCIPLINE, AND THE GROWTH OF EMPATHY

The age of justice

Children seem to notice every other child's infractions. Tattling is often a major issue with children. Help children to focus on their own behavior, emotions, and conflicts. I do two things. First, I validate the child's feelings: "That seems to have really hurt" or "I can see that you are very sad" or "That doesn't seem fair to you, does it?" I used to think that it was best to discourage what I thought was needless tattling. My attitude changed when I saw children not tattling on things that they should have. Children have a difficult time distinguishing between what is important to an adult and what isn't. Everything unjust is important to a child of this age. So how can we teach them the difference between what is tellable and what isn't? I tell my children, "If there's blood, if someone is going to get hurt or hurts someone else, if something is going to get broken, or if there is any kind of danger, tell me. Otherwise, try to work it out yourselves." If they come with something that doesn't fit into this category, I empathize and validate their feelings. Often, they'll go on their way feeling better. Of course, they need the tools to work out conflicts by themselves. They get those tools through watching you (modeling), listening to you (teaching, not preaching), and going through trial and error (having to work out conflicts on their own). Also, they need to have their feelings validated. I'll say, "That must have upset you a lot. I can understand how you feel. How can you work it out?"

Class Meetings

Goals

- To provide a forum where children's feelings, thoughts, and ideas are valued
- To teach children problem-solving skills
- To increase communication and listening skills
- To encourage self-expression in front of a group
- To create a sense of community and fellowship
- To learn about the democratic process through direct experience

Guidelines

- Class meetings must be interactive. The purpose is to facilitate discussion among class members.

- Class meetings need not only be for problem-solving. They can be used for sharing of ideas, thoughts, and feelings. They can help with planning themes around academic units, field trips, and service activities. Much of the material available regarding class meetings focuses on the problem-solving aspect. Don't become trapped into thinking that that's the only purpose of class meetings.

- Meeting length may vary between 10 and 30 minutes for lower elementary children and 30 and 45 minutes for upper elementary children. The length of the meeting depends on the age of the students, the purpose of the meeting, and the interest level of the topic. Frequency and consistency are more important than the length of the meetings.

- Meetings should be held at regularly scheduled times. They may also be held spontaneously if the need arises. Sometimes, if an issue comes up in the classroom, it is advantageous to capitalize upon that teachable moment and to hold an impromptu class meeting to discuss the issue.

- Meetings should be conducted in a circle. This allows eye contact between students and teacher and creates a warmer and more inclusive environment. Some children will consistently jockey to be the ones sitting next to the teacher. Other children will sit at the farthest point away from the teacher, amongst their friends. A simple remedy to this problem is for the children to gather in a circle first and for the teacher to join the group after the circle has been formed. In some cases the teacher may need to arrange the children so that the potential for distraction will be minimized.

- Set the agenda for the meeting. Idea: Hang a piece of chart paper in the classroom titled "Agenda Topic". Allow students to add topics to the chart during the week. The teacher can create the agenda from that chart.
- Set the rules for the meeting. Be firm about providing a safe environment for discussion. Put-downs, whisperings with secret giggles, blamings, and personal attacks cannot be tolerated if children are to feel comfortable in the meetings. Call upon the group to decide upon how these acts will be dealt with. Often, children will decide that offenders will be asked to leave the group. Do not punish the whole group for the misbehavior of a few. This creates resentment and stigmatizes the misbehaving children as the 'troublemakers'. Whatever is decided, stand firm. Any small breach of personal safety that is allowed to slide will jeopardize the effectiveness of the group. A true sense of community requires trust and safety.
- In problem-solving meetings, stay focused on finding solutions to problems. This is not the time to punish or chastise. Focus on the issues, not on individual people.
- Allow time for students to sit quietly and to think about a problem that is presented before stating solutions. This gives more introverted children time to process their thoughts before being hit by a barrage of suggestions by the extroverts. It also forces the extroverts to think before they speak.
- Go over solutions with the group. Discuss the pros and cons to various solutions. Remember, during brainstorming sessions, all ideas are accepted for consideration. Determine which solution meets the needs of the group best. Decide by consensus. Empower students to plan how the solution will be implemented. The more they are a part of the process, the more ownership they will take for the outcome.
- Establish a signal for quiet.
- End by reviewing any decisions made during the meeting.
- Do a 'whip' around the room for final comments. Children should be allowed to pass if they have no comment.
- End with a kind word.

Two children came up to me once caught in the 'he did/she did tattling' syndrome. Both kids were too busy trying to relate 'their side' of the story to me to listen to each other. I suggested that they talk to each other about how they felt. I modeled the dialog for them using "When you _____, I felt _____. The next time, would you _____ ?" They followed my modeled dialog, filled in the blanks, then walked off together to continue playing — in peace.

React with 'moral feeling'

As I mentioned in Chapter Two, it is important to react with 'moral feeling' when a child hurts another child intentionally. Again, explain how the behavior hurts the other child and point out the expressions and feelings of the hurt child. For example, if Jeffrey knocks Elizabeth to the ground while roughhousing at recess, say with 'moral feeling' "You knocked Elizabeth down! That hurt her! This isn't fun. It hurts to get knocked down! Roughhousing at recess is against the rules because people get hurt." A logical consequence should be applied to the situation. Part of that consequence should include restitution and a plan developed by the child to choose different behavior the next time. (A sample behavior plan is provided on p. 57). Ideally, you will know the children involved in the altercation. When you know the children involved, it is easier to choose meaningful and effective consequences for those individuals. The most important part of the dialogue in this situation is reacting with 'moral feeling' and encouraging children to feel empathy for the child that was hurt.

Separate the children from their behavior

Children have difficulty distinguishing themselves from their behavior. We need to help them to see that it is what they are *doing* that we don't like. Even when you tell children that it is their *behavior* that you don't like, but that you like/love *them*, they still might need reassurance. Sometimes when I am frustrated with the behavior of my children or students, I will say, "Stop acting like a ____ year-old!" I fill in the blank with their correct age. They will often respond, "But, I am a ____ year-old!" I might then respond with, "I know. I need you to act like a grown-up!" Then we all laugh. The interesting thing is they usually stop what they were doing that was driving me nuts.

This technique has a few advantages. First, it adds humor to a potential conflict situation and diffuses the tension. Second, it communicates the needs of the adults without causing the children to feel that there is something wrong with them. Sometimes a five-year-old child's developmentally appropriate five-year-old behavior drives adults crazy. If we reprimand the behavior, the child is left feeling that he/she was doing something wrong. Developmentally, the behavior is probably right where it should be. It is, therefore, only a problem from the adults' – and not the child's – perspective. It's the adult's problem. For example, five-and-one-half-year-olds pick their noses and fall out of their chairs. These two behaviors exasperate most adults. The behaviors are developmentally normal. If children understand that what they are doing is normal for five-year-olds, that it is hard being five because they have to learn not to pick their nose and fall out of chairs so that they don't get sick or hurt, and that it is something that really bothers grown-ups (although grown-ups pick their noses when nobody's looking), then everyone can get through the phase a little easier. Self-esteem stays intact. It's easier for adults to be patient when they know the behavior is typical for their child's age. I have also used this approach in the classroom with teenagers. Often, we are tempted to say to teens, "You are acting like a two-year-old!" In fact, they are acting like a teen. Again, this approach cues the child in on the expected behavior humorously without damaging self-esteem. Teens also appreciate it because they feel understood.

Provide the consistency necessary for children to feel secure in their environment

Have a set schedule and routine
It is important not to be so rigid in following a schedule and curriculum that 'teachable moments,' spontaneous discoveries, discussion, and authentic learning cannot take place.

Involve the children in establishing meaningful rules and consequences
There are many ways to do this and many resources to help you. I particularly like the behavior management system based on Glasser's Reality Therapy and Choice Theory.

REALITY THERAPY AND CHOICE THEORY

Reality Therapy
is a method of counseling developed by William Glasser, which teaches people how to take control of their own lives, to make more effective choices, and to develop the strength to handle daily stresses and problems. At its foundation is the idea that regardless of what has happened to us or what choices we have made in the past, we can make different choices today and in the future to help us meet our basic needs. By making choices to change behavior, we can change our thoughts and feelings.

Choice Theory
is based on the fundamental belief that all humans choose behaviors in an attempt to fulfill five basic needs. According to Glasser, these needs are built into our genetic structure. Glasser identifies these basic needs as Love/Belonging, Freedom, Fun, Power, and Survival. Given this theory, human behavior is determined to be internally motivated. Therefore, the only person's behavior we can control is our own.

Although each of us possess the same five basic human needs, each of us fulfills these needs differently. We develop an inner 'picture album' of how we see the world and what we want that world to be. Our behavior is an attempt to create the ideal world of our 'picture album'. A parent's or teacher's goal then is to get children to evaluate their present behavior and to determine whether it is meeting their needs.

In one example, a teacher or parent might ask a child, "Is your behavior getting you what you want?" If the child is talking constantly in class and as a consequence loses his recess, the child who wants Love/Belonging is not getting what he wants through his behavior. On the contrary, he is losing that very thing at recess. If the child is not getting what he needs with his present behavior, he will make a specific plan for change and a commitment to follow through.

The goal is for the child to determine that his current behavior is not getting him what he wants, and to choose other behaviors that will better meet his needs. The adult in the situation does not do the choosing for the child. The adult may offer suggestions to help the child come up with solutions, but ultimately the child must make the choice and commit to it. In this way, the child owns his behavior and the consequences of that behavior. The child cannot come back later and say to the adult, "You did this to me!" or "It's your fault." The child has ownership. Ownership is a critical step in effective self-discipline and moral growth.

I have found the behavior management approach based on this theory quite successful in the classroom. It utilizes an approach that promotes self-discipline, problem-solving and moral growth. A time-out procedure is used in the behavior management model. This time-out procedure may seem unworkable in school situations where a time-out room or area is not available. I have found that working with students before school and/or after school to work out solutions and develop "Win-Win Discipline Plans" can lead to fruitful results. Be creative. Another argument against this method is that it is time consuming. It is ... in the beginning. Be willing to put in the time up front. It will pay off in the long run.

The most effective way to learn the behavior management approach based on Reality Therapy and Choice Theory is to take a week-long intensive workshop. If intensive training is not available to you, the following books can help you get started.

Recommended Reading
Glasser, William

> Control Theory, New York: Harper & Row, 1984
>
> Reality Therapy, New York: Harper & Row, 1975
>
> Schools Without Failure, New York: Harper & Row, 1975

Good, E. Perry, In Pursuit of Happiness, Chapel Hill: New View Publications, 1987

Gossen, Diane, My Child is a Pleasure to Live With, Chelson Consultants, 134-110th St. E. Saskatoon, SASK S7N 1S2

Ford, Edward E. and Englund, Stephen, For The Love of Children, New York: Doubleday, 1977

Win-Win Discipline Plan

NAME: _____DATE: _____

What were you doing that was unacceptable?_____
_____

Was your behavior against the rules of the class or the school? _____
Explain: _____
_____
_____

Was your behavior helping you?_____Explain: _____
_____

Was your behavior helping your teacher?_____Explain: _____
_____

Are you willing to try a different behavior? _____

What could you have done differently in this situation? _____
_____

What is your plan to follow the rules of the class (or school)? What will
you change or improve? List things you will do rather than things you
will not do. Be specific._____
_____
_____
_____

Are you willing to accept your plan and stick with it? _____

List the consequences for not following through on your plan.
_____
_____
_____

Signatures:

Student : _____Teacher: _____

PLAN REVIEW DATE: _____Follow-up notes: ____
_____

GUIDELINES FOR DISCUSSION WHEN USING THE WIN-WIN DISCIPLINE PLAN[1]

Questions to be addressed:

What is the Problem? Or What were you doing that was unacceptable?

In Reality Therapy, the real question is "What is the problem?" I found this question led to an answer like, "There's no problem!" For me, "What were you doing that was unacceptable?" is a more direct, less vague, and more productive question. The purpose here is to list the specific behaviors that are causing the problem. Try to avoid confronting values, attitudes, and cultural beliefs.

Whose expectations are not being met?

This question is not on the plan, but it needs to be a part of the discussion. If it is the student's own expectations, you might start with "I'm concerned ...". If it is the parent's or teacher's expectations regarding rules etc., state, "Part of my job as a (parent/teacher) is to mention ... or ... to keep you safe ... or ... to create a safe environment etc." If the problem involves others' expectations, you might say, "I'm hearing things that concern me, and I want...".

What do you want as a result of the conversation?

State what you want as a result of the discussion. Word what you want in the form of a solution: "I want to work out a way that 'X' happens ..." or "I want to figure out a way that we both win, that you get _____ and I get _____." Don't get sucked into arguing about the problem. Kids are experts at avoiding responsibility and resolution by bantering, badgering, blaming, and arguing "Yeah, but...!"

What will the resolution include?

The resolution might include 1) a plan for the future, or 2) no plan (just a sharing of feelings). If there is a plan, there might be a) logical consequences, or b) no consequences. The plan must include a commitment. If it doesn't, then a new plan must be worked out that the child can commit to.

Note: When children are resistant to planning, I simply tell them that they will continue with time-out (whether that means consecutive detentions, discussions, time-outs, internal suspensions, etc.) until we 'work it out' and create a plan that we both feel comfortable with. If the plan involves restitution, it must also be acceptable to the 'victim'.

[1]The Win-Win Discipline Plan & Guidelines are based on my experience using principles of Reality Therapy and Choice Theory. They have not been endorsed by the Institute for Reality Therapy.

SUMMARY

Curriculum

- Keep the curriculum related to your students' lives.
- Use music to teach concepts of peace, cooperation, and sharing.
- Use role-play to practice conflict resolution techniques.
- If a conflict occurs in the class, when possible, role-play alternatives.
- Use children's books to teach and discuss handling emotions, behavior, and conflict.
- Use puppets to act out conflict situations.

At school and at home

- Encourage and reinforce empathy.
- Allow and encourage children to talk about their emotions.
- Hold class/family meetings.
- Help children to focus on their own behavior, emotions, and conflicts rather than on the behavior of others.

Emotions, discipline, and the growth of empathy

- Validate children's feelings.
- When a child hurts another child intentionally, react with 'moral feeling.'
- Separate the children from their behavior.
- Provide the consistency necessary for children to feel secure in their environment.
- Have a set schedule and routine.
- Involve the children in establishing meaningful rules and consequences.
- When a child hurts another child accidentally or intentionally, assist the child who did the hurting to figure out a way to make restitution.

The Resistant Child: No Peace For Me! *or*
What right *do* I have to teach children to be empowered?

No matter what you do to try to reach them, some children pull away and withdraw. Why?

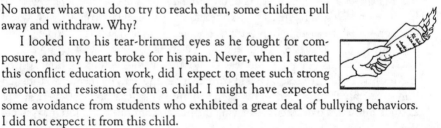

I looked into his tear-brimmed eyes as he fought for composure, and my heart broke for his pain. Never, when I started this conflict education work, did I expect to meet such strong emotion and resistance from a child. I might have expected some avoidance from students who exhibited a great deal of bullying behaviors. I did not expect it from this child.

At the beginning of the school year, this child blended in with all the other faces that I was working to come to know. He seemed like every other kid. Then, as the weeks went on and my lessons spoke more of how to be empowered and of how *not* to be a victim, he withdrew further and further into his shell. He'd sit in the back. His body language screamed with resentment and non-compliance to my requests for participation. He had the look of a hardened young man while he was just a young boy. I wondered how I could reach him. What was going on inside him? He told me he hated my lessons. I wondered why.

One day, I spoke with the classroom teacher about my concerns. I asked her what I needed to do to reach this child. I was only in the classroom once a week for my lesson. She knew this child and how to approach him. Sighing, she shook her head with concern. She had recently found out that he was being bullied at home by his older brothers. Steps were being taken to improve his situation. That day she asked me to discuss with the class what they should do if they are bullied at home. Whom should the children talk to? I spent time discussing options with the children. When everyone seemed ready to move on, I continued with my lesson.

For the next few weeks, things seemed to improve for this child. The classroom teacher praised him for his positive attitude and his progress. Over a period of a couple of months, I saw him go from wearing a hunted, stone-faced look to being a relaxed, happy child ... to being a defeated, teary-eyed boy.

It was one of my last sessions with the class. I wanted everyone in the group to participate in an assertive skill technique. This technique was to be used when two children were playing together and one child got too rough. The 'victim' would swing his/her arms to break the hold of the 'bully,' look the 'bully' in the eyes, and say loudly and clearly, "Let go! Don't ever do that again! Give me some space." This child physically moved away from the activity. He looked panicked and threatened. I tried to encourage him to participate, and he halfheartedly swung his arms, only to be greeted by laughter from some of the other children. His eyes filled with tears. He worked hard not to let them flow.

I felt at a loss. This child, more than any other child in the classroom, needed these skills desperately. The teacher strongly reprimanded the other kids for laughing, believing that the laughter had upset the boy. My sense of the situation was that this child felt defeated. He did not believe that he could succeed in defending himself. He did not even want to try. I felt that he resented me for telling him that the skills that I taught could help him. I did not understand *him*. What did I really know about his situation? Everything that I tried to teach him was in direct conflict with verbal and non-verbal messages he was getting at home. He is outnumbered at home. He is a victim, trapped. How dare I tell him to live differently?

All my lessons seemed to do was bring up powerful feelings of hopelessness and futility. Having to stand up and participate in the activity seemed to threaten him so terribly that he used all his energy to divert his attention elsewhere and to exclude himself. To do the role-playing, he had to confront his emotions – something he was not ready to do.

When I reflect upon this situation, many conflicting thoughts go through my mind. What right do I have to teach children how to be empowered, if empowerment is not valued at home? Am I setting some kids up for a bigger fall if they try these skills in a situation where they are truly powerless? In *The Dance of Anger*, Harriet Goldhor Learner writes about "Change Back!" reactions from others. In a family, each member comes to play a role. Our place in the family is to keep that role so as not to rock the boat. When one person in the family attempts to change his/her role and to think and act differently, other family members often react with strong resistance. That resistance may cause the one who wants to change to retreat back into old patterns. A young child could not possibly withstand this resistance and pressure without adult support. The "Change Back!" reactions of other family members could leave a child feeling totally defeated.

I counter these thoughts with the belief that what I am doing is helping the greater majority of kids. Most will feel more empowered and confident to defend themselves, more self-aware and able to adjust their reactions and responses in conflict situations in order to diffuse tension. Most children will use these skills effectively. Most will become more aware of the influence the media and environment have on their attitudes and reactions.

I couldn't possibly give up what I do because I believe in it passionately. However, I will now be much more sensitive to the resistant child who surfaces in my lessons. I will work to know that child, to know the obstacles he/she faces, and to adapt what I teach so that I don't set this child up for failure. Maybe what I do will help; maybe it won't. When I falter and ask myself whether it is worth it, I have to know that I couldn't live with myself if I didn't try.

Chapter 4

THE UPPER ELEMENTARY SCHOOL CHILD

A teacher's reflections: Conflict education and personal growth

I spent a year working specifically with groups of fourth- and fifth-grade students. As part of my research and experience, I kept a journal. Going back through my journal over the past year, I came across experiences in my work with upper elementary children that had special significance to me. Being able to go back, to reflect on those experiences, and to consider my reactions then and my thoughts now enables me to see the challenges, the successes, and the failures – in other words, the growth. In this section, I'd like to share those experiences and resulting insights with you. The reality of the classroom or family situation often is unpredictable and therefore difficult to plan for. Often, the best learning happens when things are not ideal and the events are not planned. The following journal excerpts are based on my year's work with fourth and fifth graders.

AWARENESS

I started the first conflict education lessons with "The Day of the Bee Sting", a story from Terrence Webster-Doyle's *Why is Everybody Always Picking On Me*. It's a true story about the author's experience with a childhood bully. In the story, young Terrence is picked on daily by the same boy. Terrence, unwilling to fight, allows this boy to beat him. One day, the bully knocks Terrence to the ground and sits on him punching. Terrence is stung by a bee. Startled and in pain from the bee sting, Terrence jumps up, sending the bully flying. Both boys realize at that moment that Terrence can defend himself.

After reading the story, we discussed how bullying affects us. We talked about the consequences of bullying for the victim and the bully over the long-term. I asked, "What takes longer to heal, bullying with punches and kicks, or bullying with words?"

After some discussion, the consensus in the group was that bullying with words takes longer to heal. They explained that bruises can heal in a week or so. Even broken bones will heal in a few months. In "The Day of the Bee Sting," Terrence says, "I sometimes feel the hurt, anger and fear from those incidents that happened many years ago. Almost forty years later, some of the effects of bullying are still with me". His bruises have healed completely, but his emotional wounds haven't. This lesson hit home with these kids. I don't think having a superficial discussion about world peace or classroom peace would have affected them as much.

One small boy had an incredible understanding of the 'bully' and the reasons bullies act as they do. Later, the teacher told me that this child is severely picked on by others in the class. They had a bullying incident in the gym that morning with this particular boy. The fifth-grade teacher expressed her belief that these kids needed to talk about 'bullies'. She said, "This is the perfect age for this curriculum. They are old enough to understand, and they have had some life experience." She told me that during the week, kids were often pointing out bullies that they noticed in stories they read or discussions they had.

I was in awe of the capability, insight, and understanding of the fifth graders. All that I have read regarding development played out in this group. They were developmentally ready for these lessons. I'm convinced that using an approach that brings concepts close to their own lives is an effective one. With this approach, children become more self-aware: they are confronted by their own behavior.

I challenged them to 'be aware' when they feel themselves getting angry and ready to react. If they could recognize it, they could stop and think and ask themselves what they could do to prevent a fight.

— The next week:

They shared with me experiences they had with siblings and friends that they handled differently because of my lessons: Sometimes, they walk away. Sometimes, they realize they are reacting and change their behavior.

The ability to follow-up is so important in this curriculum. I've considered doing one-day workshops for kids, but I'm not sure a workshop will have any long-lasting effect on the way kids think. I watched through the year as kids realized the impact of their behavior. They would try out a technique or do an awareness exercise between my lessons. When I came back to continue with the curriculum, they would talk about their experiences. They would express satisfaction about their successes and question what didn't work. Learning was an ongoing process. They didn't always succeed in changing their behavior. To do this consistently, they would need a level of abstract thought and an ability to think ahead with an understanding of the consequences of their actions that they developmentally don't have yet. However, judging from my discussions with them and the classroom teacher's observations, I believe they gained a larger overall understanding to work with.

A year later, I visited one of the teachers I had worked with using the *Why Is Everybody Picking On Me* curriculum. When I arrived, a mother was there with her two sons. One of her sons was in the fourth-grade group I had taught. The teacher introduced us. The mom asked, "Are you the one who worked with my son's class last year? Thank you! I heard so often, 'Mrs. Fitzell said...'. You would not believe how much your lessons have helped him. It has made a big difference at home!" Webster-Doyle's curriculum had made a difference for the entire family.

Pulling in the 'bully'

I read a story from Why is Everybody Always Picking on Me. *Students answered curriculum questions specifically geared toward the lesson's goals. Role-play was an important part of the activity. The most fascinating occurrence came during this first experience with role-play. All the children wanted to role-play. I told them we would be doing much of it and I would try to pick different people each week so that over the course of time they'd all have opportunities to participate.*

The role-plays focused on two types of bullies. One involved a pushing, punching bully. The other involved a sweet-talking, manipulative bully.

The purpose of the role-play is to identify different types of bullying. We often think of bullying as involving purely physical altercations. Physical bullying is one form of aggression. Verbal bullying, whether aggressive and openly abusive or sly and manipulative, is often more damaging than physical fighting, and unfortunately recognized and addressed much less.

The kids really got the point of the lesson! The neatest thing was that the class 'bully,'[1] Joey, volunteered to do the second role-play. He wanted to play the part of the bully, of course, and half-heartedly said at the end that he had wanted to play the physical bully. He had played the verbal, manipulative bully. The exciting part was that he participated! Last week, during my introductory lesson, he couldn't sit still, wanted nothing to do with the lesson or the homework, and was obviously uncomfortable. This week, even before he volunteered, I had noticed that he was attentive and more relaxed. I really feel that his volunteering to role-play was significant. The classroom teacher later disclosed that she was very surprised to see Joey's positive reaction to the lessons. He was interested and involved. He would run up and stand next to me offering to help me get started. He participated in discussion.

Because I did not pass judgment on bullies, Joey wasn't threatened by the lesson. When we teach conflict education, it is important that we do not label people as bad for having bullying behaviors. The behaviors are unacceptable – but the children are not bad. Bullying behaviors are mistakes. We all bully on occasion when we are angry, depressed, nervous, or frustrated. It does not mean we are bad people. It means we made a mistake. Mistakes are for learning. Bullying behaviors are mistakes, poor choices, or reactions without thought. If we approach teaching children (or adults) about bullying with the attitude that people who bully are bad people, we will alienate the ones we want to reach most. People who bully already have many fears and low self-esteem. If they believe that their already fragile sense of self is in danger of attack during these lessons, a wall will go up around them. They will shut down and not participate. We will lose them and all hope of making a difference in their lives. If I had passed judgment on 'bullies' in my lessons, I would not have had Joey's cooperation. He would have felt criticized, judged, and labeled 'bad'. The classroom teacher initially expected him to react this way because it was generally difficult to keep him focused and participating appropriately during the school day. When he was agitated, it was almost impossible. But now, with one exception (during the conflict education lessons), he was fine.

I took a risk with the fifth graders this week. I read a children's book to them. I was upfront with them and told them what I was doing and that I realized that they might think it was too young for them. I asked them to go with it and I'd let them evaluate me in the end. They really liked the idea of evaluating a teacher. I read Don't Feed the Green Monster *on Tuesday! (Moser, 1991). I think this book is written for adults as well as kids. The author writes to kids in the foreword and tells them to ask their parents to read the book. The kids as a whole really seemed to like it. What was surprising was Joey's reaction to the book. He's the kid with the bullying issues. He's the kid that usually can't get enough of me. He's always up front, volunteering for role-plays, etc. He HATED the book. I've seen this type of reaction from freshmen in high school that have difficulty learning. If a teacher tries to do hands-on activities or anything that appears elementary, they initially get very defensive. Usually, they are the kids who need those activities the most.*

Well, Joey has very poor self-esteem. This book suggests that every time you listen to and believe negative things about yourself, you feed the green monster. The green monster makes your self-esteem go down. It suggests that you pick one day a week, Tuesday, and decide to not feed the Green monster on that day. So on Tuesdays, you only say nice things to yourself. If you make a mistake, you tell yourself that everyone makes mistakes and that mistakes are for learning. It suggests that you make a sign that says, "Don't Feed The Green Monster!" and put it up in your room. A couple of kids were concerned that their friends might think they were weird if they had a sign like that in their room. I suggested that they put it in a place that only they would look, like their drawer or the medicine cabinet. Overall, the kids liked it. Joey, however, kept interrupting with comments like, "This is stupid!", "Yeah, right!", or "I hate this". I felt bad that the lesson affected him this way.

After the story, I told them that they were going to give a self-esteem 'gift' to each other. I handed out pieces of paper and had them fold the paper into a card I told Mrs. Arrow and her aide that I wanted them to participate also. They got in groups of four. Each person wrote their name on the front of their card. Then each person got four sticky labels. Sitting in their groups, they passed their card to the right. The person on the right wrote something kind on a sticky label about the person whose card they had. They then stuck the label in the card and passed it to the right. When they all had their card back, they wrote something nice about themselves, and stuck it in their card. The kids LOVED the activity. The energy in the room was incredible. Mrs. Arrow felt the activity was a hit. The kids were asking her if they could do it another time. I then told the class that they could evaluate the lesson and activity. I passed out the forms I had created for this and they filled them out anonymously. The evaluations confirmed that the activity was appreciated by all. A few more kids than I realized felt the story was too babyish. Many of the kids, however, said they really liked the book and it gave them some good ideas to help them build self-esteem. Several of the kids asked that we do more role-play. The evaluations were a very worthwhile activity. Mrs. Arrow even did one.

Joey never really recovered from the story. When he passed in the evaluation, he behaved rudely. Mrs. Arrow caught it and made him apologize. It was uncomfortable for all of us. Joey's desk is by the door. On the way out, I leaned over to say something positive to him. I had hoped to ease the tension. He reacted loudly, physically moving away, saying "Leave me alone." I immediately regretted trying to approach him. Mrs. Arrow reacted by calling him on his behavior. She was calm and handled it well. But I only felt worse.

I've dealt with special needs kids all of my career. My history with this kid indicated that he might be receptive to a positive comment. I didn't anticipate that he would not. I've had kids do this kind of thing before. I have been trying to remember if there was any consistency or warning in these instances. Usually, the kids were my students, and I knew how to deal with the situation. In this situation, I felt very awkward and uncomfortable.

The following week, Joey was back to his normal, friendly, participating self. Our relationship survived the Green Monster. My purpose in relaying this story is to burst the idealistic bubble that often surrounds conflict education: "If we teach conflict resolution skills, kids will solve problems peacefully, always." I've seen discouraged faces at my workshops: teachers expecting immediate and consistent results from their conflict resolution work. In reality, this doesn't happen. Sometimes, when I am in the midst of a conflict, I have to remind myself that conflict is a normal part of life. There is this little voice in my head that says, "This is what I do for a living! I shouldn't have conflict." Not so! Hopefully, most of the time, I will handle conflicts well. There will be times when I won't. Children, even when trained in conflict resolution skills, will not always handle conflict well. Children's reactions can't be predicted. Issues that push buttons can't be predicted. No one could have predicted Joey's reaction to the book. What we as parents and teachers are doing is planting seeds, nurturing those seeds, and allowing them to grow. This takes time. Sometimes, the plant will wilt. With a little care, it will stand strong once again. Joey finished the year helping me do role-plays with the second graders. He had come a long way!

ROLE-PLAYING AND REAL-LIFE SCENARIOS

We did the role-plays the students made up a few weeks ago. I had groups get together and decide how they would carry out the role-plays. I brought two with me. I had volunteers take those roles. The kids did a great job. I tied the lessons from the role-plays that they created in with the concepts we have been learning in post role-play discussion. They role-played various scenarios that have happened to them in real life. The 'victim' tried various ways of handling the bullies.

Role-playing is what the kids liked the best. I think it is also what helped them the most in acquiring skills. The most popular choices for dealing with conflict were making friends, tricking the bully, and using humor. Using humor could escalate the situation, however. Often, fifth graders mistook sarcasm for humor. I suggested that they be very careful with that technique. Even when I role-played examples to contrast the difference between using humor to diffuse a conflict and using sarcastic humor, some students could not or would not see the difference.

It was interesting how many kids (mostly girls) said that they were uncomfortable being the bully. They said that it felt strange. Yet, there were several who actually liked being the victim! One student, who is often the butt of 'bullying' in the class, said he enjoyed being the victim. I found this interesting. There is something to be gained from being a victim. Hara Estroff Marano, editor of *Psychology Today*, refers in his article on bullying to research done by Debra Pepler. He explains that a victim-bully relationship grows over time into a type of codependent relationship. They need each other, respond to each other, hate each other, yet can't stay away from each other. This relationship "validates each as a special person. If that's not quite how it goes with bullies and their victims, still these children develop a history with each other, and the behavior of each reinforces the other. Call it the bully-victim dance." [2]

THE ROLE OF THE TEACHER

There are some interesting dynamics going on in the fifth-grade group. When I first walked in, one girl came up to me and asked what to do when someone fights you and pulls your hair? All the while, she looked to the side, making eye contact with someone. She wanted someone to hear. She told me that the girl who 'attacked her' is a student in the class. I kept asking her what 'her' part was in this, eventually pointing out that there may have been many things that she could have done differently before the fight. I asked, "Did you do any of them?"

This is where the role of teachers is so very important. Often these situations are brushed off or stifled. When teachers have the awareness and understanding of all the pieces necessary for an effective conflict education program, they then have the tools to turn these situations into an effective learning experience.

At the beginning of our circle, I talked with the group about how we react to people and how those reactions escalate situations. We played some of those out — with me in the role-play. The group was very receptive. Basically, I placed ownership on all of them. If they could have done something to avoid a fight, and didn't, then they were equally responsible for the fight.

UNDERSTANDING THE EMOTION OF CONFLICT

I had them reverse roles occasionally during the role-plays. I asked how it felt to be the victim or bully. Sometimes the bullies would admit that it felt 'good'. They are almost afraid to admit this. They are very uncomfortable with admitting that it (sometimes) feels good to bully. I tell them it is important that they realize that it can feel good — or satisfying — and that that's what the bully gets out of it.

This difficulty to admit is developmental. Fifth graders are also more socially aware and consequently experience some guilt with this admission. I need to stress that feeling the emotions of the characters in the role-plays is extremely important. Unless a child understands what a bully feels when he/she is bullying, that child will not make sense of how to handle the bully. The reverse is also true.

Unless a child understands what a victim feels when victimized, that child cannot have empathy or understanding for the victim. I have students role-play a victim-bully situation, then reverse the roles. This technique works in any conflict.

An interpersonal conflict can often be better understood when the children involved in the conflict or a mediator repeats the point of view and feelings of both parties out loud. By repeating each child's 'story', both children feel heard and validated. Any misinterpretations can be cleared up. If this is taken one step further and the conflict is role-played with the children taking the opposite sides, an even greater understanding can take place. It is difficult to role-play a situation like this without getting into the emotion. Now, it may not be wise to do such a role-play in the heat of the moment. However, when children are calm and willing to work at a resolution, this technique may yield positive results.

BODY LANGUAGE

I pointed out their body language. It was great to ask, "What's her body language telling you right now?" and have the group read it correctly. The people role-playing were totally unaware of their body language or use of personal space. When it was pointed out, and they role-played again, they made major improvements.

Understanding body language is one of the most important skills that you can teach children. Kids are almost completely unaware of its importance and place in a bully-victim scenario. Body language often sends a more powerful message into the world than spoken words. Interviews with people convicted of violent crimes have reinforced the role of body language in an attacker's choice of prey.

Picture the following scenario: A mugger lies in hiding, waiting for the right moment and person to attack. Two people are walking down the street. One person is walking at a quick pace, head held high, looking straight ahead. This person displays an air of confidence in his/her manner. The other person walks slowly, shoulders slumped, looking down at the ground. This person looks unsure of where he/she is going. Which person is the more likely target? The mugger wants easy prey. He/she doesn't want to risk that the victim will turn the tables by fighting back. The latter person is the easy target.

CORPORAL PUNISHMENT

I gave the kids an assignment to look through newspaper fliers, magazines, and movie reviews and to cut out pictures that represented 'bully' to them. They could be pictures of violent toys, cartoons, etc. I wanted them to become aware of the influence their environment has on their behavior and their perception of the world.

Two girls drew pictures of what they said was child abuse. The pictures were of a parent using the buckle end of a belt on a child. I agreed that this was not peaceful and that the buckle of the belt could cause cuts and bruises. I wasn't sure what was safe to say because I would not be surprised if there are children in that class who are disciplined with a strap. I could not say it was peaceful, because corporal punishment is a violent act. In any other relationship in our society, a person could have charges pressed against them for hitting or assaulting another person with or without a 'weapon.'

As classroom teachers, we must, I think, take great care with what we say when the issue of corporal punishment comes up in the classroom. If teachers take a stand against corporal punishment in their classrooms, it may lead to children standing up to their parents or criticizing them for their actions. Children may think their parents are bad for hitting them, or say, "The teacher said you shouldn't spank." This would cause a schism between school and home. It is better to enlist parents' cooperation by working with them to find alternatives to corporal punishment. Provide parent workshops. Help parents to develop other discipline methods. (For information on how to work successfully with parents, see *At Home In Our Schools*, written and published by The Developmental Studies Center.)[3]

There is such a fine line between child abuse, which we want children to report, and corporal punishment. I tried to find a middle ground in my reactions to corporal punishment in the classroom. Some children strongly felt that it was violence. I did not pass judgment on the method, only said that some parents used corporal punishment, and some didn't. Some people believe it is wrong. Other people believe it is right. I didn't share my beliefs, with one exception.

I have shared with my high school students my opinion on corporal punishment. Again, I don't pass judgment. I simply state my beliefs. Some high school students will soon be parents. Many will parent the way they were parented. If I am giving them a different view of corporal punishment, they will make more informed choices when parenting.

Counselors and psychologists I have spoken with take a stronger, more direct approach. Many believe that teachers should tell children that corporal punishment, or at least severe corporal punishment, is not OK. They argue that if adults do not identify abusive patterns for children, children remain unwitting victims. Clearly there is no easy answer.

A final note

Teaching and using conflict resolution skills in conjunction with encouraging personal growth through understanding of the self and of others is a very rewarding path. There is hope for our future. Violence need not prevail as the norm. We need to start with ourselves, and then to teach the children a better way. As we teach in our classrooms and our homes, we need to take care not to be too hard on ourselves or to expect too much too fast. We do the best we can, observe ourselves and our students, reflect, adjust, and continue with faith that what we are doing will make some small difference in the lives that we touch.

Cognitive and Moral Development

POINT OF VIEW

While preschool and lower elementary school children are still developing their natural ability for empathy, upper elementary school children are usually able to see other people's points of view. They are less egocentric and more capable of considering other people's feelings. Children of this age are still searching to justify their own view points and are trying to coordinate their views with the views of others. Because of this, peer pressure becomes a major issue. They are highly competitive with each other, dread making mistakes, and want to be perfect in their own eyes and the eyes of others. Peer pressure is a major influence. Its impact increases as children reach the sixth grade.

WORLD VIEW

The outside world is a reality for this age group. At the younger end of this age group, children's thought processes are still very literal and logical. Thinking is still limited to physical reality. By the sixth grade, the older children will begin the transition to more abstract thought. They are able to relate world events to their understanding of themselves and their lives. They see themselves as members of a society and culture. They can reflect on their responsibility to the world. They believe in the Golden Rule: you should treat others the way you would like them to treat you. They are often at a stage Kohlberg calls the "Good Boy" - "Nice Girl" Orientation (See Appendix A for an explanation of Kohlberg's Stages of Moral Development). At that stage, they have the capacity for true altruism.

When empathy is fostered in children, when they are involved in the democratic process and empowered to make decisions, they will often choose altruistic goals and behaviors. Could we envision a future where altruism replaced adult cynicism?

JUSTICE

Fairness issues are at their peak in these older elementary school children. With the ability to look at the larger world and its inequities, they can find life's unfairness to be discouraging. Nine-year-olds may feel singled out and picked on by parents and teachers, enmeshed in the negativity of this unfairness. Ten-year-olds are more able to see unfairness and to resolve it. Eleven-year-olds may react adversely to their perception of inequity one time, and be able to resolve it the next. Intense emotions play a major role in how the sixth grader handles perceived injustice. Overall, as upper elementary school children move from Kohlberg's stage 2 to his stage 3 thinking, mercy and flexibility temper their judgments. Their view of justice is not as rigid as that of their younger peers.

RULES

Nine- to eleven-year-olds see rules as the result of decisions. The extent to which these decisions involve children's input and mutual consent determines the level of respect they will hold for the rules. At this age, children have a self-image they are intent on living up to. They sincerely want to be good. They have developed a conscience. This conscience is based on an inner standard of what they believe to be right or wrong. Because of these inner standards, rules are apt to be scrutinized for fairness and justice. If the rules evolved out of their standards, they are more apt to be obeyed.

MORAL CHOICES

Upper elementary school children make choices based on their need to be good in their own eyes as well as in those of others. They want to fit into society's norms for good behavior. Their goal is to be loved and accepted, and they may still take criticism and reprimands as rejection. They fear that if they are not 'good enough', they will lose the love and support of significant adults in their lives. Fifth graders are particularly cooperative. They are at an ideal age for conflict resolution training. They love to make deals!

Practical Approaches and Techniques

CURRICULUM

While concepts of world peace can be introduced to fourth through sixth grade students, I still don't believe it is the most effective means of teaching character and conflict education. Using the dynamics of their own personal world and of local community conflicts and issues provides a more meaningful focus.

When we deal with conflict as something that happens in another part of town or in another country, we fail to look at ourselves. Children can separate conflict and character issues from their own lives: "It's the Haitians that have the problem, not me." It is easy to theorize, discuss, and develop solutions to other people's problems. It

> Rather than waiting until violence has been learned and practiced and then devoting increased resources to hiring policemen, building more prisons, and sentencing three-time offenders to life imprisonment, it would be more effective to redirect the resources to early violence prevention programs, particularly for young children and preadolescents.
> — APA Commission on Violence and Youth

is much more difficult to look at oneself. But often the more difficult path is the path to greater growth. Fifth graders are particularly ready for conflict resolution skills. This age can be very insightful. They've lived long enough to have some meaningful experiences. They are cognitively ready to look at their role in society and their responsibility within their classroom, family, and community. Although they are still very concrete thinkers, they can think beyond themselves.

My personal preference for an age-appropriate curriculum for this age group is Terrence Webster-Doyle's *Why is Everybody Always Picking on Me?* This curriculum, complemented with self-esteem, community-building, and relationship skills activities, provides a solid base for understanding the self and its conditioning as well as for understanding why people bully, why people are victims, and what can be done to change this behavior.

Integrate music into the curriculum

As I stated in previous chapters, using music is a dynamic and creative way to teach concepts of peace, cooperation, and sharing. Children's music often addresses these concepts. Fourth through sixth graders may feel too big for this music. I think, where appropriate, it can be presented in a way that is acceptable to the group. This judgment is left to the individual teacher and the personality of the group. If the teacher is comfortable with the medium and is able to address any objections with humor, it can be successful. Popular adult music also deals with peace, tolerance, and world harmony. This music may be more difficult to find because it is not all in one place, but it exists. (Check the box titled "Music Resources for Upper Elementary Grades" on the next page). Lyrics can be the springboard for discussion. Often we allow older children to label certain "multi-sensory" teaching techniques as "babyish." Because these techniques are often essential to students' learning style, this labeling can be detrimental to their education.

Use children's literature as a tool for exploring emotions

Literature and story telling are wonderful tools for helping children to identify and deal with their emotions and behavior. It is especially powerful when we can relate events in the story to the children's lives. In *You Can't Say, You Can't Play*, Vivian Gussin Paley states the power of story beautifully: "Fortunately, the human species does not live by debate alone. There is an alternate route, proceeding less directly, but often better able to reach the soul of a controversy. It is story."

> See Additional Resources for some excellent children's books.

Music Resources for Upper Elementary Grades

The following organizations are networks of musicians who offer themselves as a resource. They have monthly songswaps.

People's Music Network for Songs of Freedom and Struggle, PMN/SFS, c/o Sarah Underhill, RR#1 Box 193, Kerhonkson, NY 12446, (914) 626-4507. Internet address: http://world.std.com/~pmn/#monthly.

Freedom Song Network (FSN), 131 Mangels, San Francisco, CA 94131, (415) 753-0245. Internet address: http://www.emf.net/~cheetham/gfrnrk-1.html.
Affirms through songs and music the right of all peoples, at home and abroad, to establish more free, just, and equal societies and to live in peace.

The Children's Music Network, PO Box 1341, Evanston, IL 60204-1341, (847) 733-8033, Internet Address:
http//www.cowboy.net/~mharper/CMN.html
"We meet and stay in touch to share songs and ideas about children's music ... to inspire each other about the empowering ways adults and young people can communicate through music ... and to be a positive catalyst for education and community-building through music."
The Children's Music Network publishes a journal called Pass It On!
Call or write for a sample.

Internet Resources:

Children's Music Web!: http://www.childrensmusic.org/
This is a non-profit organization dedicated to music for kids.

Songs for Social Change Home Page:
http://www.globalvisions.org/cl/sfsc/
Songs for Social Change (SFSC) is a network linking Los Angeles-based topical songwriters with one another, with performing artists, and with activist organizations. SFSC provides a social and organizational context for songwriters dedicated to promoting positive social change with their music. Workshops, concerts, and benefit performances are some of the activities carried out by the organization. Since its inception, more than 400 persons have shared songs and information through this nexus.

Also, do a keyword search for songs by Cat Stevens, Pete Seeger, Charlie King, Ross Altman, Jim Savarino, Kristina Olsen, Anna Fisher, Joel Pelletier, Positively Negative (Bill Rotberg and Ray Rish), Darryl Purpose, Dana Lyons, Dan Scanlon, Bob Franke, Bob Dylan, Arlo Guthrie, and Jackson Browne. Many of these songwriters have web pages.

Why Is Everybody Always Picking On Me:

Boys Will Be Boys

Author
Terrence Webster-Doyle

Illustrator
Rod Cameron

Publisher
Atrium Society, 1991

Pages
1 – 11

Reading Level
Grade 4

Interest Level
Grades 4 - 8

Synopsis

Someone hits you in the back with a ball. It hurts. You react by turning and threatening him before he can explain. He apologizes and says it was an accident. You continue to threaten him, enjoying the audience and the sense of power. The playground supervisor, Mrs. Potter, comes toward you full steam screaming about how awful you are. Never allowing you to speak, she threatens you and calls you a bully. You run off calling names behind you. You meet your friends behind a downtown store. You smoke stolen cigarettes and throw rocks at bottles. When it gets dark, you go home. Your sister immediately starts picking on you, putting you down. She compares you to your brother Jason. She says he's a better brother. You know that he's not so nice as everyone thinks he is. He gets what he wants by sweet-talking and manipulating people. When you were younger, Jason would beat you up all of the time. You turn the TV channel to watch Rambo. He's your hero. You want to be like Rambo. Your dad comes home. He's been drinking. You don't get along with him. He compares you to your brother Jason. He makes excuses for working late. You turn back to Rambo: "You fix your eyes on that flickering screen, hands sweaty, fists clenched, waiting for the big kill."

Objectives[1]

To gain the understanding and awareness that
- bullies are people who are angry
- victims are people who are afraid

Procedure

Read aloud the story "Boys Will Be Boys" in Why Is Everybody Always Picking on Me? Show illustrations.

---

[1]This lesson was adapted from Webster-Doyle, *Why Is Everybody Always Picking On Me? A Special Curriculum for Young People to Help Them Cope With Bullying* (1984). Middlebury: Atrium Society Publications

Discussion

Ask

- Who are the 'bullies'[2] in this story? Is there more than one person who bulldozes, threatens, and intimidates?
- What about

- the boy who threw the ball	- Mrs. Potter	- the sister
- Jason	- Rambo	- the father

- You
- What behaviors cause you to label them 'bullies'?
- Do they browbeat, tease, or boss? How?
- Do you think they are scared?
- What do you think each of them is scared of?
- Do you think they are angry?
- What do you think they are angry about?

Discuss

What do 'bullies' have in common? What are they feeling? Why might they act tough? How do the victims of 'bullies' feel? Do they feel any of the same emotions that the bullies' feel?

Conclude

We are all human. We all have times when we are scared or angry. That is when we are most likely to act like a 'bully' or a victim.

We are all human beings who make mistakes. It does not mean we are bad people if we make mistakes. Mistakes are for learning.

[2]The term 'bully' is used for ease of expression and readability. It is not intended to indicate that it is acceptable to label people 'bullies'. Take care that children understand that people have bullying behaviors. It is the *behavior* that is a problem. It is not OK to name-call and label people 'bullies'.

Role-play

Role-play to practice conflict resolution and social skills. Role-plays can be taken from actual scenarios that occur in the class. Students should be involved in writing their own role-plays and in acting them out. When doing this, be careful that the scripts do not single out specific children or groups. Children of this age love to dramatize and make videos of their dramatizations. Videos are an excellent tool for analysis, discussion, and improvement of techniques.

Journal entry

We have been focusing on skills. Last session, I introduced the class to the 12 Ways To Walk Away With Confidence (Webster-Doyle, 1991). I used overheads and interactive examples with the students that I spontaneously and randomly staged. The kids loved the approach. This session, I had them sit in a circle on the floor. I thought this group of shy, giggly fourth graders would resist role-play. On the contrary, they did not. I almost think my approach to choosing partners may have made a major difference. Rather than asking for volunteers, I started on my left and set the expectation that I wanted everyone to participate. I would achieve this by having the first two on my left start with a bully-victim role-play. Then after the role-play and discussion, the person who was the bully remained to be the victim in the next role-play. The next person on the left took a turn as the bully. This pattern worked well. No one refused a turn. They made up their own role-play. When they were stuck, children in the group offered options. We watched body-language and tone of voice. I demonstrated a few times how what was said "sarcastically" would sound and feel totally different if said with humor or kindness. The teacher really liked the lesson.

A SIDE NOTE: Two boys who did the first role-play seem to be two in the class who are picked on a lot, and possibly do some bullying themselves. One obviously has emotional issues. While they were role-playing, a boy directly across from me was whispering to the boy next to him, and giggling. It appeared to me that he was making comments about the two doing the role-play. I stared at him (I did not want to disturb the role-play) until he noticed I was watching. He stopped.

Before the second role-play, I firmly, and with 'moral feeling', spoke to the group about the need for everyone to feel safe to do role-play. I defined what was needed to feel safe. I specifically pointed out that whispering and giggling was not appropriate. I did NOT single out the guilty party, but I spoke to the group. I told them that I would not tolerate such behavior. I felt what I was doing was important. If they did not want to participate, that was fine, they could leave the group. All went well, without incident after that.

In order for role-play to be meaningful and effective, all the children involved need to feel safe and respected. They need to know that poking fun at people role-playing either during the session or afterwards will not be tolerated. They need to understand why such behavior will not be allowed. And they need to know the consequences of breaking the respect rule. These parameters need to be established before role-play begins. Given my experience, a reminder of the rules prior to each role-play session would be helpful. Upper elementary school children already fear the reactions of their peers. They don't want to be teased. They are afraid that if they say the wrong thing, someone will make fun of them. These fears will destroy efforts at role-play. A safe environment must be established before role-play can begin.

Use real-life scenarios

If a conflict occurs in the class, when possible, role-play alternatives. Have the class as a group come up with alternatives. All brainstormed alternatives are possible options. It is important that student responses are received without judgment. Talk about the potential positive and negative consequences of an action instead.

AT SCHOOL AND AT HOME

The media's impact on our culture

Life doesn't happen in a bubble. The world around our children forms the backdrop for developing attitudes, belief systems, fears, and reactions. This world and its impact on our culture and belief systems must be addressed with our children so they can operate from a standpoint of awareness rather than blindness and ignorance. Joel Spring, professor of education at the State University of New York College at New Paltz, denounces the impact of the media on our culture: "The government officials, educators, and foundation leaders responsible for the development of the Corporation for Public Broadcasting and the Children's Television Workshop conceded to commercial television the determination of mass culture".[4] In other words, the media are shaping American culture. If we blindly accept the images the media present (bad guys are dark, good guys are super human and their violence in the name of justice is heroic and desirable, females are sex objects, etc.), we become slaves to a money-making electronic machine. With awareness of the media's messages we can look at our reactions, attitudes, and beliefs with some understanding of their root causes. Only then can we begin positive change.

Discuss with children the influence of the media and their impact on people's belief systems and prejudices. If children are watching MTV, discuss the images portrayed in the videos. How do they portray violence, women, racial stereotypes? Explain desensitization. What is it? How does it affect our attitudes? React with 'moral feeling' to media portrayals that are detrimental to students' well-being. Explain why you feel the way you do, without preaching. Children need to know you care about how they are developing as human beings.

Encourage the growth of children's natural empathy

Praise or notice a child for sharing or showing concern for others. For this age group, it is best to praise quietly so as not to embarrass the receiver. You might say, "I noticed that you helped James with his homework today. He looked frustrated when he couldn't figure out the math problem. That was a very kind thing

Role-play scenarios

The following role-play ideas were written by
upper elementary school children.

Bully: "Give me your bike!"

Bully: "Let's go smoke behind the school."
Victim: "I can't. I'll get in trouble with my dad."
Bully: "Don't be such a daddy's boy! Come on!"

Bully: "Hey! You got the last chocolate milk in the cafe! I want it!"

Bully: "I'm thirsty, Bozo, and I have no money.
          Go get me a Coke, Bozo, now, in that store over there."

Bully: "Hey, Shrimp, give me your basketball."
Victim: "No, why should I?"
Bully: "Because I'll pound you into the ground!"

Bully: "You are so fat, you look like an elephant!"

Bully: "Your clothes don't match. They are ugly!"

to do." Be specific when noting positive behavior. Also, saying "I noticed..." takes the fluff out of the praise we habitually dish out. Pointing out emotion helps to identify the feelings with which to empathize.

Even as adults, we may not be able to identify what we are feeling in conflict situations. Nine- to eleven-year-olds still at times need help identifying their feelings. They may be angry, but what is the underlying emotion causing that anger? Help children find the vocabulary for their emotions so that they can identify their feelings. A good way to do this is to get one of those posters with all the faces on it and to name of the emotions below the faces. Even though I recommend this for the lower elementary school child, I think it is an excellent tool for people of all ages to figure out the 'word' for what they are feeling. They are available through Free Spirit Press and other sources (See "Additional Resources").

Tattling

The "It's not Fair" comment tends to peak amongst fourth graders. Children seem to notice every other child's infractions. Tattling is still common. Some children refuse to tattle because of social pressure, but they may 'get even' instead. Help them to become aware of their anger over an injustice. Teach them to stop and think before they react. What are the alternatives to tattling or retaliation?

Validate children's feelings. When children tattle, often all that they need is validation of their feelings. A question such as, "How did that feel when Janie called you that name?" lets children feel heard. To follow up with empathy regarding their feelings and options for what they can do next usually leaves them feeling like they've been heard and now have tools to handle the situation.

Teachers and parents often discourage tattling. By fifth grade, tattling is a major social taboo. The relief that upper elementary teachers and parents have from tattling holds hidden dangers, though. I asked a fifth-grade class if they would tell if they knew someone had a gun in their backpack. To my astonishment, half of the class said they would *not* tell. They explained that it would be tattling. It's social suicide to tattle. Also, telling might put them in danger. I realized that children need to be taught that telling an authority when someone has a weapon or someone is physically threatened is following a safety rule. Kids are familiar with safety rules regarding fire, going with strangers, and riding bicycles. They have a certain amount of respect for these rules. They are accepted. Personal safety needs to be addressed in the same way: when we use authority to insure personal safety, it is not tattling – it is following a safety rule. The consequences of not telling must be made clear to the children.

Cliques

Cliques are common with this age group and are developmentally 'normal'. Minimize the negative impact of cliques with community-building activities, rearranging seating periodically, and helping students to get to know each other[5]

At home, provide opportunities for children to meet other children in the community. Encourage understanding and acceptance of people's differences. When your fifth grader comes home expressing disdain at another child's failings, listen and empathize, but also help your child to see why the other child might behave or look the way he/she does. Provide varying scenarios that could result in the ostracized child's behavior. Help your child to understand why people are different rather than allowing him/her to judge them.

Hold class/family meetings

Guidelines for class and family meetings are outlined in Chapter Two. The basic structure remains the same. What changes now is the level of involvement of the children in the planning of the meetings and the types of problems that come up. By the time children are nine or ten, they can be taking turns running the meetings. This gives them another opportunity to gain a sense of leadership and empowerment. Upper elementary school children at Kohlberg's stage 3 of moral development are also challenged to consider the welfare of the whole family or class in the meetings. They will need to look beyond their own needs in the process, which will enhance the development of moral reasoning. In a family or class meeting, children and adults need to listen respectfully to each other, to allow each other to voice differing opinions, to accept each other's decisions, and as often as possible to make decisions by consensus. These are valuable relationship and conflict resolution skills for children. The modeling done at these meetings will provide lessons that will last a lifetime.

> **See Chapter Two for guidelines on setting up family meetings.**

Considerations for single parents and blended families

If you are a single parent or have a blended family, family meetings are even more critical to establishing ritual, consistency, and stability in a difficult set of family circumstances. Divorce is disruptive. Children of a divorced couple feel powerless and out of control. Having a voice in family meetings helps children to gain back some control and provides a non-threatening forum for them to express their feelings. Children of blended families inevitably face conflict between family members. Emotional issues can be intense. Family meetings will help to establish the blended family as a unified group where each member is cared for, listened to, and valued. These meetings can make a major difference in how well the family functions. (See Chapter Two for a sample of a family meeting agenda.)

EMOTIONS, DISCIPLINE, AND THE GROWTH OF EMPATHY

Bad boy! Bad girl!

Separate the children from their behavior. I cringe when I hear parents reprimand children with words that reinforce 'bad boy' or 'bad girl' attitudes. At this age, you might hear parents say, "You're no good!" or "You're just like your old man!" When parents have divorced or separated, the latter is a devastating blow and incredibly damaging to family relationships. The children really believe that they are bad children unworthy of love. Children cannot analyze these words and determine that their parents are talking about their *behavior* and not *them*. Even when you tell children that it is their *behavior* that you don't like, but that you like/love *them*, they still may be uncertain. The emotion is so much more powerful than rational thought on this issue. If you want children to believe in themselves so that they can make good choices, separate the child from the behavior.

React with 'moral feeling'

When a child hurts another child intentionally, react with 'moral feeling' (Lickona, 1992). Explain how the behavior hurts the other child and point out the expressions and feelings of the hurt child. (Some children will continue to have difficulty reading expressions, and need to learn this skill.) With this age group, I will often add a discussion about point of view and the reasons we may hurt others. This discussion may take different forms depending on the individual circumstances, but having the discussion is important. Children are beginning to reject doing what is 'right' simply because a grown-up says it is right. They need to understand how you feel about their hurtful behavior and why you feel that way. They also need to begin to think about what it may feel like to walk in the other person's shoes.

Name-calling

Don't ignore name-calling. Address it. Name-calling is a prevalent form of bullying in this age group. It is often tolerated because it is an age-old problem that seems inevitable. Even if it is age-old and inevitable, it must be addressed. Verbal bullying is often more emotionally scarring than physical abuse. Children need to understand the consequences of the behavior.

I did a survey of fourth through sixth graders. I asked them to write down which problem in their life was so important that they would like me to write to their parents and teachers about it. Many of the children listed name-calling, teasing, and being laughed at as their biggest problems. Some adults might say that these are minor problems compared to other traumas in life. Realize, however, that such verbal violence is slowly eroding the self-esteem of its victims. Name-calling and teasing cause wounds that can take a lifetime to heal. A bruise or a broken bone heals much more quickly.

Listen to their problems:

" *Somethings that really bothers me is that people call me fat and they tell me that I'm short. So sometimes I think I should go on a diet so I'm not made fun of.*"

" *I'm afraid that my clothes are not cool for my friends. I don't like to be made fun of.*"

" *Everyone calls me fat.*"

" *A lot of people make fun of me because I am part Chinese. Or because of my name. Or I am too small.*"

" *People bother me because I'm different. I'm adopted.*"

" *Peapul don't like me bekus im difrent.*"

" *I don't have any problems except the way I look.*"

Require restitution

When a child hurts another accidentally or intentionally, assist the child who did the hurting to figure out a way to make restitution. It is important that the child who caused the hurt is part of the decision to make restitution and that the other child is comfortable with it. Do not force apologies. Instead, encourage care: helping with school work, inviting the person into a game, a kind word, etc.

> **For more parenting resources on the subject of discipline, see Annotated Bibliography.**

Provide consistency

Provide the consistency necessary for children to feel secure in their environment. As I have stated in Chapter Three, it's important to have a set schedule and routine. Don't be so rigid in following a schedule and curriculum, however, that 'teachable moments,' spontaneous discoveries, discussion, and authentic learning cannot take place.

Involve the children in establishing meaningful rules and consequences. There are many ways to do this and many resources to help you. As I stated in Chapter Three, I particularly like Glasser's Reality Therapy and Choice Theory approach to discipline. The techniques based on these theories provide a solid foundation for behavior management. *Educating for Character* by Tom Lickona includes an excellent discussion of moral discipline and provides parents and teachers with a framework for effective discipline (Chapter Seven).

> **Refer to Chapter Three for a more detailed description of Reality Therapy and Choice Theory.**

SUMMARY

Curriculum

- Keep the curriculum related to students' lives.
- Integrate music into the curriculum.
- Use appropriate literature to teach and discuss handling emotions, behavior, and conflict.
- Role-play to practice conflict resolution and social skills.
- Use real-life scenarios for role-play.

At School and at Home

- Discuss the media and their impact on students' belief systems and prejudices.
- Encourage the growth of children's natural empathy.
- Quietly 'notice' when young people are caring towards one another.
- Validate children's feelings.
- Minimize the negative impact of cliques.
- Hold class/family meetings.

Emotions, discipline, and the growth of empathy

- Involve youth in establishing meaningful rules and consequences.
- Separate the children from their behavior.
- When children are hurtful or cruel, react with 'moral feeling.'
- Address name-calling.
- Require restitution.
- Provide the consistency necessary for children to feel secure in their environment.

Hear their plea!

I called a fifth-grade teacher who I previously worked with. I wanted to know what she believed was the single most important issue or problem facing upper elementary school children. Without hesitation, she announced: peer pressure. She explained that this seems to be the age where it hits: it appears to take full hold of children by the middle of the fifth grade. She suggested, however, that I ask the kids themselves. What a great idea! I did a survey of fourth, fifth, and sixth graders. I explained that I was writing a book for parents and teachers to help kids and that I needed to know what issue or problem in their life was most important for me to write about. Another way to think about the problem was, " If you could find someone to talk to your teachers and parents to help them understand something very important to you, what would that something be?"

One hundred and forty-four students answered my question. Definite themes emerged. Fifty percent of the responses involved problems with bullying and/or relationships. Approximately twenty-five percent felt that schoolwork, homework, and grades were their biggest problem. Nineteen percent had concerns about sports and fears about junior high school. Six percent didn't write any problems down.

Relationships and bullying, therefore, are the dominant issues in this age group. These kids rarely used the word 'bullying' in their problem statements, but they described it. In various ways they expressed their need to fit in, to be accepted and liked. They expressed this need when writing about their school life *and* home life.

Relationship issues are a significant concern of fourth, fifth, and sixth graders. Developmentally, however, they are in very different places from each other. Fourth graders (typically nine-year-olds) are at a transition stage, evolving from the little kid to the big kid. Fifth graders (typically ten-year-olds) are at their peak, at a stage of equilibrium, generally happy about their lives. Sixth graders (typically eleven-year-olds) are in disequilibrium, happy one minute, devastated the next! Given their developmental differences, one would expect a significant difference between the grade levels in the types of responses they gave. Surprisingly, if I took the grade levels off the survey sheets, I wouldn't be able to identify the age by the concern.

When we consider the importance of modeling behavior for children, all we need to do is read their concerns to see where we need to improve. Many children wrote of family conflicts. Most centered on sibling rivalry. Here are some excerpts from their responses:

A fifth-grade boy described a troublesome situation with his brother: "My brother is bothering me at home. He has been throwing spit at me and my parents aren't able to stop him." A fifth-grade girl wrote of difficulty with her brother: "My brother is kind of mentel and It makes me mad when he gets into a rage and when he does that, I start to tell him things that I kind of don't mean. I just want him to be normal." Another girl wrote, "My mom always yells at me when somthing goes wrong. And It's rilly my sisters falt and I get all the blame." Some focused on parent relationships. "I am having truble with my parents. My mom dose not like my dads mom. She dose not go with us when we go to her house. My mom and my dad are all ways fighting," wrote a fourth grader. One perceptive fifth grader identified her most important problem: "My dad smokes and he quit. But he started and I know but he does not know." In this situation, parent modeling has broken down.

Most of the children's concerns centered on peer pressure and acceptance. A fifth-grade boy wrote, "I hate it when kids tease and punch other people. I don't like people that are mean to others." Children expressed concern not only over other children teasing but also over the pressure of joining in the 'fun'. "When some of my friends start to fight, I don't like it because they have me fight, too," said a fifth grader. This pressure was very real. The possibility of his being ostracized by friends because he took a stand against fighting was confirmed by the statement of a fourth-grade girl: "I always thought my friends would never let me down. But one day it shocked me, my friend left me for a bully."

The upper elementary school children I worked with were extremely peer conscious. I remember the fifth-grade teacher stating that the group she had was more emotional and sensitive than any group she has ever had. My observations confirmed hers. The fifth graders were sensitive to what others thought of them and said about them. They were concerned with how others looked at them. The pressure to conform was tremendous, yet the major complaint of the girls was, "She's copying me. It's annoying!" Dagger eyes would fly across the room when subtle references to recess battles came up. Most conflicts occurred during recess, at gym class, on the bus, and during less stuctured times. As one fifth-grade boy stated, "Recess, always be on guard because every recess I get beat up." Recess is usually somewhat supervised. The bus, however, is extremely difficult to monitor. A fourth-grade girl attested to this difficulty: "I know a boy who really bugs me. He hurts me and makes fun of me. He likes to do it on the bus."

A fifth-grade girl commented: "The thing that is bothering me the most is when my friends make fun of me, pull my hair and kick dirt at me and step on my feet. The second thing is when my friend says something that you do not want anyone to know and she tells the whole world. And when you want to read your friends poem and she pinches you really hard and you tell her to let go and when she does you have this big red mark on your hand and it really hurts," laments a fifth-grade girl. What strikes me is that she referred to her tormentors as her *friends!*

As adults, we might see the incongruity in this statement. Consider, however, how often friends, young and old, find humor in putting each other down, teasing each other, and sometimes being downright cruel to each other. How often do people, especially females, young or old, know how to set boundaries for what is acceptable behavior in a friendship? Listen to a more subtle form of teasing related by a fourth-grade girl: "This is about my height. I wish I was shorter. I think I am too tall for my age. People keep teasing me because I'm tall for my age." Body image is such an issue for girls. Constant reference to body shape and size is dehumanizing and demoralizing for females. The problem is not completely limited to girls. One boy wrote, "I don't like being made fun of for making mistakes or having braces." Another boy, a fourth grader, was also taunted because of his appearance: "They like to put my neck under their arm and make me walk to certain places. People call me Chinese. But I'm not. This annoys me a lot."

I had started out with the question, "If you could find someone to talk to your teachers and parents to help them understand something very important to you, what would that something be?" You've read the answers. These answers came from fifty percent of the survey sample who identified relationship and bullying issues as their main concern. They were more important to them than academics, sports, or video games. In isolation, most of these complaints may seem trivial to an adult. They were not trivial to these children. They have asked me to ask you to understand. They need help. Hear their plea!

Chapter 5

THE JUNIOR HIGH ADOLESCENT

Pulling teeth

I'll never forget one of my first workshops for teens 'Make a Difference Today for Tomorrow'. In the early days of my conflict education workshops, I worked with a partner. We were a great team because our collected experience covered every age group and many of the interest areas of our participants. He was a martial artist and businessman with experience as a parent and youth group leader. I was a teacher and new parent with years of experience working with older adolescents. That first year, my partner John and I were scheduled to do a workshop for junior high school and high school students on verbal and physical self-defense. Although I had spent my entire teaching career working with adolescents, I had never worked with junior high students. John had worked with young teens in youth groups. He also raised four children through those years. I figured that we had the bases covered. Everything would be fine.

The high school group was scheduled first. We introduced ourselves and followed with our planned discussion and activities. The workshop consisted of some discussion, some role-play, and some instruction of physical self-defense skills. These older teens were vocal participants. It went well. John and I felt successful. At the end of the session, we were ready for the junior high school group.

They walked in, shoulders slumped slightly, in twos and threes, converging together in a corner of the room. Most were quiet. There was one student who was quite exuberant. The others laughed at his antics. They appeared to come from a different world. They were nothing like the elementary students I had worked with, and quite different from their older peers. It was disconcerting. I hoped that John knew how to speak their language.

John and I introduced ourselves to the group. They stared. Some wore sheepish smiles. The 'one' challenged us. He wanted to know if we going to show them how to beat the crap out of someone. We said no. We gave a synopsis of our hour together. We would talk a little about our attitudes and beliefs, about bullying and what it is, and about how we react to bullying. Then we would show them some very basic skills for getting out of tough situations, such as a hand or a choke hold.

With much encouragement, they slowly spread themselves out into a semi-circle. Then, they stared. We began our discussion. They stared some more. We asked provocative questions. They stared. Eventually we were able to achieve a minimum of discussion. It was like pulling teeth! We gave them a five-minute break. We needed it!

John and I looked at each other with the full realization that this wasn't working. We decided to attempt the physical skills' portion of the workshop next. At least they wouldn't be put on the spot to talk. After the break, we lined the students up in pairs. We showed them a basic move to get out of a hand hold. The boys still wanted to know how they could "beat the crap out of some-one." They made these strange noises while imitating Bruce Lee. The girls gig-gled. We explained the purpose of self-defense moves. The goal was not to hurt other people. It was to get out of difficult situations using physical defense as a last resort. Once settled, they enjoyed themselves.

I believe that they learned something. I'm not sure what. I decided that one-hour workshops — cold — do not work with this age group. They are much too fearful of making mistakes, being silly, or attracting attention to themselves. Twelve- to fourteen-year-olds need time to warm up to a situation. They need to feel safe. They need to see the relevance of what they are doing to their own lives. This can't be accomplished in an hour. — Live and learn!

Cognitive And Moral Development

POINT OF VIEW

Twelve- and thirteen-year-old children are at a major tran-sition point in their lives, cognitively, physically, and morally. They are able to see other people's points of view. They can be very empathetic. These young adolescents see their view as one of many views. They see their personal role in social and cultural terms. They can understand world issues, consider them, and be profoundly insightful. They are self-aware. They can differentiate between fact and fantasy.

RESPONSIBILITY

Children of this age group need to be seen as evolving young adults ready to contribute responsibly to society. Twelve- and thirteen-year-olds can be given responsibilities for school and community involvement and do an excellent job.

They may have excuses for why their homework isn't done or their room or locker isn't clean. Yet, they can run an after-school activity, help with Special Olympics, tutor younger children, and baby-sit.

SOCIAL AWARENESS

Twelve-year-olds are social beings. They are extremely conscious of peer expectations, judgments, and criticism. These are the years that female self-esteem plummets. Self-consciousness about appearance and other people's opinions takes tremendous mental and emotional energy for both sexes of this age. They want to fit in. They don't want to stick out. They need to feel very, very safe before they will risk opening up in discussion or role-play. Therefore community-building is essential to success when you're trying to teach aspects of character education and conflict resolution.

RULES

Rules provide a structure for cooperation. At this stage you will find the closest correlation between the consciousness of rules and the practice of them. The driving force for rule adherence at this age is the teens' desire to be understood, accepted, and involved in the decision-making process. If they are developing morally, they may choose their behavior based on rules that have been agreed upon by 'the group.' These teens, especially males, view what is right as what contributes to society or the group. They will take the point of view of the system that makes the rules as opposed to that of any individual rule maker.

MORAL CHOICES

Morally, twelve- and thirteen-year-olds have reached the 'stage of equity.' At this stage, if children receive a command that they consider unjust, they will consider other factors in their decision about whether or not to comply. Remember, the nine- to eleven-year-old might refuse to comply simply on the issue of justice. Early teens, especially girls, will consider relationships. The age of the person making the command, friendliness, and emotional attachment may figure into the teens' decision to obey. Choices are freely made. Teens may agree to obey not 'because they have to do what an adult says' but rather because it would be a nice thing to do.

Practical Approaches and Techniques

CURRICULUM

Integrate music into the curriculum

Music is still a wonderful teaching tool at this age. The trick is to find music that these young adolescents can relate to. At an age when kids are less likely to readily accept the opinions of their teachers or parents, music can open their mind. A musician is often much more impressive to pre adolescent youth than a parent or teacher. Play songs with a theme, have the students analyze and discuss the songs' message. Have a follow-up, have students write their own words to a

> *For a more in-depth discussion of music in the classroom and some excellent resources for this purpose, see Chapter Four.*

song. I have used environmental songs with young teens to encourage social responsibility and awareness. The unit has always been a highlight of my curriculum. When I have used music, students were motivated and attentive. The most rewarding result was that they remembered the lessons.

Social Studies

This is the age when conflict education and character education can be tied into current events, social studies, and literature if the relevance of the topics and issues to the students' lives is established. It is still very important to help students make the connection between what is happening 'out there' and what is happening in their lives.

The following curricula are very helpful:

- *Facing History and Ourselves*, by Facing History and Ourselves National Foundation
- *War: What is it Good For?* by Terrence Webster-Doyle
- *Violence Prevention Curriculum for Adolescents* by Debra Prothrow-Stith
- *Education for Development: A Teacher's Resource for Global Learning* by Susan Fountain

Teach conflict resolution skills

Creative conflict resolution skills, mediation techniques, and Education for Peace[1] responses to conflict are effective tools for students to acquire. These young adolescents are attempting to deal with volatile emotions, changing bodies, and loyalty shifts from family to peers – all of which creates tremendous conflict in their lives. Teens unable to deal with the conflict and changes in their lives are more at risk for substance abuse, physical fighting, eating disorders, and school failure. Providing them with tools to resolve conflict and to understand self will decrease the potential for engagement in destructive behaviors.

> *History students were significantly superior in their understanding of how individuals' decisions are affected by their society and in the complexity of their reasoning about issues such as leadership, exclusion, and conflict resolution.*
> **— Thomas Lickona,**
> **Educating for Character**

Win-win negotiation techniques and peer mediation programs provide the opportunity for students to learn valuable conflict resolution, communication, and listening skills. They are an important part of the conflict education process. When used as a part of the process rather than as the entire process, the skills are greatly effective.

When teaching conflict resolution skills, we should remember that the root of conflict must also be addressed. Unfortunately, many schools use peer mediation as the 'Band-Aid' for a bigger problem. They incorporate peer mediation programs without addressing the underlying cause of conflict. This works for a segment of the student population for a while. It does not, however, address conflict across the board. Consequently, it is questionable whether the majority of students, trained and untrained, can use the skills in the heat of the moment, or off of the school premises. If none of the other aspects of character and conflict education are addressed, long-term results will not be realized.

Role-play! Role-play! Role-play!

We can tell kids how to act, what to say, and what to think, but until they *experience* other ways of handling conflicts through role-play or in real life, they will not master the skills. A role-play can simply look like this: "We've agreed on what you want to say the next time this happens. Now, let's try it out. Say it to me like you'll say it the next time." Role-plays can be taken from actual scenarios that occur in the class. Students should be involved in writing their own role-plays and acting them out. Be careful that the role-play scripts do not single out specific children or groups of children.

If a conflict occurs in the class, role-play alternatives when possible. Have the class as a group come up with alternatives. All brainstormed alternatives are possible options. It is important that student responses are received without judgment. Talk about the potential positive and negative consequences of an action.

CONFLICT[1]

Relationships - family, friends, at work and at school - are important.
Eventually each one experiences challenging conflict.
Some survive. Others do not. Conflict can be good.
Or it can be bad. Big or small, what matters is how we handle it.
Let's grow in our problem-solving skills.
Venture into the realm of resolution.
Endeavor to work through life's conflicts.

Come to understand the root of conflict. Remember:
One solution to one conflict is not the whole answer.
New ways must be used in different situations and relationships.
Find and use different styles: a teddy bear may soothe.
Let sharks be forcers; owls will confront and foxes compromise.
In case of turtles, get out of your shell and progress is made.
Communication and compromise will help relationships grow.
Together we can make conflict work for us.

- - -

ACTIVITY
Have students earn a LICENSE FOR FIGHTING FAIR![2]
1. Introduce the rules for fighting fair[3]
2. In order to earn a license, students must
   ▪ memorize the rules
   ▪ role-play the application of the rules until proficient
   ▪ use the rules in a real situation at least once.

> ### License for Fighting Fair!
> ### Name:_____
> ### Rules:
> 1. Identify the problem.
> 2. Focus on the problem.
> 3. Attack the problem, *not* the person.
> 4. Listen with an open mind.
> 5. Treat a person's feelings with respect.
> 6. Take responsibility for your actions.
>
> _____ Date:_____

[1]Conflict box contributed by Carrie Jane Keniston, 1995
[2]Idea contributed by Carrie Jane Keniston, 1996
[3]The Rules for Fighting Fair poster and curriculum materials is available from: The Grace Contrino Abrams Peace Education Foundation, Inc. 3550 Biscayne Blvd., Suite 400, Miami, Florida 33137-3854

AT SCHOOL AND AT HOME

Encourage social responsibility, empathy, and self-esteem

Encourage students to become involved in community projects such as soup kitchens, tutoring circles, or school jobs. Such projects, either as part of the curriculum or as extra-curricular activities, have a significant impact on young teens' sense of self-worth. They also promote the growth of empathy because teens see others whose problems are 'worse than their own.'

Discuss the media's impact on students' belief systems and prejudices

If teens are watching MTV, discuss the images portrayed in the videos. How do they portray violence, women, or racial stereotypes? Explain desensitization. What is it? How does it affect our attitudes? React with 'moral feeling' to media portrayals that are detrimental to students' well-being. If young teens are watching TV, going to movies, and listening to the radio, they are exposed to countless acts of violence and sex daily. Because these incidents of sex and violence are a common diet for society's collective mind, young people are not even aware that there is a problem. They see nothing wrong with the images. They have no idea how the media are shaping their thinking. Inform them about how they mold our values and attitudes. Be persistent. Young adolescents are strongly influenced by their environment. It is critical that we challenge the environmental conditioning taking place. Explain why you feel the way you do. Children need to know you care about how they are developing as human beings. Don't preach! Preaching is tuned out. Say what you mean. Say it quickly, clearly, and emphatically, and it will be heard.

Minimize the negative impact of cliques

Cliques can be the source of strong rivalries and bad feelings. Sometimes, they can lead to violence. It is important to work on building community in schools and on reducing the formation of cliques as much as possible. When I was in school, cliques existed. There were the Jocks, the Freaks, the Squares, and the Nerds. I don't know how the names came about – we just knew them and knew who belonged in them. It seemed almost everyone was categorized. In my situation, there was not much outward conflict between the groups. Cliques primarily kept to themselves. There were hard feelings, however, a result of exclusion and gossip.

What is a clique?

1. clique (klêk, klîk) noun
A small, exclusive group of friends or associates.[2] *Or:*

2. clique

One gang researcher called a clique a "spontaneous interest group usually of the conflict type which forms itself within some larger social structure such as a gang."[3] Members of cliques tend to be similar in age.

There is a vast difference between the above two definitions. The term 'clique' as it is used in this book refers to the first definition: A small, exclusive group of friends or associates. The second definition describes a more recent term for 'gang subgroups'. Another term used is 'sets'.

Following is some helpful information on gangs found on the Internet in an FAQ (Frequently Asked Questions) on suburban gangs.[4] Some of this information may also be applicable to urban gangs.

Aren't suburban gangs just like the on-the-edge groups and cliques when I grew up?
Answer: No. When we say 'gang,' we are only talking about a group of youths banded together in a specific context who commit crimes. If a specific group of youths – regardless of their cultural facade – doesn't commit crimes, then it shouldn't be described or labeled as a 'gang'.

What types of gangs are forming?
Answer: There are three gang types that have been identified and typed by Dan Korem, and each type can have many different variants. (Four chapters in *Suburban Gangs* detail the many variants that have appeared in the US and Europe and how youth gang types are now inspiring one another across the Atlantic for the first time in history.)
Delinquent Gangs: Desire for profit and thuggery.
Ideological Gangs: Attachment to a specific ideology, which may or may not be political.
Occultic Gangs: Attachment to beliefs in occultic powers.

Is there a predictable profile of a typical gang member?
Answer: Most gang members come from a family environment where we find one of five family factors:
1. Divorce
2. Separation
3. Physical Abuse
4. Sexual Abuse (verbal abuse alone is an uncommon factor)
5. Severe parental dysfunction, such as alcoholism
Additionally, about 75% of gang youths have the Missing Protector Factor (MPF) operative in their lives, which is explained below. When the MPF is neutralized in a youth's life, gangs stop forming. The ruptured/broken home acts as a magnifying glass on a youth's rebellion, particularly on those who already have a more rebellious bent than their peers. Frustration, anger, loneliness, isolation, etc. become exaggerated, youths find those like themselves. The result: the gang. Other factors, such as destructive entertainment media, inspire gang variants, but the primal root cause of gangs is family deterioration. Regarding personality traits, there is typically no distinguishing pattern from other groups of youths: some youths will display emotional control, while others won't, some will be directive, while others prefer to be directed, etc.

Is there one key factor when layered on top of the ruptured/broken home that increases the likelihood that a youth will be recruited into a gang?

Answer: Yes, and it is called the Missing Protector Factor (MPF) referenced above. Simply stated, the MPF occurs when a youth is faced with a crisis and there is no adult that he/she can turn to for help. That is, there is no adult protector in his/her life. The MPF dramatically increases the risk of gang recruitment as is found operative in about 75% of gang youths. It is clear that more youths from broken/ruptured homes resist gang recruitment, but when the MPF is added to a youth's life, a youth is significantly greater at risk of gang recruitment, suicide, drug abuse, etc.

Who qualifies as a Protector?

Answer: A protector is an adult who sees a youth once a month in person and maintains phone contact at least once a week. An older non-adult sibling typically doesn't qualify. Youths need protection provided by those who are older and wiser. The protector, who lives conveniently close to a youth, simply responds to a youth's call for help. This doesn't mean that the protector will be able to solve all of a youth's problems. Not even parents can do that. A protector simply tries to help, counsel, guide, or seek outside help for a youth – just like a concerned parent.

Is the gang just a replacement for the family?

Answer: The root need is even more primal than the need to have a family: it is the desire to be released from pain, anger, anguish, etc., spawned by the broken/ruptured home. Youths hope that the gang will provide one of three devices or payoffs: *The Mask* – You put on your gang regalia, swagger, look imposing, fire off your secret hand signals – and you can pretend that you are something that you are not. *The Distraction Device* – Join a gang, become absorbed in the crazed culture – and you don't have to think about what is going on at home. You can avoid dealing with the real issues in your life. *The Empowering Device* – This is particularly common for females in gangs who have been molested or abused. For them, the gang can give them power over others. (Female membership in suburban gangs is typically 5% -10%.)

Should I be concerned that my child is likely to get into a gang?

Answer: Most parents only need be concerned if their child has one of the five factors detailed earlier and/or the MPF is operative in their child's life.

What are some of the indicators that a youth might be involved in a gang?

Answer: Below is a sampling of potential indicators which might indicate gang interest. None of these items by themselves is a sure-fire indicator, but if there are several of these indicators in an at-risk youth's life, it is wise to start asking questions. If in doubt, local juvenile officers, school teachers, social workers, and youth pastors are good sources of information regarding local gang attire, activities, etc.

- Severe change in grooming, such as shaved or spiked hair
- Severe change in attire, such as baggy pants always worn below a youth's underwear, wearing a waist bank
- Extreme forms of music with violent or extremely provocative lyrics
- Excessively secrecy
- Excessively rebellion and defiance – typical teen rebellion doesn't qualify

- Hand signals used between friends in a group
- Graffiti-like drawings in notebooks

Aren't small towns less vulnerable to gang activity?
Answer: No. Gang-related crimes, such as homicides, are occurring in small towns across the US. Sometimes this is due to gang members moving to a community. More commonly, however, the number of at-risk youths in small towns has risen to intolerable levels, and these youths are then inspired by youth subculture media (movies, music, magazines) just like their counterparts in large metropolitan cities. There is no evidence that this trend will reverse itself anytime soon.

If I suspect that gang activity is present in my neighborhood, what should I do?
Answer: First, let your exposure to this new gang activity encourage you to get involved in a youth's life preemptively before he/she joins a gang. Become educated about this new gang trend. Second, unless you have proven experience dealing with juvenile delinquency, don't directly confront gang members; rather contact your local juvenile officer and the appropriate school officials for assistance.

Are there any gang prevention/intervention programs that can be implemented in my neighborhood?
Answer: An excellent program that educates kids about the dangers of gangs is the GREAT (Gang Resistance Education and Training) PROGRAM. The Phoenix Police Department has teamed up with Alcohol, Tobacco, and Firearms to create the first gang education program taught in neighborhood schools. Over 1500 juvenile officers have undergone rigorous training and are currently presenting this program in schools throughout the US. If your local community doesn't have a juvenile officer trained to present the GREAT PROGRAM, encourage your local police department to contact GREAT at South Mountain Precinct, 400 W. Southern Ave., Phoenix, AZ 85041, (602) 495-5004.

THE BOYS AND GIRLS CLUBS has developed a successful program that directly reaches out to gang members who are predominantly from urban areas. In 1994, in Ft. Worth, Texas, it helped implement a gang intervention program that helped reduce gang-related homicides by 25% in the first year.

Books on the Subject

Canada, Geoffrey. (1995). *Fist Stick Knife Gun: A personal history of violence in America.*
    Boston: Beacon Press
Korem, Dan. (1995). *Suburban Gangs – The Affluent Rebels.* Richardson:
    International Focus Press
Wooden, Wayne. (1995). *Renegade Kids, Suburban Outlaws:*
    Wadsworth Publishing Company
Miller, Maryann. (1993). *Weapons and Violence In Our School and On Your Streets.*
    New York: The Rosen Publishing Group
Arthur, Richard. (1992). *Gangs and Schools.*
    Learning Publication
Bender, David L. et al. (1992). *Youth Violence.* San Diego:
    Greenhaven Press

EMOTIONS, DISCIPLINE, AND THE GROWTH OF EMPATHY

Allow young teens time to deal with their emotions

Young adolescents can be very volatile. If a student comes to class upset because of an argument in the hall, your class and what you are teaching will not be first and foremost on his/her mind. With students who have a tendency to lose control of their emotions, I usually establish a signal or a procedure ahead of time, for that student to recollect. Sometimes, we would establish a mutually acceptable place to 'chill out' for ten minutes. The student would return to class when his/her emotions were back in control.

Use upsets as opportunities for learning

Use upsets as opportunities to learn about feelings, expectations, and communication skills whenever possible. Remember, developmentally, teen students focus on upsets. We may have a different agenda. We would not expect a two-year-old to share well, to see others' points of view, or to ride a two-wheeler. A two-year-old's developmental stage is obvious. We adjust our expectations accordingly. Twelve- and thirteen-year-olds are also in a very definite developmental stage. We need to consider their developmental position when we are teaching and parenting. The curriculum can wait.

React to peer cruelty with 'moral feeling'

It is still important to react to peer cruelty with 'moral feeling'. When students are caught up in their own emotional viewpoints, help them to see the other side.

Talk about and demonstrate respect

The word 'respect' can be powerful with this age group. Connect unacceptable behavior with its effect on self-respect and respect for others. I have been amazed at how well students relate to this concept. In my classroom, I have a rule: "Respect yourself, your teacher, and your peers." Students understand very quickly how many behaviors fall under the category of respect.

Require restitution

When an adolescent verbally or physically hurts another child accidentally or intentionally, assist the one who did the hurting to figure out a way to make amends to the hurt youth. It is important that the one who caused the hurt is part of the decision and that the other person is comfortable with the arrangement. Don't force apologies. Instead, encourage caring behavior, such as assisting with a difficult assignment, offering some positive words (encouragement, sincere compliments), or replacing a broken or missing item. If disruptive behavior has cost the class time, suggest a special presentation on the subject being currently discussed, or assistance with paperwork. Restitution as a consequence teaches much more than an insincere apology or an unproductive detention.

Separate young teens from their behavior

It is still important to separate youth from their behavior because self-esteem is fragile for this age group. I was working on a behavior plan with a student recently. An important part of the planning process is for children to acknowledge their own behavior. This young man would not own his own behavior. He denied, blamed, pointed to other people's behavior, and feigned ignorance. Finally, I stated that we would not be able to resolve our 'conflict' without his cooperation in acknowledging his behavior. His reply stunned me with its honesty. He said, "I don't want to admit that I was doing that because that will mean I'm bad. I don't want to be bad." I spent the next ten minutes talking with him about my views on misbehavior, people who make mistakes, and the use to which mistakes can be put. When he seemed convinced that I didn't and wouldn't think that he was a bad person, he worked with me to resolve our 'conflict.'

Involve adolescents in establishing meaningful rules and consequences

The Reality Therapy and Choice Theory approach that I describe in Chapter Three is an excellent starting point for behavior management with teens. As a rule of thumb, keep the number of rules to a minimum. If you come up with a list of many rules, intelligent young people will manage to find all the behaviors that should be on the list, but are not. Much to your chagrin, they will use that list to their advantage. It is better to have four broad, simple rules than countless detailed rules. There are many ways to do this and many resources to help you.

> *See Chapter Three and Annotated Bibliography for sources.*

Hold class/family meetings

As I have previously stated, it is still important to have an agenda. All family or class members can contribute to this agenda. Consistency is important. If teens have had exposure to family or class meetings through their elementary years, they will accept the meetings more readily than if they have had no exposure. This is especially true in a family situation. A family will have to explain the value of the meetings by placing emphasis on the parents' desire to listen to what the teens have to say (without lectures, judgment, and reprimands). The parental commitment will need to be proven over time. Teens are at a precarious age where they want to reject such family involvement and yet desperately need it at the same time.

Family meetings should be held at least once a week, but may be called by a family member at any time. Again, reinforce the importance of the meetings by not allowing interruptions. The teen years pose a greater challenge to the continuity of the meetings because of extra-curricular activities and peer interests. It's also a time when parents are misled by their children's independence and self-sufficiency into thinking that 'family' activities are unnecessary or impossible to maintain. Parents must remember that it is

> *See Chapter Two for a family meeting agenda.*

the teenagers' job to fight for separation and autonomy, but that it's the parents' job to provide a safe and supportive environment for that autonomy to develop. That environment needs to include discipline, boundaries, and continued family rituals, traditions, and closeness.

Class meetings as part of the adolescents' educational environment are invaluable for airing problems, dealing with developmental concerns, and providing a forum to discuss teen risk factors such as drug use, peer pressure, premature sexual activity, and bullying. [5]

> **See Chapter Three for more information on how to set up and conduct class meetings.**

SUMMARY

Curriculum

- Integrate music into the curriculum.
- Use Social Studies as a catalyst for discussion of conflict.
- Role-play to reinforce and practice conflict resolution skills.
- Teach conflict resolution skills.

At School and At Home

- Encourage social responsibility, empathy, and self-esteem.
- Discuss the media's impact on students' belief systems and prejudices.
- Minimize the negative impact of cliques.
- Hold family/class meetings.

Emotions, Discipline, and The Growth of Empathy

- Allow teens time to deal with their emotions.
- Use upsets as opportunities to learn about feelings, expectations, and communication.
- React to peer cruelty with 'moral feeling'.
- Talk about and demonstrate respect.
- Require restitution.
- Separate teens from their behavior.
- Involve teens in establishing meaningful rules and consequences.

The Adolescent Girl:
Implications For Conflict Education

I get so confused
From day to day.
One minute I'm falling,
Then, again, I'm steady on
My feet,
Far from emotion with
My head in the clouds,
Confused
Over feelings from the past
And feelings of the present.

It's funny how I used to know
Myself.
But didn't.
I'm trying to be good…
— Anne, 8th grade

✦✦✦✦✦✦✧✦✦✦✦✦✦

"As the 'I' who spoke clearly at eleven becomes in
adolescence 'confused,' so the resolution of that confusion
occurs through the discovery that responsiveness to
self and responsiveness to others are connected
rather than opposed."
— Carol Gilligan, 1993

✦✦✦✦✦✦✧✦✦✦✦✦✦

Lori walks down the hall of the junior high school between classes.
Three girls corner her by her locker. "Where did you get those shoes?" they jeer.
"Are they a K-Mart special?" The girls laugh. Others join in the
laughter as they walk by.

✦✦✦✦✦✦✧✦✦✦✦✦✦

Corrina used to live in Springfield. She and her family moved out west several years ago.
She returned to her old neighborhood in the fall of her junior high year. She luckily reunited
with one of her old childhood friends, Amy. She was relieved that she at least knew someone
at the junior high. Things seemed OK the first few days of school. Then trouble started. No
one would talk to her but Amy. When Amy wasn't around, she was left alone to watch and
hear the whispers and snickers of the other girls. School quickly became a very uncomfortable
place to be. Amy discovered that another close friend, Sandy, was jealous of the time Amy
was spending with Corrina. Sandy had been spreading vicious rumors about Corrina to ruin
her chance of making friends and to pressure Amy into rejecting her.

✦✦✦✦✦✦✧✦✦✦✦✦✦

In my 'Character and Conflict Education' workshops, the majority of questions from teachers and parents involves bullying and violence between boys. According to Webster's New World Dictionary (1988), 'to bully' means "to hurt, frighten, or tyrannize over, as a bully does". In *Bullying at School,* Dan Olweus defines 'bullying' this way: "A student is bullied or victimized when he or she is exposed repeatedly and over time, to negative actions on the part of one or more other students." But parents and teachers are rarely concerned with girls' bullying. Occasionally, a situation with a girl will come up for discussion. However, female conflict is seldom the focus. I think we are often very unaware of the interpersonal conflict and bullying that goes on with girls. This lack of awareness has, I believe, three reasons. First, girls are more subtle with their bullying. Bullying between girls often takes the form of exclusion, gossip, and name-calling. It's often done quietly. Second, girls are often the victims of bullying by boys. So the problem remains a 'boys' problem. Third, girls eventually lose their voice. Their conflicts are not taken seriously. They are not listened to. Bullying of girls typically doesn't involve fist fights, blood, or broken bones; therefore, *it's not really a problem.* But girls *are* physically fighting today, much more than in years past, although this behavior is not typical.

When looking at girls through a developmental lens, we see that bullying (including sexual harassment) and conflict are critical issues for girls as they enter adolescence. The strength, straightforwardness, and confidence girls demonstrate in the early elementary years begin to diminish. As they reach the seventh and eighth grade, they become quieter, unsure of themselves, confused, and more vulnerable. They begin to read and believe the messages the media and society send: Girls must be good. Girls must be kind, cooperative, and quiet. If girls are too smart, too loud, too competitive, too spirited, or too aggressive, they may not be accepted and liked, especially by the boys. It is at this time in their lives that it is most important to understand *how* girls develop and, with that understanding, to teach them to reclaim their voice: "Adolescence is a critical time in girls' lives — a time when girls are in danger of losing their voices and thus losing connection with others..."[6] Another study describes the female sense of self this way:

> "Jean Baker Miller, writing in the mid-1970s about women who came for psychotherapy, noted that women's sense of self is built around being able to make and then maintain connections with others and that a loss of relationship is experienced by many women as tantamount to a loss of self".[7]

So, how do girls develop? And why is the way they develop significant to conflict education? Until Carol Gilligan's studies of girls' development in the 1970's and 1980's, child development theories were based solely on studies of boys. Freud, Piaget, and Kohlberg based their theories on boys. Kohlberg's six stages of moral development were derived from data gathered in a study of 84 boys over a period of twenty years. As boys develop, they begin to make moral decisions based on the rights of individuals and on justice. Kohlberg's higher stages of moral development involve making decisions based on individual rights and justice. When girls did not demonstrate behavior consistent with these theories, the general consensus was that there was something wrong with the girls. The next assumption was that girls did not reach the higher stages of moral development, whereas boys did.

Gilligan observed through her interviews with girls that they base their moral decisions on different factors than do boys. Girls develop differently. Girls generally do not value individuation and separation as do boys. Rather, girls value connection. They need to be connected to others. Girls base their moral decisions on care and responsiveness to others. Their moral conflicts are not black and white; they're not about justice and rights. Their moral conflicts are about caring, not hurting, and maintaining relationships and connectedness. Kohlberg determined that this lack of separation and need to consider other people's feelings exemplified his third stage of moral development. Describing Kohlberg's third stage, Gilligan says, "At this stage, morality is conceived in interpersonal terms and goodness is equated with helping and pleasing others".[8] Remember, however, Kohlberg's studies did not include girls. Girls do not operate on a lower level of morality; rather, they operate from a different perspective. That perspective is one of care and responsiveness to others and the importance of maintaining relationships and connectedness in the world.

To be clear, I think it is important to note that studies of boys and girls and of men and women have shown that both sexes may be capable of seeing and understanding both perspectives.[9] Also, men sometimes make moral decisions based on a care and responsiveness perspective, and women sometimes make decisions based on a rights and justice perspective. To totally separate boys' and girls' development in black and white terms is misleading.

So what kind of impact does this new understanding of female development have on character and conflict education curricula? Bernadette, a woman in her 30's, has shared concerns with me about the level of cruelty adolescents can encounter at the hands of their peers. Her interest stems from a deep empathy she has for the victims of such ill-treatment. Through journal writing, she was able to get in touch with the pain of her own junior high years. She shared the story with me for inclusion in this book. Finally, she will be heard. Let's look at Bernadette's story and see where education failed:

My seventh- and eighth-grade years were the worst years of my life. Every day of those junior high years brought pain, humiliation, and a disintegration of self under the onslaught of name-calling, spit, and laughter. I was called dog, mutt, and canine. I would find bones on my desk and tacks on my seat. I felt worthless, frustrated, and helpless. I'd tell the teachers what was going on. They could see what was going on. They told me to ignore 'them'. When I couldn't bear it and lashed back, I was told it was my fault because I didn't keep quiet about the abuse. They didn't listen to me. They didn't hear me. I had no voice. I was alone, disconnected, struggling with my sense of self, fighting to hide the pain and the shame. I knew I didn't belong. I was a misfit. I was ugly. I was a 'dog'.

The message from my teachers was loud and clear. I had no right to a voice, no right to defend myself, no right to dignity. Years later, the self-doubt and the fear instilled in those years still surface to plague me in my weaker moments. Few know *of this part of my life because of the shame that emerges when I try to share the story. At some deep primal level there lies an irrational belief that somehow, it was my fault. I wasn't good enough. I should have been silent.*

— Bernadette

Bernadette's story, although extreme, is an example of what can happen when we don't understand female development. Bernadette lost her voice, her self-worth, her self, in part because of a lack of awareness and understanding of her teachers. At a time when girls need to be empowered to speak for themselves, to feel connected, and to feel cared for, she was silenced, isolated, and dismissed. Girls weren't supposed to fight back. They were supposed to be quiet and good.

Bernadette needed her female teachers to model assertiveness and strength. She needed them to model caring and responsiveness to both boys and girls. Bernadette needed teachers who could work with the class on relationship, communication, and listening skills. She needed to be listened to. She needed to be treated with fairness.

Bernadette needed help in understanding her own reactions to the boys' bullying. The class as a whole needed the skill of an insightful teacher to help them look at their own behavior and determine where it came from and why it was there.

So how can we help Bernadette, Corrina, Lori, and other girls like them? How can we help them reclaim their voice, maintain and build on their confidence, and resolve conflicts peacefully? The following sections will address this question. I outlined five components necessary for a complete Character and Conflict Education Program in Chapter One. Let's look at each of these components and consider them in light of female development.

A CHARACTER AND CONFLICT EDUCATION PROGRAM FOR GIRLS

Modeling the desired behavior

The women in an adolescent girl's life play an important part in shaping her attitudes and beliefs about the role of women in society. Girls need role models who base their identity and self-worth on who they are as people, rather than on how pretty or fashionable they are. These female role models are confident because of their talents and interests rather than their popularity or sexuality (Pipher, 1994). They are honest and open about talking to girls about those beliefs and values. They live according to those values. These role models can be teachers, mothers, or other significant women in a girl's life. Given the power behind the media and the negative messages about women that they send to our girls daily, we cannot be too assertive about sharing our views with our girls. They need us desperately at this point in their lives. Our North American culture sends countless messages to girls to encourage them to pull away from their mothers and to become glamorous Barbie-like sex objects in a world that increasingly subjects them to abuse and takes away their voice. If we don't intervene, who will? What will become of our daughters?

Alissa, 14, is incredibly confident for her age. She does well in school: "I'm not super popular, but I have my friends and I get along with most people. I don't care about being super popular." Alissa is athletic. She plays volleyball and softball, runs track, and does martial arts. I was surprised at her strong voice, her lack of concern about being the victim of bullying, and her candor. When she spoke about conflicts she had with friends and school mates, she was clear in her understanding about her role in the conflict. It was important to her to handle it so that she maintained relationships and connections with people when possible. She was able to act on her own behalf to resolve conflicts with peers. She had the understanding, the confidence, and the skills to resolve conflict peacefully. She described situations where she was proactive in her approach to avoiding conflict. When I asked her what helped her the most in developing these skills, she recalled her martial arts teacher, Ms. Park: "I think girls should be taught to resolve conflict the way Ms. Park taught me. She explained to us why people might start a fight. She taught us ways to handle it if kids tried to start a fight." Alissa went on to explain how she was taught. Ms. Park used role-play and discussion based on current research regarding conflict resolution, criminal behavior, and victim statistics. She empowered her students with physical and verbal self-defense skills. What was loud and clear to me was that Ms. Park was a major role-model in Alissa's life. Alissa had studied martial arts at Ms. Park's school since she was three. The experience hasn't taught her to be violent. It has given her the confidence and the skills NOT to fight. I know Ms. Park personally. Soft-spoken and assertive, she is a strong female role model. She respects her students and values their individuality, yet she sets high standards for character and self-discipline. She's a ballerina and a martial artist. Ms. Park made a difference for Alissa.

Relationship

Because relationships and connectedness are so important to females, they will often conform to society's expectations rather than stick up for their true selves. From my discussion with girls and my research into their development, I have come to believe that providing an affirming and safe environment for girls to develop relationships and relationship skills is most important. If girls do not feel safe to speak, share, or participate in their environment, the moral values they hold most dear – relationship and connectedness – will be a source of continual conflict and pain.

Leslie, 13, is soft-spoken, reserved, and a bit shy. She speaks thoughtfully and carefully. I had known Leslie since she was six; however, I hadn't visited with her in well over a year. I had known her as confident, imaginative, outspoken, and vivacious. I never knew the shy, reserved Leslie until now. I was struck by the change. I told her that I had done a lot of reading that says that girls lose their voice in junior high. I explained what I meant by that and asked her if she believed it was true. She answered, "Yeah, a lot, because they always worry that if they say one thing, someone might think it's stupid and tease them or make fun of them or something, but when they're younger, everyone is just like, doing the same stuff and it doesn't really matter." I asked her what might be the cause of some of the teasing. Her answer surprised me: "Sometimes in my junior high, a lot of the teachers will put boys against girls if they do questions and it makes me and my friends uncomfortable because the boys will pick on us. But then again, it goes the other way. The girls will pick on the boys."

I found this same situation identified as a source of conflict by the other girls that I spoke to. The girls represented two different junior highs. Girls were pitted against boys in math games and gym sports. The girls unanimously expressed dismay and discomfort at this system of division. At a time when girls lose their voice because of the mere presence of boys and their dominant expression in the classroom, because of documented favoritism towards boys by teachers, and because of media devaluation of the female, girls are put in a position that reinforces their defeat and encourages conflict with boys. The girls I interviewed described situations where a female honor student who got straight A's would not volunteer to give any answers towards the success of her all-female team. They said the boys would yell out the answers in these games. The girls didn't answer as quickly or at all. The boys would often win. In gym, the boys 'always' won, therefore reinforcing the stereotype that 'boys are better'. The girls suggested mixing up the teams to include both boys and girls, so they would be more even. In *Raising A Daughter*, Jeanne and Don Elium write, "Because many girls lack the early training that makes them 'at home' in their bodies, they feel overwhelmed by games that go too fast and are dominated by players with greater skill. Too often, teachers fail to equalize play opportunities and team memberships in order to make the girls' experience more positive and successful".

Myra and David Sadker explain in *Failing At Fairness* that the majority of schools follow a traditional model of education. This model is rife with the miseducation of boys and girls. The traditional model is one that "promotes competition over cooperation, aggression over nurturing, and sports victories rather than athletic participation." They add that although there may be some benefit to be gained from this type of education, it is lacking balance and consequently unhealthy: "From their earliest days at school, boys learn a destructive form of division – how to separate themselves from girls. Once the school world is divided, boys can strive to climb to the top of the male domain, thinking that even if they fall short, they still are ahead of the game because they are not girls".

As a high school teacher, I have never divided teams along gender lines. The girls I interviewed stated that their elementary school teachers did not pit boys against girls in games. I find it ironic that it is done with regularity at the age when it should be most avoided. Pitting boys against girls does not help to insure a safe environment for building relationships or positive communication.

Chelsea, 13, is also quiet and shy. She described herself as different than when she had been in the fifth grade. She said, "With people that I don't know really well, I'm kinda quiet and shy. In fifth grade, I was not like that at all. I was a lot louder, outspoken, and I didn't care what other people thought. It's weird." I asked her what she thought had caused the change in her. She replied: "I guess I'm afraid I'll screw up. Because, they ask for an answer and you're not sure if it is right, and if it isn't, you worry about that stuff. You worry about what people will think. You don't try to be funny. You don't try to answer. You just sit there." Chelsea also felt that the large number of students in junior high creates more social pressure and conflict. She noted the difference between the smaller population of her elementary school, where she knew everybody and felt safe, and the larger numbers in the junior high. She liked the possibilities for meeting more people and developing relationships, but that fear of expressing herself among "people I really don't know that well" caused her to be "quiet and shy."

I asked the girls, "If you could design a school that met girls' needs, what would it be like?" Alissa's first requirement would be to have school uniforms. She felt that uniforms would eliminate much of the conflict that occurs in the school. She explained that kids often get into physical fights over teasing about clothing. She felt that if everyone looked the same, it would make things more "even". Chelsea also liked the idea of uniforms as long as they were comfortable. Uniforms brought images of uncomfortable dresses to some of the girls, so they were unsure if they would like them. Most agreed that if they were attractive and comfortable, uniforms would be a good idea.

Clothing created major divisions between groups of students. It was a crucial external factor responsible for the inability of the girls to feel safe. If they did not have the "right clothes", many relationships could not be formed. The importance placed on clothing feeds into 'lookism' which is the evaluation of a person solely on the basis of appearance. Lookism is rampant in our culture. It is reinforced by the media, by our attitudes towards unattractive people, by our comments, jokes, and beliefs about appearance. Lookism devalues women. It was described as the primary source of conflict by the girls I spoke with.

Chelsea smiles easily and displays a quiet inner strength that I find admirable. She has perfected the art of 'blending in'. But for the issues that are most important to her, such as smoking, drugs, and dating, she stands strong. When I asked her whether clothing was an issue, she agreed that it was a primary source of conflict: "Girls worry about what they look like. You don't want to look babyish. And you don't want to look wicked sophisticated. You've got to be right in the middle, follow the trends and stuff, and if you don't, you'll be laughed at. Other kids will talk behind your back. And that doesn't feel good at all. You gotta be with everybody else or you'll look wicked different. And some people won't talk to you at all so you'll be a loner. During the summer it's OK because you don't see half the people, so you can do whatever you want, basically. But when you get back to school, you change. This way you won't get picked on. You'll stay friends with all your friends. You don't get stuck by yourself."

For parents and teachers, the clothing issue is probably difficult to address. Few schools have a uniform policy although the idea is being tried at some schools across the country. The results seem to be positive. What we can do, however, is address these attitudes in our classrooms and homes. We can talk about lookism. We can point out how the media manipulates viewers to value appearance. We can discuss how this establishes a barrier to relationships and creates conflict. We can educate our children about the consequences of placing so much value on appearance at the cost of relationships and the self. Eating disorders are rampant in our society partly because of the importance our culture places on appearance and thinness. The teasing, isolation, and stereotyping that result from the value junior high students put on designer clothing and appearance, along with the lack of education centered on understanding relationships and the conditioning effects of the media, create an unhealthy, emotionally unsafe environment for our girls. Consequently, girls caught up in the expectations of society and unsure of their ability to successfully conform are quick to ridicule and make scapegoats of girls who clearly don't conform.

In *Reviving Ophelia*, Mary Pipher writes: "Many girls can describe a universal American phenomenon — the scapegoating of girls by one another. Many girls become good haters of those who do not conform sufficiently to our culture's ideas about femininity." She adds, "This scapegoating functions as the ultimate form of social control for girls who are not sufficiently attentive to social pressures. Scapegoats are shunned, teased, bullied and harassed in a hundred different ways." Putting someone down lowers the status of the victim (in the bully's mind) and makes the bully 'feel' better. As teachers, parents, and adults who work with girls, we have a responsibility to educate children about the culture that feeds this form of alienation. In junior high, where relationship and connectedness are so critical to girls, we are allowing it to continue by default.

Conditioning: Understanding its role in shaping our attitudes

"Adolescent girls come of age in a culture preoccupied with money, sex and violence, a culture with enormous problems — poverty, pollution, addictions and lethal sexually transmitted diseases," says Pipher. She adds, "The ways the media have dehumanized sex and fostered violence should be the topic of a national debate. After a five-year study, the American Psychological Association found that watching television can lead to antisocial behavior, gender stereotyping and bad grades in school. The APA warned that television has become a dominant and disturbing influence on the national psyche." The APA also warns that "repeated exposure to scenes of violence against women in movies and TV creates a callousness toward women in both males and females" (Strauss, 1992).

I believe that the best immediate defense against the conditioning effects of the media and our culture is to be aware of society's influences on our development as human beings, and to educate ourselves and our children about those influences. I say children, rather than girls, because to help girls, we need to help both sexes to understand what they think, and why they think the way they do. As individual parents and teachers, we often feel helpless against the barrage of outside influences on our children. What we must remember is that if we work to understand how *we* are affected by the media and culture and, with that understanding, learn to revive our true selves, we can help our children to see these conditioning effects as well.

How we can help

So how do we begin to see ourselves so that we can help our daughters and female students? I recommend starting by reading Mary Pipher's *Reviving Ophelia: Saving the Selves of Adolescent Girls*. I read this book before interviewing junior high girls. I wanted to believe that Pipher was talking about a harsher world than the one I lived in. I wanted to believe that my community wasn't as damaging to girls as the book claimed our entire culture was. But when I interviewed the girls, it felt as if I was hearing an echo. The reticent voice Gilligan speaks about and the damaging effects of our culture and media were reflected in the interviews. There were few surprises. At times, *Reviving Ophelia* brought me to the verge of tears. I agonized for my daughter and what lies ahead for her. I look at her vibrant self and dread the changes that seem inevitable in adolescence. On the positive side, I am now aware of the impact of our culture and the media on her development: only if I am aware of the problem can I do something about it.

After reading *Reviving Ophelia*, look at yourself. Look at your attitudes and beliefs. Assess where they come from. Are they the result of media influences? Of society's expectations about the role of women? Of your upbringing? Of cultural influences? Two other excellent books to help with this process are Emily Hancock's *The Girl Within* and Belenky, Clinchy, Goldberger, and Tarrule's *Women's Ways of Knowing: The Development of Self, Voice, and Mind*.[10] Again, only once you understand your own attitudes, beliefs, and behaviors can you help young females. If you can't see where the messages are coming from and what impact they have on you, you won't be able to identify them and discuss them with your children or students. Jeanne and Don Elium argue in *Raising A Daughter*, "To begin to use cultural forces for the good of our daughters, we must first shake ourselves awake from the cultural trance we all live in. This is no small matter, to untangle our true beliefs from what we have been taught to believe about who and what girls and women are".

Watch the movies, TV shows, and commercials that teenagers are watching. Listen to the music they are listening to or, if you can't bear to listen, read the CD or cassette jackets where the words of the songs are often written out. Talk to girls about the way women are portrayed on television, in movies, or in music. Ask them what it teaches them about the roles of women. And also educate boys.

Involve adolescent girls in work with the homeless, the elderly, or the handicapped. Service with the disadvantaged feeds adolescent girls' need for community and relationship, gives them a sense of purpose, and gets them out of the poisonous media culture. Service builds self-esteem and responsibility. They will also gain a more positive view of their own lot in life. Let girls know that *they* are OK. It's our society and culture that's all messed up.

Empowerment

One of the clearest memories from my junior high years is the resentment I felt when people, especially men, would tell me to smile. I can't tell you how many times I heard this. I learned a pat response: "There's nothing to smile about". The sad part is that that was how I felt. I lost myself completely in junior high. I remember going into seventh grade confident and self-assured. By ninth grade I was hiding in doorways when peers walked by because I didn't want them to see what I 'looked' like. I feared being the target of jeers because of my 'hand-me-down' clothing and appearance. I felt powerless against the world. I had a small group of friends that I trusted. Everyone else was suspect. I couldn't understand what changed. I was incredibly confused about what I was doing 'wrong'. I wanted to fix myself, but didn't have a clue how. Somehow, even when I tried to stick up for myself or to demonstrate what I could do well, it backfired.

Pipher writes about a student, Cayenne, who says, "'Girls are supposed to smile. If I'm having a bad day, teachers and kids tell me to smile. I've never heard them say that to a guy'." Pipher adds, "Girls who speak frankly are labeled as bitches. Girls who are not attractive are scorned. The rules are reinforced by the visual images in soft- and hard-core pornography, by song lyrics, by casual remarks, by criticisms, by teasing and jokes." When I was in junior high, the media messages weren't sent as abundantly and degradingly as they are today, but the message was still clear: Boys were allowed to be loud, vocal, and aggressive. Boys' looks weren't particularly important. Girls were supposed to be quiet, reserved, passive, pretty, and accommodating. And things haven't changed for the better. They've gotten worse.

So how do we empower our girls? Modeling empowered behavior for our girls, providing a safe environment for them to develop relationship skills, and helping them to understand the conditioning effects of the media – all this lays the foundation for self-empowerment. Excellent resources available to help with this process include Jeanne and Don Elium's *Raising A Daughter: Parents and the Awakening of A Healthy Women* and Caryl Rivers, Rosalind Barnett, and Grace Baruch's *Beyond Sugar and Spice: How Women Grow, Learn, and Thrive*.[11]

Girls need to develop competence and problem-solving abilities in order to feel empowered. They need opportunities to develop critical-thinking skills, decision-making skills, and leadership skills. From an early age, these skills need to be encouraged and reinforced.

Encourage girls to keep a journal. This journal can include poetry, short stories, thoughts about the day, or favorite activities. A journal can provide a wonderful link to the past as the young person grows. It is also a very useful way to sort out feelings, to express emotions in a nonthreatening way, and to make time for quiet reflection. In knowing and expressing oneself, one is empowered. One has a voice. Avoid those little diaries that provide very small spaces to write under the date. I kept a diary such as this when I was a young girl. It did two things. It frustrated me because I wanted to write more and there was no room to write. It limited me in what I wrote because I did not want to mess up my book by writing 'over' other dates. A journal with a handsome cover, preferably one that the teen picks out herself, and completely blank, lined pages is best. If you have a child who would like unlined pages to draw in the journal, those are available too.

Encourage physical activity. Both individual and team sports have their value. Involvement in sports enables girls to see their bodies as a functioning, healthy part of their whole selves. If a girl is uncomfortable with sports, I suggest a martial art. It's individual – anyone can learn it and progress. Girls involved in sports see their bodies as something other than sex objects. I also think that team sports prepare girls to deal better in a 'man's world'. I diverted from teaching for a few years to enter business. I worked in a large computer company which was male-owned. The male language alone was an obstacle and barrier for me because men spoke in sports and military terms. Because my exposure to sports was limited, I was at a real disadvantage any time men spoke. I found myself attempting to learn a 'new language' and regretting that I never had been encouraged to play sports.

I feel very strongly that every girl should have *self-defense training*. This training should include practical physical self-defense, conflict resolution strategies, and assertiveness training. If the interest is there, I would encourage girls to take martial arts training. I simply cannot comprehend why in martial arts classrooms 70 - 80% are still boys and only 20 - 30% are girls. Where are all the girls? In dance class! My daughter takes dance. She also takes a martial art. Pipher states, "On any given day in America, 480 women and children will be forcibly raped, 5,760 women will be assaulted by a male intimate partner and four women and three children will be murdered by a family member." She adds, "Rape is the 'tragedy of youth' because 32 percent of all rapes occur when the victim is between the ages of eleven and seventeen." I am a high school teacher in a middle class suburban town. It is not a large urban city. Several of my students have been raped or sexually assaulted. I know these girls personally. It happens. For us as parents to close our eyes and to pretend that it can't happen to our daughters is foolish. It can. Girls need the skills to defend themselves in this world. Why aren't they in martial arts classes? Why aren't they in self-defense? What cultural stereotype are we buying into when we sign our little boys up for karate and our little girls for ballet?

Leslie, a tall girl who, with some training, could possibly defend herself verbally and physically quite well, said she could not defend herself as well as she thought she should be able to. She worried that there were kids who could beat her up or pick on her. She believed that she could defend herself verbally against some people, but did not have overall confidence in this area. When people picked on her, she just shrugged it off to avoid a conflict. Although she said that this worked for her because she didn't get into a fight, she also declared that it "really brings you down".

Chelsea, a petite girl, believed she was not very strong: "If someone came after me (to physically fight), I'd be really scared because I'm not that strong." That belief in itself puts Chelsea at a big disadvantage with anyone who may try to physically bully her or who she may think could escalate verbal bullying into physical violence.

As an adult whose only athletic experience before the age of thirty-three was one semester of basketball and one semester of field hockey in college, I can't even begin to tell you what the martial arts have done for me. I've come into my own with martial arts. I've learned to care for my physical self as I never have before. I see my body as a living, working machine rather than as something I have to constantly fight with to keep slim. I feel more confident in my ability to verbally stick up for myself with adult 'bullies'. When I walk alone at night, I'm more confident and aware of my surroundings. I'm sure it shows in my walk and stature. The experience has been incredibly empowering for me.

Alissa, the fourteen-year-old I spoke of earlier, exudes a confidence unusual in a girl her age. As I said, she has studied martial arts since she was three. Her parents encourage and support her athletic interests. She told me of an incident with a girl in her school who was bullying her. She said, " I don't know why this girl didn't like me. She was out to get me. One day she spit on me. I didn't do anything back to her because I didn't want to fight. I kept trying to make friends with her. But she just didn't like me. She called me names. One day she pulled my hair. Nothing I did to try to get along with her worked. She just didn't like me. One day she punched me. At that point I had to use my self-defense. It was horrible. I don't ever want to go through that again." She went on to add that the girl never bothered her again. She also said that if she had not had the skills to defend herself, she thought it would have really hurt her self-esteem. She would have felt powerless.

Skills

I think it is especially important to teach girls how to be assertive. Junior high school girls usually do one of two things when in conflict: they passively retreat or they loudly curse, threaten, and sometimes physically attack. The majority are passive. Recently, I used a student handbook and teacher's manual written by Gerri Johnson, Gershen Kaufman, and Lev Raphael called *Stick Up For Yourself: A Ten-Part Course in Self-Esteem and Assertiveness for Kids.*[12] What I like about this course is that it not only teaches assertiveness skills, it also helps kids to realize that they own their own behavior. Everything they do is a choice and has consequences.

Teach girls about becoming clear, focused, and centered. This can be achieved through a meditative art such as T'ai Chi or Yoga. Controlling one's breath and 'emptying the mind' are also means to achieve this clear, focused, centered state. Quiet time and space are important. One method is to sit comfortably in a quiet room, to close your eyes, and to focus on your breath. If your mind wanders, simply watch your thoughts and let them go. If you catch yourself thinking, stop thinking and refocus your mind on your breath. Don't judge your success in this process. Just be.

Teach girls about body language. Our bodies send out messages about how we perceive ourselves. Prisoners who have been jailed for muggings and rapes have described how they determine who their victims are. They look for body language that signals easy prey: a bowed head, eyes looking at the ground, slumped shoulders, a lack of eye contact, hands in pockets, and a slow, hesitant stride. Peers in school or the neighborhood will see the same signals. They may not be able to analyze and dissect them, but the non-verbal language is there and understood. Role-play scenarios with different body language. Discuss what comes across as confident and effective and what does not. If a girl shouts a weak "no," with head and shoulders slumped and cringing, the "no" will not be taken seriously.

Teach girls to shout "NO" firmly, with direct eye-contact and a straight posture. Even if they never have to shout it in real life, the fact that they have done it will help them to assert themselves in other areas. I found girls as young as eleven unable to shout. Also teach them to shout "STOP!" and "FIRE!" It is better to yell

"FIRE!" than "HELP!" because people will come out to see a fire.

Take a women's self-defense class with your daughter. If you are a teacher or someone who works with girls, educate the girls and their parents about its value. Make sure the course goes for at least eight weeks. The one-hour sessions at local police stations are informative; however, they are not meant to teach physical self-defense in a way that is internalized for real use. Two weeks after the session, most of what you have learned will be forgotten. Even longer workshops and courses should offer refresher courses periodically.

Sometimes when we look at today's violence against women, the sexual innuendoes in our speech, the degradation of women in movies and the media, and the objectification of women through advertisements and TV, we can become jaded and discouraged. But I believe we *can* make a difference. Just think back to your own adolescence. Close your eyes and try to remember one person in your life who made a significant difference for you in your teen years. For most of us, there is at least one. That difference may have been made by a teacher, a coach, a parent or neighbor, a minister, a counselor, or some other significant person. It may have happened in the course of a single incident or conversation, or in a long-term relationship. Now ask yourself, does this person know what a difference he/she made in my life? Many times he/she doesn't. Many times the lessons learned weren't even realized by you until you were much older. If you get discouraged in your attempts to help your girls, remember this person in your life. One person CAN make a difference. We just need to believe we can.

Chapter 6

THE HIGH SCHOOL ADOLESCENT

Verbal bullying

Jen was soft-spoken and frail in her appearance. She walked with a slow, short stepping gait. Her handwriting was neat but pained and laborious. People who knew her appreciated her sweet, gentle personality. Jen learned that she had a debilitating, progressive, incurable neurological disease. The news was a devastating blow to Jen and all who knew her.

One day, Jen physically attacked another girl. This behavior was totally uncharacteristic of her. Jen, however, had been cruelly and continually taunted by this girl and a few other students for at least two years. Jen and her parents had notified her school administration of the problem. She had sought help from a school counselor to deal with the harassment. The students were spoken to. No direct disciplinary action had been taken. There were no specific consequences attached to this verbal bullying. Finally, distraught over the news about her illness and tired of silently enduring the verbal abuse of her tormentors, Jen physically lashed out. She was suspended. Jen showed up to class one more time after that incident. Then she disappeared. She attempted suicide. Fortunately, she did not succeed. She didn't return to school. She feared the taunting. She didn't feel safe. The high school failed to provide a safe learning environment for this student. Consequently, she sat home alone. She couldn't get an equal education. Who is responsible?

The sad news is: most faculty at Jen's high school were unaware of what happened to her. The majority of the school's student population didn't know. If we randomly asked teachers whether teasing, taunting, or harassment were a problem at that school, the majority of faculty and students might say no. Demographically, the school population consisted of middle to upper middle class kids in a small New England town. This was not an inner city. No knives or guns were used. The weapons were words, expressions, and gestures. Were they any less damaging? The emotional scars for Jen will last much longer than it takes for a physical wound to heal. Jen was a victim of verbal bullying.

Jen's story is a drastic example of verbal bullying. What about the kid who jokingly puts down another student in the name of friendly bantering? Sometimes it ends after a few sarcastic remarks. Sometimes it comes to blows when one of the players no longer sees the humor in the situation. I'm not talking about playful teasing that doesn't cause hurt feelings. I'm talking about 'put downs,' words that can be taken as insults — even when the players are laughing about them.

I've taken a stand on this type of humor in my classroom and home. I simply don't allow it. I explain to my high school students that my classroom is a safe haven. It is a place for them to come where they do not have to worry about being put down. When they defend their humor, I explain that teens have to take a lot of garbage from too many people. Too many people are quick to put them down. So why should they have to listen to put downs in my classroom. I want them to feel good when they are in my room. I encourage them to say kind things to each other. I remind them how important respect is to me. I tell them that they deserve respect. 'Put downs' are not respectful. What's interesting is that once they hear the rationale for the rule, they accept it. I also give them permission to call me on my behavior if I ever break the rule. (I suggest they do it politely.) I rarely hear insults in my classroom.

When people think of a bully, they think of a punching, kicking, physically aggressive person. If they had to give a bully a gender, it would be male. This narrow view of bullying causes us to only react strongly to physical bullying in our society. In reality, verbal bullying, which includes harassment, taunting, mocking, exclusion, and shunning, can have equally devastating consequences. Unless extreme, physical bullying heals rather quickly. The consequences of verbal bullying can last a lifetime.

J. Jarvis

I hesitate to refer to verbal bullying as anything other than verbal bullying because I find that there is a tendency to minimize it as a social problem. People react to the word 'bully' with a certain sense of alarm. People don't react to taunting, mocking, exclusion, or shunning with the same degree of concern. I think the alarm should sound just as loudly for verbal bullying as it does for physical bullying.

Consider the typical disciplinary procedures for physical fighting in our schools. They usually involve suspension or expulsion. In contrast, verbal bullying, with the exception of sexual harassment, is often dealt with very lightly and inconsistently. Often, the only consequence is a reprimand. Many teachers ignore verbal bullying even though it is much more prevalent than physical bullying. It is a major problem in our schools and our society.

Verbal harassment is not only played down as a problem by school faculties and administrations, some school personnel use verbal bullying as a disciplinary or motivational tool themselves. In specific settings, it is accepted and even expected. You only need to go to the locker room or the football field to see verbal bullying at peak performance. In *Boys Will Be Boys*, Myriam Miedzian writes, "The language of sport is filled with insults suggesting that a boy who is not tough enough, who does not live up to the masculine mystique, is really a girl or homosexual." She cites football player David Kopay as saying, "like many other coaches, Dillingham [fictitious name] used sexual slurs — 'fag,' 'queer,' 'sissy,' 'pussy' — to motivate (or intimidate) his young athletes". I'll never forget the look of dismay on a friend's face when she told of standing on the sidelines of a high school football field shocked at the language being used by the coach to reprimand the team during practice. She was horrified at the example being set for her son by an adult role model: "My husband and I didn't bring him up that way. We taught him to respect women. This isn't right, but there is nothing I can do. My son would never forgive me if I complained about it."

Once during a spirit rally, a football team brought out a stuffed dummy representing the opposing team. They threw the dummy on the field and proceeded to attack it, tearing it to pieces. 'Take 'em apart' was the epithet. The opposing team was dehumanized by being symbolically abused before the entire student body. The message was clear: "Bullying in the name of winning and sports is OK." But the reality is that it's *not* OK. In order to play the game, boys, and in many cases also girls, must work hard at repressing empathy. They must steel themselves to the humanity of the other team. They must hide their own humanity and feelings to endure the abuse of the coach they are supposed to look up to(Miedzian).

High school teachers, coaches, and parents of adolescents need to be aware of the price society pays when we ignore or, at worst, participate in verbal bullying. I rarely speak to a parent or teacher who is not concerned about the fate of our society. Disrespect, rudeness, selfishness, bullying, and a lack of regard for other human beings are rampant in our culture. Before we become discouraged and throw up our hands in resignation, remember that we can set an example for our youth. We can set limits and boundaries for them to live by. We can make the difference in our society through our words and our actions.

Cognitive And Moral Development

COGNITIVE DEVELOPMENT

At approximately thirteen years of age, teens enter what Piaget defines as the stage of "Formal Operations". This stage is characterized by the ability to think abstractly. As with all developmental stages, some children reach this stage earlier, some later – and some never (this depends on their life experiences). When teens reach the Formal Operations stage of cognitive development, their reasoning skills develop substantially. They can now think in terms of possibilities. They can deal more flexibly with problems they encounter, whether these are academic, practical, or social. Teens can identify a problem, make an educated guess as to how to solve the problem, experiment with potential solutions, and determine a conclusion. Obviously, such abstract thinking and social reasoning are significant developmental milestones in adolescence.

According to Erikson, a teenager's energy is spent on his/her "Search for Identity".[1] This identity is primarily tied to choosing a career. Teens are trying to work out how they will contribute in a meaningful way to adult society. If they cannot do this, they are in a state of identity confusion and more likely to become involved in early sexual activities, drug use, and delinquent behavior.

When my first-born was two and a half, I read several reference books on the 'terrible two's'. I was a new mother anxious about being a 'perfect' parent. I remember a statement in at least one of those books that likened the two-and-a-half-year-old to the teenager. All I had to do was go to work the next day to see the commonality. The behavior of the teens in my freshman and sophomore classes was not that much different from that of my two-year-old. Both were egocentric. Both were fighting for independence. Both were screaming "NO!" to my requests. Both would say "No," but mean "Yes." (Or say "Yes" and mean "No.") Neither knew what they wanted. But instead of looking at these teenagers with disgust for their immature behavior, I could understand.

In *All Grown Up and No Place To Go*, explains that teens exhibit typical behaviors and characteristics that are provoked by the development of abstract thought.[2] Teens are fault-finding, argumentative, self-conscious, indecisive, self-centered, self-conscious, and rebellious. They also tend to tout idealistic virtues, yet do the opposite. If this sounds discouraging, remember that all these traits can be channeled in a positive direction. How adult role-models respond to adolescent behavior strongly influences what path teens will take. Helping adolescents make purposeful commitments is a positive step toward resolving the identity crisis. Teens who make meaningful, personal commitments to causes, hobbies, or a sport are shaping their lives in a positive way. These endeavors lay the foundation for the adult self-image.

Teens must sort through the chaos of their lives to determine the values and belief system that they will carry into adulthood. They must learn how to deal effectively and maturely with other members of society: "Adolescent goals (conscious or not) include establishing identity, giving up dependency, becoming emancipated from parents, choosing a career, and developing a commitment to responsible citizenship and to a particular role and place in society".[3] All adolescents are aware of these challenges at some level. The angst they produce colors their view of the world. Sometimes the path for them seems hopeless and the world overwhelming.

Point of view

Adolescents see life in terms of black or white. They typically don't see shades of gray. Their perception is also biased by their own self-involvement. As they mature, they become less self-centered and show greater concern for others. They are capable of seeing others' points of view but because of their black and white thinking, they are quick to pass judgment. Children who have had adults in their lives who modeled caring, compassion, and empathy, and who taught relationship skills and self-awareness, will be able to see others' points of view. I have worked with individual students, however, who are incapable of understanding other people's viewpoints. More sadly, they have absolutely no empathy for the 'victim' in any given situation. This reminds me of a TV documentary on youth crime. The teens interviewed for the program had all been convicted of violent crimes. What I saw in their faces as they recounted details of the crimes was frightening. They had absolutely no remorse, no empathy, and no understanding of the social impact of their actions. And yet these children were born with a natural sense of empathy. What happened?

Social awareness

"What I look for in a friend is someone who is upbeat, energetic, outgoing and just fun to be around because I can let loose and have fun without worrying about my parents being on my case all the time." — Hot Rod, age 16

I remember being an adolescent. I remember how grown-up I felt, how idealistic I was. At that time of my life, I believed that most adults could not possibly understand me. Only my friends could relate. Relationships with my peers overshadowed any other relationships in my life. My friends were everything. My family was there, present and important, but in the background — or in the way. I understand now that these feelings are typical of the adolescent years. As I work with teenagers, it helps if I can remember what I felt as an adolescent.

Peer relationships are so critically important to the adolescents' conception of themselves that the self-image evolving from those relationships may remain generally unchanged throughout life (Lauton and Freese). When we consider how cruel and intolerant young adolescents can be towards anyone who does not fit in or who is different, it becomes apparent that this cruelty and intolerance, if not addressed, can create emotional scars that can take years to heal. According to Erikson, this intolerance is a defense mechanism against identity confusion. Teens are constantly asking the question "Who am I?" and in the process vehemently reject any reflection of who they believe they are not.

We need to do a better job helping teens through social issues and conflicts. Because of the structure of secondary education, students are exposed to little, if any, instruction focussing on social education. They are on their own to resolve this inner turmoil through trial and error. Anthropologist Margaret Mead noted that adolescents from cultures that provided a more peaceful, serene transition from childhood to adulthood did not encounter the "storm and stress" so typical of Western teens.[4] In a less complicated and more sheltered world, formal social education may not be necessary. In an industrialized, media laden high-tech world of disconnected communities and families, excluding social education leaves kids vulnerable to external pressures and victimization.

Moral choices

According to Lawrence Kohlberg, adolescents make moral decisions based on a sense of justice and values. Most are at Kohlberg's level II (*Morality of conventional role conformity*). At this stage, teens conform to social conventions and support the status quo. They want to please others, especially their peers. Most teens want to obey the law. Some teens, however, may be at level I (*Preconventional morality*) where behavior is controlled by external influences: desire for reward or fear of punishment. Some few may be at level III (*Morality of autonomous moral principles*). At this level of moral reasoning, people follow internally held moral principles and decide between conflicting socially accepted standards. Development to a level of higher moral reasoning is influenced by culture, gender, and family background. It is important to note, however, that Kohlberg's levels may not apply to other cultures or to females. His studies were based on males.

Carol Gilligan on the other hand studied female moral development. Critical that Kohlberg based his study on males, yet generalized his theories to include females, Gilligan determined that females base moral judgments on an ethic of care. In such an ethic, caring for others takes precedence over justice. Human emotion is valued and considered. Conflicts arise over the issue of hurting others. For most adolescent girls, responsibility involves considering the feelings of others.[5]

> **In one study, adolescents who followed their consciences when faced with a moral dilemma had parents who took their children's moral transgressions seriously.**
> **— Thomas Lickona, Educating for Character**

Beyond generalities

Now that I have described high school adolescents – from freshmen to seniors – as one homogeneous group, I have to admit that the description does not tell the whole story. There is an incredible developmental difference between a fourteen-year-old and an eighteen-year-old. Betty Staley understands this developmental difference. In *Between Form and Freedom: A Practical Guide to the Teenage Years*, she presents a view of the adolescent more accurate than any other that I have read. Everything that I have experienced in working with teenagers over the years is written and clarified in her book.

Practical Approaches and Techniques

CURRICULUM

Social Studies

Social Studies courses at the high school level are an ideal place to teach conflict resolution, peace education, tolerance, etc. An aware teacher can tie conflict education topics into current and historic events, psychology, and anthropology.

For example, choose a conflict in history. Ask students to analyze how the parties resolved or escalated the conflict. Discuss the contributing attitudes, prejudices, and cultural or religious beliefs that may have influenced how the conflict was handled. Then rewrite the script. Consider what would have happened if the conflict had been handled differently. Take it one step further and find a parallel in modern life.

Social Studies courses can provide a wonderful forum for students to learn about what they think and believe:

> The study of anthropology involves a close look at ethnocentrism. Ethnocentrism is the belief in the superiority of one's own ethnic group. It causes conflict. When adolescents study anthropology, they learn to view the differences of other cultures without passing judgment. They learn to understand, not to judge.

> The study of current world political issues, e.g. the tribal wars of West Africa, can involve an investigation of how our individual lives and environments are affected by violent responses to conflicts. The dynamics of warfare can be analyzed.

> The study of democracy and democratic values involves the study of human rights. Democratic values – respect for the dignity and freedom of the individual, responsibility, tolerance, equality of opportunity, and justice – can be affirmed.

> The study of mythology also offers a vehicle for understanding self. In *Between Form and Freedom: A Practical Guide to the Teenage Years*, Betty Staley writes, "Studying the myths of a culture allows youngsters to understand the ways people think. Studying their values provides the youth with a possibility to reflect on his or her own cultural values. Such an interest often leads to greater understanding of humanity and an enhanced sense of brotherhood."

By delving deeper into the "Why's," "How's" and "What if's?" of history and culture, adolescents will have to look at themselves. Their thinking will be challenged. Conflict education will be a part of the curriculum.

Supplementary curricula appropriate for high school students (see bibliography) are

- *Facing History and Ourselves* by Facing History and Ourselves Foundation
- *War: What is it Good For?* by Terrence Webster-Doyle
- *Violence Prevention Curriculum for Adolescents* by Debra Prothrow-Stith
- *Educating for Human Dignity* by Betty A. Reardon
- *Arming the World: The International Trade in Arms* by Pippa Bobbett and Stephany Koorey

- *Peace and War: A Resource for Teaching and Learning* by Peace Education Project
- *Looking for Peace* by Sarah McCrum (cassette tape and booklet)

Drama

Drama touches the core of the human heart. Adolescents involved in dramatic productions can experience powerful emotions in the safety of another character: "Through drama, adolescents are able to try out roles, to experiment with anger, confrontation, sensitivity, compassion, and sacrifice, and to vicariously experience what happens to people in different life situations"(Staley).

Drama is often reserved for the Drama Club or the school theater group. This is unfortunate because drama can be a dynamic tool for teaching in the classroom. I know of a French teacher who uses drama to involve her students in the French language and culture. The students create and present a French musical. A Law Studies teacher runs a mock trial. An English class enacts Julius Caesar. A science class role-plays a land use debate. The students *feel* what they learn. The learning is deep.

Playwriting also can absorb the students in simulated conflict situations, e.g. students could be asked to write a dialogue between two soldiers – one might be a captive POW, the other his captor. Students can act out conflict situations for students in lower grades and then draw from the children how the problems can be resolved peacefully. Some high schools have theater groups run by students who write scripts to address teen issues. These teens perform their mini-plays for other schools, for parent groups, and at community events.

Conflict resolution skills

It is still critical to teach conflict resolution skills to high school students; however, the set-up of most high schools makes teaching those skills extremely difficult. There is seldom a way for high school students to get consistent daily lessons on conflict resolution. If conflict resolution is taught, it is usually done as a unit in health education. While this is a good idea, such units usually span a maximum of a few weeks. Those few weeks may be the only formal conflict resolution training the students get in all four years of high school. Mediation programs are often successful; however, the only students who get substantial training on how to mediate and resolve conflict are the mediators. The students trained as mediators comprise only a small percentage of the total student body. While many students may take advantage of the mediators, I wonder what conflict resolution skills the non-mediators are getting.

> One of the unanticipated results of having so many parents involved in our Beacon program is that it has reduced the level of violence in the school itself. When we began to think about it, this made sense. Young people are less likely to act violently in a setting where their mother, or their friend's mother, might be.
> — Geoffrey Canada, Fist Stick Knife Gun

Given the structure of the system, I choose to teach 'conflict resolution' through modeling, talking through conflict incidents that occur in my classroom, suggesting other ways to solve problems, and devaluing fighting as a solution. I don't know how much of what I say and do gets through, but I hope that I plant seeds that will grow while my students' maturity blossoms. For the short term, high expectations of behavior in my classroom provide for a safe environment in order for students to learn and grow.

AT SCHOOL AND AT HOME

Encourage social responsibility, empathy, and self-esteem

Dr. Sheila Davis, a professor of lyric writing at New York University, states that songs "are more than mere mirrors of society; they are a potent force in the shaping of it ...[P]opular songs... provide the primary 'equipment for living' for America's youth."
— Sheila Davis,
"Pop Lyrics: A Mirror and Molder of Society"

Adolescents today have the attitude, "If I'm not getting paid for it, I won't do it." This is possibly a reflection of our societal attitudes as a whole. Groups that depend on volunteers have a smaller and smaller pool of people to count on. This is in part the result of both parents having to work. With more people in the workforce, fewer are available to volunteer. Even those who can volunteer often don't. We are a 'for pay only' society. Our children are a reflection of this.

I have stopped paying my children an allowance based on the work they do in the house. They get an allowance regardless of the work they do. I realized that by paying my children to do work around the house, I was encouraging this 'for pay' attitude. The reward is external. There is no encouragement for an internal sense of satisfaction for a job well done. My children are expected to contribute to all aspects of keeping the house. They have jobs assigned to them based on their ability level. We are a family, a team. None of us are paid for what we do in the house. We do what needs to be done because we are a part of the team. Logical consequences exist for work not done.

Adolescents benefit from involvement in community projects, soup kitchens, tutoring, school jobs, etc. Such projects, either as part of the curriculum or extra-curricular, have a significant impact on young teens' sense of self-worth. In their identity search, adolescents draw on these experiences to get a sense of who they really are. Interest in social issues also helps adolescents become free from self-preoccupation (Staley). Service activities promote the growth of empathy because teens see others whose problems are 'worse than their own.'

Discuss the media's impact on students' belief systems and prejudices

Recently, I posed a question to a group of students who were adamant in their opinion that the media do not change attitudes. I asked, "If the media do not change attitudes, then why were Marilyn Monroe and Elizabeth Taylor considered beauties forty years ago, when by today's standards they would be considered too fat? Who or what caused our attitudes towards weight to change?" My students gave this question some thought. They could argue that violence in the media did not have an impact on them because it is difficult to determine the sources of violent attitudes. The fashion industry, however, is obviously promoted by the media. The results are visible and obvious. If television did not exist, could Twiggy ave changed the image of female beauty almost overnight?

Again, discuss with your teens the cultural impact of graphic violence, sex, and drug use in movies. Provoke their thinking on these issues. They will often argue that they know what is real and what is not, that they are not affected by the media. Don't accept that argument. How would they know how much they are affected? They know no difference unless you tell them. Explain your viewpoints. Teens have to make choices regarding their beliefs, but they cannot make informed choices in a moral vacuum. Don't 'impose' your views, rather give them information based on fact or Universal Values[6] so that they may make informed choices.

> **Another possible source of guidance for teenagers is television, but television's message has always been that the need for truth, wisdom and world peace pales by comparison with the need for a toothpaste that offers whiter teeth and fresher breath.**
> **— Dave Barry,**
> **Kids Today: They Don't Know Dum Diddly Do**

Conflict resolution skills in the home

"I think that all adolescent problems stem from the home. A child isn't going to have the esteem and strength to defend and believe in himself if he can't even get help and comfort at home. No matter what parents or teachers say, we are going to follow what you do." — Jennie, age 17

First, we must ask ourselves, "What are we modeling for our children?" Our children have been watching how we deal with conflict from infancy. Many of their patterns of dealing with conflict come from what we, as parents, have modeled. We need to look at how we, as parents, handle conflicts in relationships *and* conflicts in discipline. It is difficult to change our patterns for handling conflict without a commitment to education and practice. This education can come in the form of family mediation services, community parenting workshops, counseling, or reading and research (See Annotated Bibliography for reading resources).

Second, how do we teach our teens to handle conflict? Adolescents will learn by our example. When I say example, I mean our methods of resolving conflict directly with them and our insistence that they work through conflict with us in an appropriate way. We can also encourage adolescents to take specific coursework on conflict resolution or mediation or to become involved in specific activities that promote such learning.

This is a good time to encourage a quality martial arts program if the kids are not already in one. Find a program that emphasizes the non-violent philosophy of

What teens have to say about the media

Media violence has only affected me in a minor way. It has only left me numb to violence in general. I do not feel as bad now as when I saw it before. — John, age 16

I think that violence on TV and visual media has somewhat desensitized me to violence. It's impossible not to be. — Sara, age 15

Media affect every aspect of our lives. They dictate how to dress, how to act, and how to think. Media gives us a set of false morals to live by. I used to hate it when my friends would use bad language. I would remind them of this whenever they used a swear word. They were using these words because in movies etc. the stars all use profanity. It is seen as cool. A few months ago, I was shocked to discover that I didn't mind the swearing anymore. I had become accustomed to it by hearing it all the time in the media and in my own life. Along with this, I am no longer affected by the deaths of people I don't know. It is so common in the media for people to die, that it's no longer tragic to our society. It's just a fact of life that so many people die violent deaths, just like it's a fact of life that mosquitoes are smashed by people every day.
— Leah, age 16

I feel that TV has a negative effect on American culture but has the potential to have a very positive effect. We tend to be visual creatures. The visual element in our lives is very important and pertinent. Determining that, TV, no doubt, has an effect on the mind. Its influence is great. — Uma, age 15

The media focus on pretty women who are skinny and have the perfect body. I feel this escalates the problems that young women are facing. I have many friends who want to lose weight when they are already too thin. The media are not the only source of this attitude. Sports coaches and, in my case, ballet teachers are pressuring teens to look good in order to do good. — Trish, age 16

The media do no good for American culture. They have had a very neg-ative influence with their portrayal of skinny, sexy girls. Personally, it makes me very self-conscious. I feel as if, without consciously knowing it, my body is always on display. Truthfully, this is probably mean to say, but it makes me view the male sex as hormone-crazed pigs.
— Melissa, age 17

Media violence only gives me a bad feeling toward the world, my future, things that are yet to come. It makes me worry that the world won't be a safe place to live. — Jeff, age 17 the traditional martial arts. But be careful! Many schools place ads in the yellow pages claiming to teach discipline, respect, etc. Yet what they teach is fear. It is crucial during these years, while teens are defining their identity, that they do not attend a program that uses a militaristic drill-sergeant approach to teaching the martial arts. This will only teach teens to use power to control through fear. It will not teach them how to resolve conflict.

Look for a school that offers a complete martial arts program. Such a school will understand that in order to cope with conflict successfully, the student has to be taught to address conflict on all levels:
1. Prevention – to understand and avoid conflict
2. Resolution – to prepare the mind to resolve conflict through nonviolent means
3. Management – to humanely and skilfully quell conflict through physical means.

In this holistic way, the martial arts become peaceful.

Discipline

"We can help young people develop character by bringing them face to face with themselves and helping them set things right. By doing this we are communicating that there are objective standards of moral behavior and we expect youngsters to live up to them … If … parents focus on protecting the youngster from the punishment, they often do disservice to their children.… For teenagers to grow and develop their character, they need the courage of adults to help them face an unpleasant situation and to develop from it."– Betty Staley

Two common misconceptions come to mind when I think of teenagers and discipline:
1. Teenagers are old enough to be left unsupervised, especially after school.
2. Now that teens are old enough to take care of themselves and demanding to be allowed to do so, the parenting job is basically over. There's not much a parent can do at this point anyway.

Let's look at the first myth. Most teenagers get into trouble after school, before parents get home from work. That is when most sexual activity, delinquency, and drug use occur. A study of approximately 5,000 eighth graders found that students who had no supervisor for eleven or more hours a week were at twice the risk of substance abuse as their peers.[7] In addition, Metropolitan Life's 1993 national survey found that teachers and law enforcement officials agree that the lack of parental supervision at home is a major contributing factor to violence in schools.[8]

I have found many parents all too quick to save day-care expenses and to buckle under kid pressure to leave them home alone as early as third grade. Most of these parents really believe that their child would not break the rules or get into trouble. By the time these kids are in high school, they have had hundreds of hours of unsupervised time to experiment with breaking the rules. The parent, who may be vigilant at monitoring the younger children with phone calls and neighbor feedback, relaxes with the older children. Leaving them alone is old hat. The older kids get, however, the more expert they become at manipulating the situation to get away with misbehavior. I listen to their conversations in the school halls and classrooms. Their parents would be appalled if they knew what they were doing — and getting away with.

How to Choose A Martial Arts School[1]

The martial arts teach the importance of choosing carefully. The selection of the right school requires that you make a careful choice. There are many different kinds of Martial Arts schools, and you must sometimes visit more than one to find the right one for you.

It is important to see how the instructor teaches so you can see what kind of person he/she is. If the instructor is interested only in teaching self-defense, then you will only be taught how to fight. If the instructor is interested in helping you understand yourself and end conflict by nonviolent means, then he/she is teaching Martial Arts in a helpful way — a way that will help create peaceful relationships between people. Use the following checklist as you visit schools and observe classes:

1. Ask the students what they think of the classes.

2. Observe the classes.

3. Ask the teachers many questions and observe how they respond to your asking questions.

4. Ask if you can try a class or two.

5. Be aware of the 'vibrations' you get from the instructors. Are you afraid? Do you feel you can trust them? Listen to your feelings.

6. Ask how much lessons cost and what the payment schedule is. If the instructor asks for a lot of money in advance and you must sign a contract for many months of lessons, ask if you may have a three -month trial membership. It takes at least three months to get a good feel for whether you like it or not.

7. Look around at all the options. Don't feel pressured into taking lessons at one particular school.

8. STAY AWAY from schools that control students through fear (they often call it 'discipline') and a quasi-military environment. What they are really doing is bullying.

9. STAY AWAY from schools that encourage young people to emulate violent Martial Arts 'action heroes'.

Trust what you see and feel. If you take your time, you will find the right teacher and school. Choose with care.

[1]Adapted from *Facing the Double-Edged Sword*, 1988 and *The Shuhari Journal*, 1994 by Dr. Terence Webster-Doyle. Copyright 1997 by Susan Gingras Fitzell
Free the Children! Conflict Education For Strong Peaceful Minds. New Society Publishers. This page may be photocopied.

What can a parent do? Staying home is not an option for many parents. If possible, arrange work hours so that one parent is home during the after-school hours. Insist that teens become involved in after-school activities. If transportation to and from activities is a problem, try to network with other parents and share the responsibility. I cannot stress the need for supervision of adolescents enough. According to a study cited in the *Journal of Social Work*, strict supervision can protect children from violence and crime even in the most adverse environments.[9]

> **According to a Justice Department study, parental supervision, attachment to family, and consistency of discipline were the most important barriers to delinquency and drug abuse.**
> **— Stuart Greenbaum, "Drugs, Delinquency, and Other Data"**

The second myth – that the parenting job is now basically over – also yields serious consequences. Teens may need a different type of involvement. Parents need to allow teens opportunities to develop independence; however, this does not mean abandoning all limits, boundaries, and expectations.

The lack of consistent societal values and expectations in our culture has seriously undermined the ability of parents to hold to their ground rules. It has also created incredible confusion as to what the ground rules should be. Often, parents simply don't know what to do. When everyone else's child is doing x, y, and z, and you disapprove, how do you keep from buckling under the pressure to conform? Or how do you keep from asking yourself, "Am I being too strict? Too overprotective?" Some parents and most teens would have you believe that if you are 'too strict', there is something seriously wrong with you. You are left wondering if you need a therapist.

If we listened to what teens say when they are disciplined, we would think that discipline is the last thing they want. We fear we might lose them if we discipline them too much. Or worse, they might turn on us. In one survey of children aged ten to seventeen, however, 39 percent said they "sometimes" wished their parents were stricter or kept a closer watch over them and their lives (National Commission on Children).

Adolescents, especially between the ages of thirteen and sixteen, need adults to set reasonable rules and limits and to stand firm on them. They will push back, kicking and screaming against the boundaries. If parents yield to them, teens will eventually believe that their parents do not care (Staley). Teenagers admire strength, not weakness. They do not need a parental friend. They need a parent they will respect. I never worry that my students may not like me. What matters to me is that they respect me and believe me to be fair.

Hold class/family meetings

Family and class meetings are still important. The special considerations for adolescents discussed in Chapter Five remain the same, with variations in the magnitude of teen involvement outside the home. Without a homeroom period or morning meeting, the high school teacher will have much more difficulty implementing the class meeting approach. As a high school teacher, I used a weekly meeting, usually fifteen minutes on Fridays, to carry out the goals and ideals of a class meeting. It was a challenge to remain consistent. Curriculum demands often threatened to usurp my class meeting time. The scope of the meetings was less formal. We discussed concerns that came up during the week, or a topic of the students' choosing. I believe in the value of these meetings despite their limited scope.

> **See Chapter Five for special considerations for adolescents.**

The benefits were social interaction and teacher-student bonding. This relationship is so difficult to encourage and establish at this age and yet so necessary for the moral and social development of the student and the morale of the teacher. High school teachers generally minimize the importance of social interactions and teacher-student bonding. They focus on the curriculum. Many feel their only purpose as teachers is to teach content so as to prepare students academically for the future. I contend that when students and teachers form relationships based on caring and trust, much more academic learning occurs. In my workshops I ask teachers to close their eyes and remember one coach or teacher who made a positive difference in their lives during their teen years.

> **See Chapter Two for a sample family meeting agenda.**
>
> **See Chapter Three for details on how to set up class meetings.**

What they remember about that teacher is a relationship that fostered growth through caring.

EMOTIONS, DISCIPLINE, AND THE GROWTH OF EMPATHY

Allow teens time to deal with their emotions

As I've stated in previous chapters, it is important for students to have time to deal with their emotions. Teenagers are often ruled by their emotions. Emotions override their good judgment, dominate their peer relationships, and physically exhaust them. If they find a new love, their world is an emotional high. If they break up with a boyfriend or girlfriend, their distress can be all-consuming. Arguments can become volatile. Protests are passionate. The fight for independence is powered by intense emotion. When teens are in a state of extreme emotion, it is difficult for them to focus on academics or household responsibilities. Often, they simply cannot function beyond talking endlessly with friends about their feelings or withdrawing to their room to sleep or listen to music.

A little patience and care can go a long way when teens are overpowered by the turmoil of their emotions. In the classroom, try to foster an environment where teens feel comfortable enough to ask for what they need, whether that means seeing a guidance counselor or the nurse, or a trip to the lavatory to pull themselves together.

At home, be present for your teens, letting them know that you are willing to listen without judgment and without telling them what to do. Listen, empathize, offer suggestions, and if necessary share how you feel. A good verbal technique to use is to say, "How you deal with this is your choice. Make a good choice for yourself." Avoid lecturing or telling them they are being too sensitive. Avoid telling them how much worse it was for you. They don't care and can't relate. The only message they will get is that you don't understand. If they believe that you don't understand, they won't come to you the next time.

It's easy for us to trivialize some of the problems that teenagers get upset about. To them, however, their problems are all-consuming. Their emotions are intense. They don't have the maturity to keep these things in perspective. They need us to be understanding, to give them space to deal with these emotions, but also to set boundaries and limits so that we are not victims of their outbursts and they are protected from clouded judgment.

React to peer cruelty with 'moral feeling'

It is still important to react to peer cruelty with 'moral feeling' (Lickona, 1992). When students are caught up in their own emotional viewpoints, help them to see the other side. Simply don't tolerate disrespect for others. There are respectful ways to convey opinions and attitudes. Teens will make a greater attempt to be considerate if the expectation is firmly there from parents and teachers. If the expectation is not there and adults resign themselves to the inevitability of teen vulgarity, taunting, and disrespect, adolescents will pay the price in poor moral growth. I see adults turn their heads on this behavior all too often. Maybe they feel it is normal. Maybe they don't know what to do. Maybe.... The bottom line is that if we turn our heads, we are giving our silent consent. Set expectations and stand firm.

Talk about and demonstrate respect

As I stated in Chapter Five, the word 'respect' can be powerful with teens. Use teachable moments to connect unacceptable behavior with its effect on self-respect and respect for others. Teens rarely plan to be disrespectful. They react. They don't think the consequences through. This is partly a result of their emotions taking over. If disrespectful behavior is checked and discussed, teens become more aware of it. They also respond to the high standard of behavior that is being set. When disrespect is ignored, teens get the message that it is acceptable and common.

Require restitution

As I stated in previous chapters, restitution is an important component in character development. It holds youths accountable for their behavior. Restitution encourages responsibility, ownership, empathy, and remorse. When it takes the form of service, the experience is positive and often builds self-esteem. Restitution takes more time than simply imposing a 'sentence.' Investing that extra time yields great benefit: restitution 1) promotes an understanding of consequences, 2) is more likely than punishment to build self-esteem, and 3) yields a lower rate of recidivism.

RESPECT

1. Listen carefully when students speak. Remain open-minded and objective. Consider their messages carefully. Avoid interrupting a student or offering unsolicited advice or criticism.

2. Respect students' personal space. Students may feel threatened and become agitated if you violate their personal space.

3. Use friendly gestures, not aggressive ones. Avoid 'finger-pointing'. Open, upturned palms may be more appropriate and effective.

4. Use preferred names. Ask each student how they would like to be addressed in the classroom. Only in rare instances would their chosen name be inappropriate.

5. Get on their level. Try to adopt their physical level. If they are seated, try kneeling or bending over, rather than standing over them.

6. Ask questions rather than make accusations. This assumes that the student is a responsible person. "Are you ready to begin?" works better than
"Put your magazine away. It's time to start class." Use a concerned and kind tone.

7. Address problem behaviors privately. Reprimanding students in front of their peers may embarrass them unnecessarily. Speaking to them privately helps preserve their integrity and self-esteem.

Reprinted with permission from Teacher Talk. *Center for Adolescent Studies at the School of Education, Indiana University, Bloomington, IN., http://education.indiana.edu/cas/tt/v2i3/respect.html*

Copyright 1997 by Susan Gingras Fitzell
Free the Children! Conflict Education For Strong Peaceful Minds. New Society Publishers. This page may be photocopied.

Separate teens from their behavior

It is still important to be sure to address the misbehavior of the children and *not* the worth of the children themselves. When we are dealing with small children, it is easier to remember not to put them down while disciplining. It is not as tempting to 'tell that child just what I really think' to let off steam. Why? Because the smallness of the child is a reminder to us that we are dealing with *a child*.

Teens, however, are often as tall as adults. Some tower over you. They speak with adult words and adult vulgarity. They think abstractly, expressing themselves in ways we wish they wouldn't. When they have frustrated us to the very edge of our limits, we don't look at them and think, "They're just little children." Instead, their sarcasm and put-downs invite our sarcasm and put-downs. Unless we are careful, we can easily fall into the trap of labeling them no-goods. Personal attacks and generalized statements flow easily from angry mouths. This not only escalates conflict, it destroys relationships and the self-esteem of all involved.

I have a student who frequently yells, "I hate you!" when he doesn't get his way. I respond, "That's OK. But you still must treat me with respect. Your behavior is inappropriate." He is baffled by my acceptance of his hate and my refusal to retaliate with anger and hate. He does not need me to reinforce his lack of self-esteem. He needs me to set standards for his behavior and to hold him to them.

Involve teens in establishing meaningful rules and consequences

As I stated in Chapter Four, keep the number of rules to a minimum. Again, it is better to have four broad, simple rules than countless detailed rules. In my high school classroom, students defined the rules through class discussion and consensus. The are 1) Respect others, yourself, and school property, 2) Do the best job that you can, 3) Come to class on time and prepared, 4) Follow school rules as identified in the student handbook. This list works. Students soon learn that 'respect' is a very big word. Most classroom behavior falls under the category of respect. My behavior management methods have their foundation in Glasser's Reality Therapy and Choice Theory (refer to Chapter Three for details on this approach).

SUMMARY

Curriculum — At School
- Use Social Studies as a catalyst for discussions of conflict.
- Introduce Drama as a way to explore emotions and beliefs.
- Have students develop and put on interactive skits for lower age groups.
- Teach conflict resolution skills.

At School and At Home
- Encourage social responsibility, empathy, and self-esteem.
- Discuss the media's impact on students' belief systems and prejudices.
- Teach conflict resolution skills in the home.

- Don't underestimate the importance of consistent discipline.
- Hold class/family meetings.

Emotions, Discipline, And The Growth of Empathy

- Allow students time to deal with their emotions.
- React to peer cruelty with 'moral feeling'.
- Talk about and demonstrate respect.
- Require restitution.
- Separate students from their behavior.
- Involve teens in establishing meaningful rules and consequences.

Relationship Violence

Daddy, where are you?
You are sleeping. You can't hear me
as I cry here alone in bed all night.
Daddy, where are you?
It happened again.
He yelled at me
and called me names
like bitch
and slut
and others that hurt so much
it hurts just to say them.
Daddy, where are you?
Tonight was the worst.
He pushed me against the wall
and hit me.
My face is black and blue.
But, I was in too late for you to see.
Daddy, where are you?
Then he said he was sorry.
He told me that he loves me.
Now what should I do?
Daddy, where are you?
I need you.

— Susie, age 17

❖❖❖❖❖❖✿❖❖❖❖❖❖

My boyfriend and I were having a big fight. He was furious because I made plans to go on an overnight beach trip with my friends. He started calling me all these names. Then he hit me. He screamed that I'd better not go, or else.

— Jessie, age 18

I regularly present workshops on conflict education, empowerment, mental self-defense, etc. As a result, I was approached by the advisor for the Student Council of a suburban high school to do a presentation or workshop for the high school's Student Council members. Given that I would only have an hour or two to present a topic of consequence, I wanted a critical subject with a presentation that would make an impact. I proposed a workshop on dating violence during which I would show a video on the subject. Afterwards, there would be time for questions and answers. A school counselor, a psychologist, and I would be available for the discussion period. My proposal was rejected. The reason: the topic was considered inappropriate for the Student Council group. I was told that the decision was made by the council officers and the advisor. In light of the fact that one out of four teenagers reports having been involved in at least one abusive relationship, it seems to me that the topic is very appropriate.

I don't think, however, that the Student Council's attitude is unusual. First, relationship or dating violence and date rape are loaded topics. This is especially true because many people view the subject as feminist and anti-male. School administrations may be fearful of repercussions from parents of male students. The reality is that although male students are potential victims of relationship violence, female students comprise the overwhelming majority of victims. Date rape is almost exclusively a crime against females. Considering the statistics, I have in this chapter used the male gender for the abuser and the female gender for the victim. It is important to realize, however, that both sexes can be victims of dating violence and that both sexes are capable of being abusers.

Another reason schools may be reluctant to address the problem of relationship violence is a lack of awareness regarding the prevalence of the problem. Relationship violence is a secretive act. Victims of relationship violence rarely go to adults for help. They may be afraid that they will be further victimized by either losing freedoms, or by being blamed. Consequently, adults are unaware of the increasing incidence and magnitude of the problem. If school staff and parents don't believe the problem is significant, they won't address it. Human nature is such that if we are not personally touched by a crisis situation, we aren't moved to do something about it. Well, it's time we take our blinders off. The problem does exist. We need to act *before* it reaches epidemic proportions.

UNDERSTANDING RELATIONSHIP VIOLENCE

Societal/cultural values

My rude awakening regarding the drastic change in teen attitudes towards dates and relationships came in the spring of '95. I overheard several fourteen- and fifteen-year-old boys talking about their girlfriends. They were a clean-cut group. They were talking shamelessly, as a matter of course, and almost boastful. What they were talking about shocked me. They weren't talking about sports, sexual conquests, or female anatomy. They were talking about hitting and slapping their girlfriends. They made it sound like a normal, acceptable thing to do. The male

**There are nearly three times as many animal shelters in the United States as there are shelters for battered women and their children.
— Senate Judiciary Hearings, Violence Against Women Act**

supervising the group ignored the conversation. The lack of action on the part of the adult disappointed me. I can only guess at the reasons for his passivity.

Could it be that we, as a culture, have become apathetic towards the increasingly discourteous attitudes of our youth? Do we feel that our efforts to try to change the negative and violent beliefs of our young people are an exercise in futility? Have we bought into the 'Good Ol' Boys' world where women should be passive sexual objects? Are we unsure of what attitudes and values we should teach? Are we wary of being accused of imposing our values on our students? Are we worried about stepping on someone else's familial and cultural toes?

It's impossible to separate family values from cultural attitudes in general: "We can't talk about families without talking about culture, values, beliefs and traditions. And we can't talk about taking action to confront dating violence without challenging traditional values and beliefs regarding the family, courtship and marriage, male/female relationships and seeking help" (Levy and Giggans). Family values about appropriate feminine and masculine behavior have a strong influence on dating relationships. For example, in a family where girls are brought up to please and cater to men, female victims of relationship violence may be blamed for failing to appease the men. Religious beliefs about the head of household as well as about marriage and divorce may trap families in patterns of behavior that hide, encourage, or dismiss abuse. Consequently, "people in conflict within their cultures and between cultures must make choices. Using culture as an excuse when in conflict is avoiding responsibility" (Levy and Giggans).

North American society values power and control. Our culture's 'tough-guy' image equates physical and emotional violence with masculinity. From John Wayne to Chuck Norris, North American male heroes consistently demonstrate aggressive ways to resolve conflict: fists, guns, threats, and intimidation: "In our society, teenagers can learn mistaken ideas of what is normal in a relationship from what they see in movies, television and advertising. They see many situations in which a strong person or group maintains their power by using violence to control people who are less powerful."[10]

Movies, television, and music videos portray violence against women as a common fact of life. This is our entertainment. The more graphic it is, the better the ratings. The sad news is that it sells. The media's presentation of women as objects of sex and abuse is desensitizing our society to the violence. Boys are especially prone to this desensitization because of their identification with violence and masculinity. We are being conditioned to view violent behavior as normal, acceptable, and natural. Consider the definition of brainwashing, a well-known means of dealing with prisoners during times of war:

Brain·wash·ing (brân wòsh ˆîng, -wô´shîng) *noun*
the application of a concentrated means of persuasion, such as an advertising campaign or repeated suggestion, in order to develop a specific belief or motivation[11]

What are today's media presentations if not 'repeated suggestions' and 'advertising campaigns'? Do advertisers use sexy, excessively thin models for any other reason than to create a specific belief or motivation? Face it: the media are brainwashing our culture. None of us remains unaffected.

Our culture glorifies macho men. It views women as sex objects. We accept stereotypes of powerless, submissive women and idolize powerful, controlling men. This makes relationship violence seem more normal. Donald Sabo, co-author of *Sex, Violence and Power in Sports: Rethinking Masculinity*, writes, "Boys are encouraged to live this model. Be a man by being violence-prone. Be a man by keeping your feelings inside all the time. And be a man by using women as sexual trophies. This is not a feminist issue, but a public-health issue."[12] This social model is especially confusing to the adolescent who is searching for identity and using cultural messages to establish that identity.

We are also quick to blame the victim in our culture. Friends and relatives often blame the victim of relationship violence. They may discourage her from prosecuting. They'll tell the girl that it's not a big deal, or claim it will ruin the guy's future. They often make the victim feel guilty and responsible. Think of how quick people are to question the rape victim's whereabouts, dress, and behavior. In a violent marriage or dating relationship, it is often the woman who is faulted for staying in the abusive situation. The focus is on the abused woman, not on the abusive male.

This focus is a result of our fear of victimization. If we can find fault with the victim, then we can mistakenly believe that it can't happen to us. If we don't do the things the victim did, we won't be next. For example, if we can find fault with a victim's dress, and we don't dress that way, we are safe. If we can find fault with the choices the victim made regarding where she was, what she was doing, or who she was with, and we make different choices, then we can feel safe. That is why we feel so much more vulnerable, threatened, and outraged when an elderly woman is a victim of rape because we can't separate ourselves from the possibility of our own victimization by blaming it on actions or appearance. The elderly woman probably wasn't dressed like a 'slut' or on the street after midnight. It is more difficult to blame her.

This attitude of blaming the victim has become the norm for our young people. I have heard teenagers take an unwavering stand against victims of violence and crime: "If you leave your calculator on your desk and walk away, and it gets stolen, it's your fault!" or "If a girl is a victim of relationship violence or rape, it's her fault for not doing something about it!" or "If you don't lock your car, it's your fault if your CD player gets stolen!" or "She deserved to get slapped!" or "If I lose my wallet in the mall, and someone finds it and takes the money, it's my fault for not being more careful!" These aren't only the attitudes of a 'street-wise' minority. These are the attitudes of youth across the board. They may very well be the attitudes of your students and your children.

Who is at risk for relationship violence?

I have friends who have been through emotional and physical violence with a date or boyfriend. The cause might be that the abuser has no power in his own life, so he feels that he can be powerful if he can control another person. Parents and teachers might help by giving their children enough control over their lives so that they can build up their self-esteem. — Female, age 16

It is natural to want to separate ourselves, our students, and our children from the 'at-risk' group. In actuality, relationship violence can happen to *anyone*. Abuse can happen in *any* type of relationship: male/female, male/male, or female/female. It crosses all economic, ethnic, religious, racial, and gender groups. There is no specific 'type' of person that becomes enmeshed in relationship violence. No one is immune. That fact is the most frightening aspect of the problem. No parents can rest assured that it won't happen to their child. It can.

Here are some statistics (these statistics are understated because many or most girls never speak up):

- "In studies of adolescent violence, researchers are finding that physical abuse among dating teens seems to be a rising trend. Twenty-five percent of teenagers responding to a recent survey said they have experienced physical violence in a dating relationship. Other researchers estimate that this figure is conservative, and that the percentages of young people who are victims of dating violence are even higher."[13]

- "In a 1992 study conducted by the University of Illinois at a representative high school outside Chicago, 36 percent of students reported some form of violence in a dating relationship. Only 4 percent had talked about it with an authority figure."[14]

- Studies show that approximately one out of every three high school and college students has experienced sexual, physical, verbal or emotional violence in dating relationships. Date rape accounts for more than half of all reported rape cases."[15]

- Ninety-five percent of reported abuse is male violence toward women.[16]

- Victims of domestic violence often report that the violence started while dating. Domestic violence is the primary cause of injury to women, producing more injuries to women than rapes, muggings, and auto crashes combined.[17]

These facts are sobering. To bring the message close to home, consider the following: if you have twenty-four students in your classroom, six will be victims of dating or domestic violence. If you are the parent of four children, one will be a victim of dating or domestic violence. The potential is there even if you have sons, although it is probably reduced.

Why are our teens vulnerable to relationship violence?

Teenagers desperately want to be in a dating relationship. Lori Casey, a crisis intervention worker at the YWCA in Manchester, NH, explains that couplehood is very important in our culture: "Society doesn't celebrate being yourself." It applauds and romanticizes couples. As we spoke, words to a love song on the radio echoed this sentiment. Even our most self-assured girls can fall victim to this cultural attitude. Girls will stay in an abusive relationship rather than be without a date. A lack of confidence in being independent is a major factor. Girls become dependent or codependent rather than independent. Women are trained from toddlerhood to be nurturers, fixers, and caretakers. Even girls brought up by progressive parents who try to minimize this conditioning are bombarded by cultural messages defining appropriate female behavior. All the girls have to do is turn on the radio or TV or step outside their door to be influenced.

Domestic Violence is the leading cause of injury to women between ages 15 and 44 in the United States — more than car accidents, muggings, and rapes combined. — Uniform Crime Reports, Federal Bureau of Investigation, 1991

Boys are also victims of cultural expectations: "There is a lot of peer pressure on guys to be sexually active, so sometimes they are sexually aggressive with girls. Guys feel it is their role to be dominant and to control their girlfriends' activities and behavior" (Levy, 1993). Again, this is the 'macho' male image glorified by our culture. Think of the words men use to taunt the guy who is believed to have a strong, powerful, or dominating wife or mother: he is "pussywhipped," he is "henpecked," he has "no balls," he's got "a ring through the nose," he's a "wuss," he is "momma's boy." I can't tell you how many times I have been asked by family and friends, "Who wear's the pants in your relationship?" I always found that to be a distasteful question. I felt uncomfortable. No matter what I said, it wouldn't be the right answer. I would reply, "We are equals." Then I would get a litany of comments about women's lib. I always knew that the 'right' answer was "Him."

Vicarious learning also plays a major role in forming male abusers. Many young men who are abusive in relationships are simply repeating patterns that they have witnessed at home. They've watched and listened as their mothers were verbally or physically abused at home. They believe this violence to be a normal part of a relationship.

While gender roles and expectations cultivate relationship violence, inexperienced teens romanticize relationships. They believe that jealousy and possessiveness are signs of love. They have mistaken ideas about sex and relationships. Many teens believe that if a guy takes out a girl and spends money on her, she owes him sex. She may not want to have any sexual contact; however, there is tremendous pressure on her to comply with his demands (Levy, 1993).

Several years ago, I took a women's self-defense course. There were five teenage girls in the class. One night, the instructor read down a list of dating myths and asked for 'true' or 'false' answers. The myths covered situations when a girl could say no to sex. I was astounded at the girls' answers. They really believed that at certain points in any given situation, they could NOT say no to sexual intercourse.

People don't choose to become battered in a relationship. Two people fall in love in the seduction stage of a relationship. During that time a very intense bond develops. The girl or boy feels that the other person is the perfect romantic part-ner. These romantic feelings about male/female roles in a relationship influence how the partnership is perceived.

Teens are susceptible to exploitation. They are confused about what is happening and have difficulty identifying the behavior as abuse. Lori Casey, the YWCA crisis intervention worker in Manchester, NH, explains that the abusive person is a master at manipulation. He finds his victim's weak spot and goes for it. You can have a girl who is president of her class, a successful athlete, and an honors student, yet she becomes involved with a boy who is abusive. Suddenly, she finds herself trapped. Why? He has found her weak spot. Everyone has one. Such weak spots are needs or beliefs held deeply within the girl's psyche that make her vulnerable to the abuser. He uses her weakness against her to control her.

Weak spots or risk factors that make women susceptible to relationship violence may not be apparent to parents and friends. They include low self-esteem regarding a girl's perception of her appearance or her ability to get and keep a boyfriend. She may feel great about her academic, sports, or music ability, yet feel terrible about her attractiveness to the opposite sex. Gender role identity is another weak spot with ramifications in dating relationships. Girls who have 'feminine' gender identities, particularly emotional excitability and relationship dependence, are at risk to experience abuse.[18] They have accepted the male and female stereotypes that make them vulnerable to male violence and female passivity.

Another risk factor is what Howard M. Halpern in his book *How To Break Your Addiction to a Person* describes as Attachment Hunger. When attachment hunger is great, people are prone to staying in relationships even when they know they are bad for them. Halpern explains that relationships can be addictive in the same way that people become addicted to substances or behaviors like gambling: "What makes a particular relationship an addiction is when these little addictive 'I need you' elements expand to become the controlling force in [a person's] attachment."[19]

Halpern describes attachment hunger as the basis of being addicted to another person. The roots of attachment needs lie in the mother/infant relationship: "Even the most devoted of mothers cannot be perfectly tuned in to the child, cannot be with him at every moment, cannot be always and immediately responsive to his needs." Halpern explains that a person's dependent attachment is likely to be based on an early and unresolved need to attain oneness with the mother of the early years. The clinging seen in abusive relationships, he believes, is based on an old illusion: "The mother or father to whom you looked to make you feel good, secure, and strong exists in the person with whom you are now involved; therefore, if you can get that person to love you, everything will be okay" (Halpern).

Parental use of corporal punishment also sets the groundwork for males and females to accept physical violence in a relationship as a deserved act of love. The girl looks for the parent in the boy, and his violence is accepted as punishment for her misbehavior. Also, according to Murray Straus's studies on corporal punishment, children who were spanked frequently are more likely to be aroused by sadomasochistic sex.[20] The buttocks are an erogenous zone: "Spanking of the buttocks can stimulate immature sexual feelings in some children. They have no control over those feelings, nor do they understand what is happening to them. The tragic consequence for some of these children is that they form a connection between pain, humiliation, and sexual arousal that endures for the rest of their lives".[21]

Teenagers experimenting with sexuality and confused in their search for identity are further troubled by the open display of sadomasochistic clothing, jewelry, and body piercing in vogue today. Again, violence in relationships appears normal. More sadly, it may be filling a deep psychological need stemming from early childhood experiences.

Why the victim can't get out of an abusive relationship

By the time the abuse starts in a relationship, a dependent or codependent relationship between the partners has been formed. The relationship is so intense that the victim feels trapped. Even when her rational self knows that this relationship is bad for her, her emotional self can't let go. She may be financially dependent on the abuser. Emotionally she is so dependent on her partner that to be without him would be devastating to her sense of self. Without him she would feel an emptiness, despair, and sadness that she believes can only be alleviated by her connection to him. Her world revolves around the whims of her partner. He expertly manipulates the situation to remain in total control. She romanticizes his jealousy and possessiveness. She focuses on all the charming things he does during the seduction period, equating his behavior with love. She fears his rejection.

When he becomes abusive, the victim thinks the violence is somehow her fault. She starts believing that she deserves the abuse. He reinforces this belief by repeatedly abusing her verbally. He tells her it's her fault he lost his temper, it's her fault he had to hit her, no one else would put up with her, she's lucky to have him. He plays mind games by saying one thing and doing another, by giving her the silent treatment, by manipulating her with kind words, and then with accusations and threats. He unloads his problems on her. She bears the brunt of his emotional rollercoaster.

> I would make up my mind that I'd had enough. I wouldn't stay with him if he continued to act this way. I decided to tell him. We talked about how he hurt me. I told him that I wouldn't stay with him if it continued. He got all little boyish. He was full of apologies. He made excuses for his behavior. He talked about all the people in his life that weren't there for him. I knew these things were true. He had a rough life. I was the one person in his life who believed in him. I felt sorry for him. He asked me to give him a chance. He promised it would get better. The emotion was so intense between us. So, I gave him another chance. I knew my mom and my friends would think I was crazy. I didn't care. I believed him. I knew I could help him. I had to keep trying.   — Samantha, age 18

> **Women who leave their batterers are at a 75% greater risk of being killed by the batterer than those who stay.**
> — Barbara Hart, National Coalition Against Domestic Violence

Samantha couldn't get out of her relationship with an abusive partner because she believed that she could change him: "If only I can convince him that I love him, he'll change." She hoped it would get better. Because women have been conditioned to be selfless caretakers, nurturers, and protectors, they are prime targets for manipulators who are skilled at identifying these traits as weak spots. If a girl's self-esteem is largely dependent on her ability to care for others, that self-esteem is seriously in jeopardy in an abusive relationship. Her ability to be good enough is constantly attacked by the abuser. If a girl's self-esteem is dependent on caring for others, she has no internal sense of positive esteem. She looks for esteem outside herself. Without self-esteem, she is unable to develop and maintain mutually rewarding relationships.

Sometimes family and friends encourage the relationship to continue by ignoring the signs of abuse or by siding with the abuser. Mothers who grew up in abusive, male-dominated environments and who accept this as normal, may fault the daughter for not conforming to the demands of the male. In this situation, the girl's voice is stifled. She receives the message that her feelings are wrong or invalid. She questions her identity and doubts her own beliefs. She accepts the verdict that she is the guilty one. Or she develops hostility and anger that she represses, suppresses, or otherwise internalizes. All of this will leave her confused and mistrusting.

It is difficult to leave an abusive relationship. Victims become emotionally dependent on their abusive partners. Victims need non-judgmental support, safety, and assistance in order to leave. Criticism and blame will further undermine their self-esteem and make it even more difficult to make the break.

Signs and symptoms of relationship violence

How do you know if you, or someone you know, is in a violent relationship? What signs do you look for? The following are some of the signs and symptoms of relationship violence. Not all these behaviors are necessarily present. In the early stages of a relationship, only the milder symptoms will be obvious. These indications are warning signs of the violence ahead. As the relationship progresses, the violence escalates. Some relationships don't become physically violent for years. It is important to realize that verbal violence is just as damaging to the woman, if not worse. Don't assume the relationship is not abusive simply because there is no physical violence!

- **He has low self-esteem.** He believes, "I'm nothing without you."
- **He is extremely jealous.** Jealousy is not a sign of love. It's a sign of a serious lack of trust. This lack of trust stems from low self-esteem and deep insecurity. This insecurity is manifested in jealous, controlling behavior. He gets mad if she talks to other people. He spies on her. He watches where she is, what she is doing, and who she is talking to. He accuses her of flirting and calls her a 'whore.' He is jealous of her family and friends. He won't accept breaking up.

- **He is severely possessive.** He treats her as if she was property. He sweeps her off her feet. He forces her to commit to the relationship before she is ready. The pressure he puts on her may be subtle. He can be very manipulative.
- **He is controlling.** He completely rules the relationship and makes all the decisions. He tells her how to dress, how to wear her hair, who she can be with, and where she can go. He believes men should be in control and women should be passive and submissive.
- **He has unpredictable mood swings.** His behavior shifts dramatically between being jealous, controlling, or angry to being sweet, charming, and loving.
- **He is explosive.** He yells loudly, calls names, threatens others with violence. He loses his temper frequently and more easily than seems necessary. He becomes enraged when she doesn't listen to his opinion or advice.
- **He experiences physical or verbal violence at home.** He is abused or his parents' relationship is physically violent. He may have been, or still is, beaten by his parents, particularly by his father. Children from abusive homes are affected. Boys tend to become aggressive whereas girls become passive and submissive. Many abusers were witnesses to family violence as children. They saw their fathers beat their mothers. Consequently, they view this behavior as normal and acceptable. But not all boys who grow up in violent homes become violent. Some boys hate the violence and grow up to be loving, non-violent husbands.
- **He is violent towards animals or things.** He kicks or hits pets. He punches walls, throws objects, breaks things in anger.
- **He is physically violent towards her.** He may slap her, pull her hair, twist her wrists, arms, or fingers, push, shove, or punch her.
- **He is using alcohol and drugs.** Alcohol lowers a person's self-control. He uses alcohol or drugs as his excuse for violence. He pressures her to use drugs or to drink with him.
- **He does not respect women.** He expresses derogatory attitudes towards women, calling them "bitches," "chicks," or "broads."
- **He ignores her feelings, wants, concerns.**
- **He uses guilt to make her do what he wants.**
- **He forces or manipulates her into having sex.** She is afraid to say no. He ignores her personal boundaries. He won't accept "NO" for an answer. He makes her perform sexual acts that she doesn't enjoy.
- **He uses fear, intimidation, and humiliation to control her.** He embarrasses her in front of other people.
- **He isolates her.** He uses lies and criticism to alienate her from friends and family. If she has male friends, she is a "whore". Support systems cause trouble. He coerces her into skipping school.
- **He has unrealistic expectations.** She is expected to meet all his emotional and physical needs. He won't settle for anything less than perfection. The definition of perfection changes from day to day.

- **He blames others for his problems.** It's the teacher's fault he's failing. It's his parents' fault he takes off. People are out to get him. He tells her everything that goes wrong in their relationship is her fault. It's her fault he got angry. He has a history of bad relationships that he blames on others.

The abuse cycle

Things would be going great. I felt like I was on a high. Then he would start picking on little things that he said I did wrong. I could almost predict it by the calendar. He would get angrier and angrier over the smallest things. The tension would build. Then something would happen and he'd explode. I felt totally defenseless against his attacks. They destroyed something inside of me. When he finished his tirade, he'd leave. I was left with all this hurt, totally confused about what to do. Then, when we got together again, he'd be so sweet. He'd do anything for me. I tried to talk to him about what happened, but he'd start apologizing, saying he couldn't help it because I made him so mad. He promised it wouldn't happen again. Then things would get better again. I just hoped it would last.   —Carrie, age 18

Relationship violence is rarely an issue at the onset of a relationship. The couple meets, flirts, and begins to define their relationship. During the initial courting period, the boy is charming, often doting and caring. The girl is 'swept off her feet' by the attention her boyfriend is giving her. She falls in love with him and the illusion that he will take care of her, understand her, and be there for her whenever she needs him. He falls in love with her and the illusion of her total and complete adoration. She could not predict that this perfect, romantic relationship would turn violent. She is hooked. This is critical for the boy. He can later say, "Look what we had." She will later say, "If only we could get back to where we were." These illusions make it hard to end a violent relationship.

The cycle of violence goes in phases. The **first phase** is the tension-building phase. In this stage the boyfriend becomes moody and critical. He finds fault with his girlfriend's actions, with her looks, with what she says or doesn't say. He is on edge waiting like a cat perched to attack. She tries to figure out what is wrong. He can't tell her. She tries harder and harder to be 'good.' She can't seem to please him. If she tries too hard, he may start to feel smothered and actually withdraw from her emotionally.

The **second phase** is the violence stage. Something sets off his anger and he explodes in a tirade. He verbally assaults her, blaming, accusing, name-calling, and humiliating her. He becomes passive, ignoring her. He gives her the silent treatment as an attempt to control her. He starts throwing things, punching walls, looking for objects to take his anger out on. He may push her and hit her. Sometimes he sexually attacks her. Many times her sobbing will stop his attack. He starts to feel guilty, apologizes, and tries to make up.

The **third phase** is the seduction stage. They reconcile. Their relationship is intensely happy, romantic, and sexually satisfying. During this time the girl begins to believe that things will be different. She forgets the hurt he has caused her and focuses on all the wonderful things he says and does for her during this phase. She excuses his violent behavior. She is constantly explaining to her friends and family all the reasons she loves him and stays with him. She often denies his violence.

A **fourth phase** sometimes ensues. If the girl tries to break up with him or he is angered again before they reconcile, his violence may escalate to deadly proportions. This is a very dangerous phase. He may think that if he can't have her, no one else will. This phase can lead to serious injury or even the girl's death.

Love, hope, and fear keep the cycle in motion and make it difficult to end a violent relationship (Peace at Home, see Additional Resources). The couple believes that they are deeply in love. During the seduction phase, the victim focuses on the relationship's good points and convinces herself that it is not all bad. Hope keeps the relationship intact. She hopes that he will change. The relationship didn't begin like this. She only wants it to go back to the way it was in the beginning. Everything was perfect then. Fear paralyzes her from moving out of the relationship in its worst moments. She fears that the threats to kill her and her family will become a reality.[22]

VICTIM NO MORE! WHAT YOU CAN DO

How to protect yourself from relationship violence

Young women can take positive steps to protect themselves from victimization. Education is the first step. If girls are aware of the signs and symptoms of relationship violence, they are more likely to recognize those symptoms before becoming trapped. With awareness comes the ability to take action to prevent becoming a victim.

Linda Murphy, Empowerment and Self-Defense Instructor at Murphy's Inc., teaches a women's self-defense course intended to reprogram women to think assertively, to think quickly, and to think defensively – both verbally and physically. She believes one of the key elements to preventing being a victim is practicing verbal assertiveness and body language that demonstrates strength and confidence. "Strengthen your voice," she says, "every day! Practicing these skills every day feeds into your ability to fight (verbally or physically) and to defend yourself. Plus, you are validating to yourself that you are worth fighting for and that it's OK to stand up for yourself."

If you find it difficult to assert yourself through voice, words, or body language, she suggests you imagine that someone is doing something to your kids. "How would you feel and act," she asks, "if someone were attacking your kids? Allow yourself to get in touch with your primal self." I asked her if this example would work with teens. She explained that she uses this example with young people frequently. They usually can relate to protecting small children. It is often easier to summon our most aggressive self to help children. Often, speaking up for ourselves is the hardest thing to do. "When we speak up for other people," Murphy explains, "it validates our strength."

Murphy believes that the best way to avoid relationship violence is to focus on what you want in life, even if it means asking yourself, "'How much time do I want

THE CYCLE OF RELATIONSHIP VIOLENCE[1]

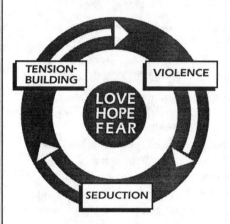

The Cycle of Relationship Violence shows how relationship violence often becomes a pattern made up of three stages:

TENSION-BUILDING

criticism, yelling, swearing, using angry gestures, coercion, threats

VIOLENCE

physical and sexual attacks and threats

SEDUCTION

apologies, blaming, promises to change, gifts

It also explains how three dynamics – love, hope, and fear – keep the cycle in motion and make it hard to end a violent relationship.

LOVE / HOPE / FEAR
keep the cycle in motion

Love for your partner, the relationship has its good points, it's not all bad.

Hope that it will change, the relationship didn't begin like this.

Fear that the threats to kill you or your family will become a reality.

THE VIOLENCE WHEEL

The violence wheel helps link the different behaviors that together form a pattern of violence. It shows the relationship as a whole – and how each seemingly unrelated behavior is an important part in an overall effort to control someone.

[1]Reprinted with permission from Peace At Home, Inc., A Human Rights Agency, 95 Berkeley Street, Suite 107, Boston MA 02116, 617-482-1851

These diagrams and their descriptions in their original form, refer to domestic violence. Relationship violence falls in the same category as domestic violence. Relationship violence is termed domestic violence when partners begin to live together. These diagrams are just as relevant to relationship violence as domestic violence.

to spend with one person, my friends, my family, etc.' By asking yourself this question, you are much more focused on what *you* want to do. You are in charge of yourself. It takes you away from feeling like a victim. Confident people serve other people, too, but because they want to, not because they feel like they have to."

What you can do if you are a victim of relationship violence

- **Tell someone.** Develop a support system. Confide in a friend or relative who you trust. Find a support group.
- **Remember that you are not alone.** You are not the only person who is in this type of situation. You are not a bad person because you are caught in this relationship.
- **Document injuries.** Take photographs. Keep a journal describing what is happening. Place documentation in a safe place: with a friend, a trusted relative, or a counselor. Don't leave this information where he can find it.
- **Seek counseling.** Contact a local crisis centre to get information about resources such as shelters, counseling, and legal assistance. Do this *before* you think you'll need the information.
- **Go to a hospital.** If you are injured, get medical attention.
- **Report the assault.** You can get a restraining order to provide some protection for yourself. This is a court order signed by a judge stating that for a specified length of time, he cannot harass, molest, or harm you. They may forbid any contact. If he stalks you or tries to make contact with you in any way, the police have legal cause to arrest him.
- **Press criminal charges.** If you feel intimidated by the difficulty of proceeding in a criminal case, try the civil court instead. It is easier to win a case in civil court. Bring someone with you who can support your testimony during the trial. Judges and State attorneys are sometimes biased, hostile, or indifferent towards domestic violence.
- **Understand that you *cannot* stop the violence.** You cannot change the abuser!
- **Look in a mirror, look into your eyes, and say, "I deserve to be treated with respect."** Say, "I deserve to be loved without being hurt! I am strong and courageous! I am a survivor!" (Levy, 1993)
- **Plan for your safety.**
- **Take a self-defense course.** As I said earlier (and it really merits repeating), this is one of the most empowering things that you can do to help yourself. You will not only learn physical self-defense skills, you will become strong mentally and emotionally. The physical fighting skills become secondary in importance. Emotional strength and empowerment are the primary goals. Choose your school carefully. Be careful not to choose a school with a drill-sergeant instructor. You need an instructor who helps you to feel safe. Observe classes. Choose a style that can give you practical self-defense skills. Take note of how many female students are in the classes. Stay away from schools that can't keep female students. Are there any female instructors? You need to feel comfortable and safe. Your partner may strongly disapprove of your participation in a self-defense course. Be strong! Do what is best for *you*.

PROTECT YOURSELF FROM RELATIONSHIP VIOLENCE!

- **Practice verbal assertiveness skills and strong, confident body language – every day!** Strengthen your voice. This increases your ability to fight and defend yourself.

- **Be aware of male/female stereotypes.** Our culture encourages men to be dominant in a relationship. It conditions women to believe they should be passive and please a man. Accepting this cultural message makes you vulnerable to victimization. Stick up for yourself!

- **Set limits and boundaries.** Decide what behavior you will accept in a relationship and go with this decision. Communicate these expectations to your partner clearly through words, tone of voice, and body language. Do not back down!

- **Trust your gut.** If behavior in your relationship does not feel right, it probably isn't right. Don't ignore your feelings. Do what it takes to care for yourself and to keep yourself safe.

- **Back out at the FIRST sign of temper.** It will not get better. Relationship violence escalates and becomes more serious after each cycle. If you must stay in the relationship, insist that you both go to therapy to learn to communicate effectively and to manage anger appropriately.

- **Avoid alcohol and other drugs.** Incidents of relationship violence increase when partners are under the influence of alcohol or drugs. If your thinking is impaired, you won't be able to make good, quick decisions to ensure your personal safety.

- **Take a self-defense or traditional martial arts course.** Don't wait until you are threatened or in danger. Self-defense for women, young or old, is a wonderfully empowering activity. It builds self-confidence, self-discipline, inner strength, and control. It also provides women with an opportunity to succeed in a traditionally male sport, equalizing male/female roles.

- **Say NO! to any unwanted sexual behavior.** Any sexual behavior forced onto you after you have said NO! is an assault!

WHAT YOU CAN DO IF YOU ARE A VICTIM OF RELATIONSHIP VIOLENCE

- Tell someone.

- Remember that you are not alone.

- Document injuries.

- Seek counseling.

- Go to a hospital to get care for your injuries.

- Report the assault.

- Press criminal charges.

- Understand that you cannot stop the violence.

- Look in a mirror, look into your eyes, and say, "I deserve to be treated with respect."

- Plan for your safety.

- Take a self-defense course.

- Be strong. Do what is best for you.

How to help a victim of relationship violence

When your best friend is being abused and she tries to hide it, it hurts more than just herself. We all knew something was wrong when she said she didn't know where the bruises came from and when we saw him hit her all the time. She acted as if it was fine and nothing was wrong with their relationship. Just because he buys her gifts all the time it does not make up for the abuse that he gives her. When confronted by family or friends, they deny that anything is wrong because they think it's all right. No one has the right to hurt another human being. Both females and males need to be taught how to handle their anger better than some of them do. – Jennifer, age 17

Teens don't go to adults for help because they are afraid choices will be taken away from them. "Studies have shown that teens rarely seek help from adults about this problem. Parents don't expect these kinds of problems with children of this age, and often don't recognize the violence for what it is. When not recognized and actively confronted, violence that starts at this critical stage of a young person's life may have damaging effects for years to come" (Levy and Giggans). Parents and teachers need to set up lines of communication and parameters to work *with* them, so that the teens don't lose all control. Levy and Giggans emphasize that it is important to educate teens in a non-threatening way. Give them all the accurate information. Don't lie to them. Don't break trust.

So, what can you do to help victims of relationship violence? Don't deny the problem! Be willing to accept what is happening and open your mind to the options.

- **Educate yourself.** Learn as much as you can about relationship violence. Some excellent references are listed at the end of this chapter.
- **Listen without judging.** Support her as a friend. Allow her to tell her story. Encourage her to express her feelings.
- **Don't blame her.** If you do, she will avoid you. If she avoids you, you can't help her.
- **Believe her and let her know that you do.**
- **Tell her that she doesn't deserve to be abused.** Girls and women who ended abusive relationships said that this statement was most influential in helping them to leave.
- **Let her know that you care and are concerned about her welfare.** Be there for her even if she doesn't leave the relationship. Let her know that she can always come to you – no matter what.
- **Tell her that the abuse is not her fault.**
- **Be sensitive to her feelings.** Fear, ambivalence, anger, denial, and helplessness are all normal reactions to relationship violence. Acknowledge her courage to tell someone.
- **Help her to see her strengths.** Her self-esteem is low. She needs to see her value as a human being.
- **Don't spread gossip.** It could be dangerous for her, and for you.
- **Encourage her to get help.** Offer to go with her to talk to someone: a teacher, a counselor, a crisis center worker.

- **Help her to make a safety plan.** Help her to prepare for an emergency. Never encourage her to follow a safety plan that she believes will put her at greater risk. The most serious battering occurs when the woman breaks off the relationship.
- **Give her good information about abuse.** Give her the number for a Battered Women's hotline.
- **Be patient and supportive.** Don't try to save her. She needs to make the decision to leave on her own. She won't leave until she is ready.

WHAT WE AS INDIVIDUALS CAN DO
FOR OURSELVES AND SOCIETY

I have experienced relationship violence myself, not to the extent of date rape, though. I've been there to listen to girls who have been in the same situation... The cause could possibly be jealousy or possessiveness...I'm not sure family or teachers could do anything to stop it. I think the only way it would stop would be if the guys saw first hand what they were doing. For example, stage a violent fight between a man and a woman and see what the guys' reaction is.

There is no need to have someone who supposedly cares about you degrade you and put you down and tell you that you aren't worthy of anyone else. This is a huge problem. It needs to be dealt with before any more women are murdered by overprotective men. – Kira, age 17

You can do something to fight the increasing frequency of relationship violence. There are, according to H. Lindgren, two ways that you can help: [23]

Work on yourself, your beliefs, and attitudes

If violence exists in your family or your relationships, get help to work the issues through. Changing ingrained behaviors and patterns takes time and guidance. It is extremely difficult to do it on your own with a self-help book. The problem does not go away by itself.

Be a role model. Do not accept and support the cultural stereotypes that encourage dominant-submissive relationships. Walk your talk. Model appropriate behavior and accept nothing less from your children and students. Set the standard for your community.

Work in the community to get the message out

Get involved in a community effort to reduce family violence. Support private and public efforts to address family and youth violence. For example, contact your local YWCA, University Extension Service, churches, mental health centers, battered women's shelter's, etc. for ways to help. Encourage these organizations to offer educational workshops.

Motivate local schools to begin a comprehensive program to educate students about the roots of conflict, the sources of violence, and the solutions to the problem. At the junior high and high school level, specifically address relationship violence.

Teachers – use teachable moments to address the issue of relationship violence! Don't shy away from the discussion. If dealing with the topic helps one person, it's worth it.

Where to get help

In the USA

- **The Mental Health Association**, 1-800-969-6642 (offers referral to the Mental Health Association in your area that has counselors and support groups for young people)
- **National Coalition Against Domestic Violence**, 1-800-799-7233 (offers referrals to counselors and support groups in your area)
- **National Coalition of Agencies Against Dating Violence**, 303-839-1852 (offers referral to support groups, videos on dating violence, and reading materials)
- **YWCA, United Way, Salvation Army, National Organization for Women** They have resources that offer help for victims of dating or domestic violence.
- **National Domestic Violence Hotline**, 1-800-799-SAFE
- **Family Violence Prevention Hotline**, 1-800-363-2873
- **Native American Women's Health Education Resource Center**, PO Box 572, Lake Andes, South Dakota 57356, 605-487-7072. For $1.30, they will send you a booklet called *Date Rape*. The booklet is available in quantity.
- **Peace At Home, Inc.**, 95 Berkeley Street, Suite 107, Boston, MA 02116, 617-482-1851. They publish a booklet called *Domestic Violence: The Facts*. This handbook shatters myths, identifies warning signs, and encourages help in order to stop violence.

In Canada

Health and Welfare Canada and the National Clearinghouse on Family Violence can provide information and education on spousal assault. They also provide specific information for multicultural and ethnic populations. This recognizes that while wife abuse is universal, the 'symptoms' may not necessarily be so.

- **National Clearinghouse on Family Violence**, Family Violence Prevention Division, Health Programs and Services Branch, Health Canada, Ottawa, Ontario, K1A 1B4
  Tel.: 613-957-2938, Toll-free: 1-800-267-1291, Fax: 613-941-8930, TDD users: 613-952-6396, Toll-free: 1-800-561-5643

British Columbia

- **Battered Women's Support Services**, PO Box 1098, Stn. A, Vancouver, BC, V6C 2T1, 604-687-1867
- **Victims' Information Line**, 3102 Main St., Ste. 202, Vancouver, BC, V5T 3G7, 604-875-6381 or 1-800-563-0808
- **Pacific Centre Family Services Association - Victoria, B.C.**, Victoria, BC, V9C 1Y8, 250-478-8357. They offer individual and group counseling for women who have experienced violence in their adult relationships or who were sexually abused as children. Support and advocacy for women, with priority placed on client safety. Service restricted to women resident in the Western communities.
- **Victoria Women's Sexual Assault Centre**, 306 - 620 View Street, Victoria, BC, V8W 1J6, 250-383-5545, Internet address: http://www.islandnet.com/~vwsac/

Ontario
- **Abused Women's Helpline**, 1-800-265-4305, sponsored by Violence Against Women Services Elgin County, 76 Wellington Street, St. Thomas, Ontario, N5R 2R1, 519-633-0155
- **Metro Action Committee on Public Violence Against Women and Children (METRAC)** METRAC is a community organization and resource that promotes the rights of women and children to live free from violence and threats of violence. METRAC is supported by the Toronto Council.
  Tel.:416-393-3135, Internet Address: http://www.interlog.com/~metrac/
- **Women's Place**, 905-684-8331
- **The Niagara Regional Sexual Assault Centre**, 905-682-7258

Manitoba
- **Family Dispute Services**, Department of Family Services, 114 Garry St., 2nd Fl., Winnipeg, MB, R3C 1G1, 204-945-1705

Saskatchewan
- **Victims' Services**, Saskatchewan Justice, 1874 Scarth St., 7th Fl., Regina, SK S4P 3V7, 306-787-3500

Alberta
- **Alberta Council of Women's Shelters**, 12739 Fort Rd., Ste. 2, Edmonton, AB T5A 1A7, 403-456-7000
- **Office for Prevention of Family Violence**, 10030-107th St., Seventh St. Plaza, 11th Fl., Edmonton, AB T5J 3E4, 403-422-5916

North West Territories
- **Department of Health, Social Services**, PO Box 1320, Yellowknife, NT X1A 2L9, 403-920-6255

Yukon
- **Family Violence Prevention**, PO Box 2703 (J7), Whitehorse, YK Y1A 2C6, 403-667-3581

Quebec
- **Indemnisation des victimes d'actes criminels**,1199 rue Bleury, 9ieme etage, C.P. 6056, succ. Downtown, Montreal, QC H3C 4E1, 514 873-6019

New Brunswick
- **Family Services, Department of Health and Community Services**, 520 King St., Carleton Place, Fredericton, NB E3B 5G8, 506-453-2040

Prince Edward Island
- **P.E.I. Human Rights Commission**, PO Box 2000, Charlottetown, PE C1A 7N8, 902-368-4180

Nova Scotia
- **Nova Scotia Human Rights Commission**, 5675 Spring Garden Rd., 7th Fl., PO Box 2221, Lord Nelson Arcade, Halifax, NS B3J 3C4, 902-424-4111

Newfoundland and Labrador
- **Provincial Association Against Family Violence**, PO Box 221, Stn. C, St. John's, NF A1C 5J2, 709-739-6759

On The Internet

- **http://www.rtvc.org/helplink/ab-btrdw.htm** or write HelpLink, 6350 West Freeway, Fort Worth, TX 76150. Their counselors will correspond with you confidentially and free of charge.
- **http://violet.umfacad.maine.edu/~shin/fem/nhope/teen.html** or write New Hope for Women, PO Box 642, Rockland, ME 04841-0642.
- **http://ianrwww.unl.edu/ianr/pubs/nebfacts/nf244.htm** provides information and references regarding recognizing a potential abuser in a dating relationship and figuring out what you can do.
- **http:// lifestylesmag.com/jew-family/4friends.txt.** The source is Jewish Women International, 1828 L Street, NW, Suite 250, Washington, DC 20036, 202-857-1300.
- **http://www.cs.utk.edu/~bartley/saInfoPage.html.** The Sexual Assault Information Page (SAIP) is a not-for-profit information and referral service created and maintained by Chris Bartley. SAIP provides information concerning acquaintance rape, child sexual abuse/assault, incest, rape, ritual abuse, sexual assault, and sexual harassment. Information is provided via the WWW, e-mail, a bi-monthly electronic newsletter as well as occasional hardcopy mailings for specific requests. All information, including the newsletter, is provided totally free of charge.
- **http://www.acjnet.org.** (Canada) Access to Justice Network (ACJNet). The ACJNet opens doors to Canadian legislation, people and organizations, publications, databases, and discussion forums on justice and legal issues.
- **http://www.achilles.net/~council/visavis.html** (Canada) Vis A Vis Newsletter.
- **http://www.women.ca/women-study.html#vaw.** Canadian Women's Internet Association, Resources for Women's Studies. Contains a large list of resource links for women.

Books

- *The Battered Woman* by Lenore Walker
- *Battered Woman Survivor Guide* by Jan Stateman
- *Dating Violence: Young Women in Danger* by Barrie Levy
- *The Emotionally Abused Woman* by B. Engel
- *Getting Free*, by Ginny NiCarthy
- *In Love and In Danger: A Teen's Guide to Breaking Free of Abusive Relationships* by Barrie Levy
- *Next Time She'll be Dead* by Ann Jones
- *Shattered Dreams* by Charlotte Fedders
- *What Parents Need to Know About Dating Violence* by Barrie Levy and Patricia Occhiuzzo Giggans
- *You Are Not Alone* by Susan Rouse

PERSONALIZED SAFETY PLAN[1]

Use the following fill-in statements as a guide in developing a safety plan.

While you are in the relationship

- I will have important phone numbers available for my parents, a close friend, and myself.
- I can tell _____ and _____ about the violence and ask them to call the police if they believe that I am in immediate danger.
- If I leave my boyfriend, I can go (list four places): _____, _____, _____, or _____.
- I can leave extra money, car keys, clothes, and copies of documented abuse with _____.
- To ensure safety and independence, I can keep change for phone calls with me at all times, open my own savings account, rehearse my escape route with a support person, review safety plan on _____ (date).

When the relationship is over

- I can (or parents can) change the locks, and install steel/metal doors, a security system, smoke detectors, and an outside lighting system.
- I will inform _____ and _____ that I am no longer dating my partner and ask them to call the police if he/she is observed near my home.
- I will tell _____ at work about my situation and ask _____ to screen my calls.
- I can avoid stores, banks, and hangouts that I used when dating my abusive partner.
- I can obtain a protective order from _____. I can keep it on or near me at all times as well as leave a copy with _____.
- If I feel down and ready to return to a potentially abusive situation, I can call _____ for support or attend workshops and support groups to gain support and to strengthen my relationships with other people.

Important Phone Numbers:

Police _____
Hotline _____
Friends _____
Shelter _____

[1] Adapted from "Domestic Violence: The Facts" -- A Handbook to STOP Violence, courtesy of Peace At Home, Boston. Copyright 1997 by Susan Gingras Fitzell
Free the Children! Conflict Education For Strong Peaceful Minds. New Society Publishers. This page may be photocopied.

The Junior Reserve Officer Training Corps (JROTC)

I was at a community parade recently when I was struck by a scene that might make some members of society proud, but which saddened and discouraged me. I witnessed a JROTC troop marching to cymbals and twirling guns. The young, impressionable teens clad in military garb looked disciplined and controlled. This must be good, right?

It didn't feel 'good' to me. I work with teens. I understand the sentiment that military discipline is the answer to troubled youth and delinquency. I can accept this route as the answer *after*, but not during high school. Because of the identity crisis and developmental needs of the teen years, JROTC is not a responsible choice for 'straightening out' our youth. Dr. Leo Sandy, Veterans For Peace, a professor at Plymouth State College, clearly identifies the problems associated with JROTC. Following is a memo he sent to all the high school principals in the state of New Hampshire. Some were not pleased with his message. It is human nature that we don't always like what we need to hear. Dr. Sandy's message provokes thought. I think its inclusion in this chapter is appropriate, since high school youth have to make decisions about such institutions.

MEMORANDUM: JROTC

Date: 30-Oct-1996
From: LEO ROBERT SANDY, Ed.D., NCSP
        VETERANS FOR PEACE
To: Susan Fitzell
Subject: JROTC

DEMOCRACY, SECONDARY EDUCATION, AND JROTC

In 1957, General Omar Bradley said, "We know more about war than we do about peace. We know more about killing than we do about living." In 1955, General Douglas MacArthur wrote, "The next great advance in the evolution of civilization cannot take place until war is abolished." Albert Einstein in 1934 said, "Schools ought to be intent on presenting history from the point of view of progress and the growth of human civilization, rather than using it as a means for fostering in the minds of the growing generation the ideals of outward power and military successes ...[and] that in the teaching of geography and history a sympathetic understanding be fostered for the characteristics of the different peoples of the world, especially for those whom we are in the habit of describing as 'primitive'." In 1980, Dr. Gene Sharp wrote, "If freedom is to become a reality, students need to learn how to think for themselves, to reason, to seek fresh solutions to problems, to challenge with reason their 'teachers' and text books, to learn from the knowledge, experience, and authority of others, but also to be willing and able to go beyond established knowledge and authority when needed to seek *greater knowledge and understanding... A society made up of such people would be unpalatable both to would-be internal tyrants and to foreign conquerors."* This testimony brings into question the JROTC program – a growing movement to militarize our schools and to indoctrinate our students.

The encroachment of the military in public schools has met stiff opposition. For example, a resolution was passed at the 9th Annual Convention of Veterans for Peace, in August 1994, in opposition to high school JROTC and other military programs. In the summer 1994 issue of VFP Journal, Dick Tyler, a West Point graduate and veteran of 10 years of military service, wrote an article entitled, "School Boards Should Cancel JROTC Programs." In 1992 at Long Beach Polytechnic High School in California, a gang emerged out of the JROTC program. This gang, the Ace of Spades, killed a student. The manner in which they killed the boy was modeled from a Special Forces technique learned in the JROTC program. One of the gang members said, "We love the way the military works. All of us just wanted to take it a little farther."

On 12-20-89, the New York City School Board said "No" to the implementation of a JROTC program at Martin Luther King High School in Manhattan. Their decision was based on the skewed history lessons in the JROTC curriculum; for example, serious errors of omission. Also, Martin Luther King himself urged the US away from a dependence on military solutions. Why should we embrace something that during the 1940s Japan and Germany used to brainwash its youth and to then send them off to their deaths? Several other reasons were given including the indoctrination of impressionable youth, the promotion of a Rambo-type mentality, the lack of funds for better purposes, and the military curriculum which is at odds with educational goals and good pedagogy.

There are sound developmental objections to JROTC as well. For example, adolescents, viewed from three major developmental theories, are seen as being capable of developing a self-chosen identity, a higher level of thinking, and a moral perspective that includes conscience, human rights, and universal ethical principles. However, experiences must be in place to actualize these accomplishments. Schools, therefore, are in a position to foster or retard these areas of development.

In order to accomplish these developmental outcomes, students need to be exposed to situations in which they can question, analyze, critique, challenge, debate, and argue. They need to learn to be self-reliant, to make decisions, and to solve conflicts nonviolently through effective communication and conflict resolution skills. They need to be exposed to nurturing, scholarly, and nonviolent models, and to be cared about as individuals. Their school experience needs to ensure that they give of themselves to others, be presented with controversial issues to discuss and work out, engage in cooperative learning activities, have an in-depth assessment of their strengths, weaknesses, learning styles, and career interests.

It is my opinion that the values, beliefs, and methods of the military are in direct conflict with those of education. It is more likely that the identity that is fostered by JROTC programs is what James Marcia refers to as "foreclosed", i.e. ready-made. In terms of higher thinking skills, the military emphasizes following orders and a concrete or black/white level of thinking rather than an abstract or gray one. In terms of moral development, the military's emphasis is on stage 4 thinking which emphasizes conformity and loyalty only to the immediate reference group and not to our common humanity, to individual conscience, to environmental issues, or to basic human needs and rights.

According to the world famous expert on intelligence Jean Piaget, one major goal of education is "to form minds which can be critical, can verify, and do not accept everything they are offered. The great danger to today is of slogans, ready-made trends of thought. We have to be able to resist individually, to criticize, to distinguish between what is proven and what is not." The very things that make the military work efficiently cause havoc in a democracy. Presenting issues of guns and power to adolescents who, for years, have been negatively influenced by violence in the media amounts to nothing more than a perpetuation of violence indoctrination. Even though JROTC instructors may be nice people and the program helps some off-track students to get their lives in order, the bottom line of the military is still violence.

If violence is going to be greatly minimized in our society, every time it rears its head in varied forms, from war toys to JROTC, it should be eliminated. Every potential source valuing violence should be examined and dealt with through citizen action. JROTC has a subliminal message that is dangerous to a free society. A democracy can only be viable if the military assumes the role for which it was intended but which it may now be exceeding: the defense of the borders of the US.

High school graduates and college students are in a much better position to decide on participation in the military. Impressionable adolescents are not able to discern as well as older youth. Leaders of bellicose countries in recent history also knew this and did much to indoctrinate youth. On examination of JROTC educational materials and practices, there is evidence of American cultural arrogance, discrimination, justification for dehumanization of different people and cultures, promotion of violent solutions, blind obedience to authority, and an emphasis on punitive methods to enforce 'orders'. How many parents really want their children in the future to sing this pilot's ditty from the Vietnam War:

"Strafe the town and kill the people,
Drop napalm upon the square,
Get out early every Sunday
And catch them at their morning prayer"

FACTS BEHIND DR. SANDY'S MEMO

The American Friends Service Committee commissioned an important academic study of the Army JROTC curriculum entitled "Making Soldiers in the Public Schools." This factual report is especially useful to give people who are concerned about JROTC in public schools and to share with school board members and curricular committees that are re-evaluating JROTC programs.

What follows are some excerpts from the JROTC textbooks themselves. This is what our JROTC teens are learning:

Bigotry

Author's Note: What attitudes are being promoted towards other cultures? Are we promoting understanding, tolerance, and peace when we allow JROTC into our schools?

"Fortunately for the Army, the government policy of pushing the Indians farther west then wiping them out was carried out successfully." – LET 3 (*Leadership Education and Training*, US Army JROTC textbook, 3rd year), p. 185.

"One must be aware of cultural differences between peoples. For instance, Americans generally place a high value on human life. This may not necessarily be the case in other cultures or countries that might be willing to gamble lives for political or economic gains, for example certain of the terrorist-sponsoring nations of the Middle East." – Naval Science 4, Naval Institute Press, Annapolis, MD, 1990 (4th year NJROTC), p. 141.

Guns

Author's Note: Is our goal to get guns *out* of the hands of our youth, or *into* the hands of our youth?

"The study of marksmanship...is intended to improve self-confidence and self-discipline." – LET 1, p. 246.

Note: Army Regulation 145-2, Appendix P, orders JROTC instructors to encourage students to join the National Rifle Association: "Modern advocates of gun control, registration, and the banning of gun ownership should at least be aware that their efforts, well intentioned as they may be, are probably unconstitutional." – Careers in Aerospace, Center for Aerospace Doctrine, Research, and Education, Maxwell Air Force Base, Alabama, 1985 (Air Force JROTC), p. 76.

Recruitment

"...this chapter will give you the four-step process needed to enlist in the military." – LET 2, p. 220.

"Recruiting Office personnel should be invited to the annual N[avy] JROTC military ball. The recruiters are good people to get to know. They can answer many questions about the Navy...." – Naval Science 1, p. 90.

Author's Note: We must ask ourselves, "What is the fundamental purpose of the Government's push to get JROTC in our schools?"

Loyalty, Drill, and Discipline

Author's Note: These teachings promote freezing moral development at Kohlberg's Stage 4: Law and Authority Orientation – where one blindly accepts social rules.

"Soldiers are trained to obey orders instantly, without questioning them." – LET 2, p. 217.

"Respect for authority and discipline go hand in hand, but the first one to be acquired must be discipline. Self-discipline involves full and voluntary acceptance of authority." – LET 1, Air Training Command, Maxwell Air Force Base, Alabama, 1989(1st year AFJROTC), p. 65.

"When troops react to command rather than thought, the result is more than just a good-looking ceremony or parade. Drill has been and will continue to be the backbone of military discipline." – LET 1, p. 87.

"Among the traits of a good follower, loyalty is at the top of the list. This means loyalty to those above us in the chain of command, whether or not we agree with them." – Naval Science 1, p. 24.

Vietnam

Author's Note: Is this an accurate representation of history?

"At the same time, the United States become [sic] involved in the war in Vietnam and drafted large numbers of young people who seemed to be more interested in reforming America than in fighting for it.... .In addition, despite the activities of radicals, the American people in general knew that the military establishment had been blamed for things which were not the military's fault." – Careers in Aerospace, p. 66.[24]

ALTERNATIVES TO JROTC[25]

JROTC programs are based on an ideology which conflicts with the philosophy and mission of public schools. JROTC, however, is embraced in communities because of its promise to teach teamwork, leadership, citizenship, and service. Communities want a program that will instill discipline, reduce violence, and build self-esteem. The promise of career training and scholarships is seductive. But communities must not be blinded to the fact that despite its promised rewards, JROTC is *not* a program for peace or conflict resolution. It is *not* a program that encourages empowerment. Most importantly, it is *not* a program that promotes high-level moral reasoning.

I am not opposed to the military. We need a military for national defense. I simply believe that adolescence is the wrong time to impose militaristic conditioning on our youth. As teens approach their eighteenth year, they begin to solidify their identity. Only then can they consider the military as an option with some understanding of who they are. If they are subjected to military conditioning before then, they may never know who they really are.

So what can we do to address the very real concerns that the JROTC programs use as their platform for entry into our public schools? We can consider other programs that embrace the same goals, yet achieve those goals through peaceful ideology. Communities will argue that they don't have funds for additional activities. What many people don't realize is that JROTC costs communities between $30,000 and $70,000, with the costs increasing after the second or third year. I would wager that we could fund several of the programs below with those same tax dollars. For the sake of our youth, let's consider the options.

Teamwork, leadership, discipline, self-esteem, achievement, and physical challenge

- **YouthBuild USA** is a national program in which at-risk youth learn construction skills and work together to build affordable housing, exercise leadership skills, and further their education. **YouthBuild USA**, 58 Day Street, Third Floor, West Somerville, MA 02144, 617-623-9900
- **Outward Bound** engages in wilderness training. Teams of young people learn survival skills and respect for the environment by traveling to wilderness areas.

- **Outward Bound National Office**, Route 9D R2 Box 280, Garrison, NY 10524-9757, 800-243-8520, Expeditionary Learning Division: 617-576-1260

Preparing for the future

- **Upward Bound** is a federal program that helps students with exceptional need improve their chances of getting into college, through tutoring, mentoring, and financial aid counseling.
- **Support school music and arts programs.** On an individual, local level, young lives are often turned around by youths learning to excel in school bands, orchestras, dance classes or art workshops. Yet arts programs are often the ones most threatened by school budget cuts
- **Internship and Mentorship programs.** Contact the **National School-to-Work Learning and Information Center**, 400 Virginia Avenue, Room 210, Washington, DC 20024, 1- 800-251-7236, stw-lc@ed.gov, http://www.stw.ed.gov
- **Partnerships with community colleges** offer work-based education and a window into higher education, opening up a world of possibility for students who might not have realized it was possible.
- **National Association of Partners in Education (NAPE)**, 209 Madison Street, Suite 401, Alexandria, VA 22314, 703-836-4880

Citizenship, self-esteem, achievement, and service learning

- **National Association of Service and Conservation Corps (NASCC)**, 666 Eleventh Street, NW, Suite 500, Washington, DC 20001, 202-737-6272, emonascc@igc.apc.org.
- **ACT for Citizenship Today Close Up Foundation**, 44 Canal Center Plaza, Alexandria, VA 22314 , 1-800-336-5479 x 640.
- **Constitutional Rights Foundation**, 601 South Kingsley Drive, Los Angeles, CA 90005, 213-487-5590.
- **Corporation for National and Community Service**, 1201 New York Avenue, NW, Washington, DC 20515, 202-606-5000, http://www.cns.gov
- **National Service-Learning Cooperative**, University of Minnesota, 1954 Buford Avenue, Room R-290, St. Paul, MN 55108-6197, 1-800-808-SERVE, serve@maroon.tc.umn.edu, http://www.nicsl.coled.umn.edu
- **The National Society for Experiential Education (NSEE)** houses the National Resource Center for Experiential and Service Learning which contains publications, research materials, program information, and other resources on experiential education and service-learning. 3509 Haworth Drive, Suite 207, Raleigh, NC 27609-7229, 919-787-3263, nsee@interpath.com.
- **The Youth Volunteer Corps of America (YVCA)** is a national network of over 40 local affiliates that promote civic responsibility through structured volunteer service among middle school and high school students. 6310 Lamar Avenue, Suite 125 Overland Park, KS 66202-4247, 913-432-YVCA
- **Public/Private Ventures (P/PV)** has developed a wide variety of model curricula,

tool kits, resource guides, and other resources useful to practitioners of service-learning programs. One Commerce Square, 2005 Market Street, Suite 900, Philadelphia, PA 19103, 215-557-4400, ppvg@dolphin.upenn.edu

- **Urban Gardening groups.** Often coordinated through your county's BOCES (Bureau of Cooperative Extension Services), they're active in inner cities and smaller communities alike. Teams of inner-city youth are restoring blighted areas, performing a needed service, and garnering job skills at the same time. Often, urban gardening programs are combined with multicultural education and tutoring and motivate their young members to stay in school!

Preventing gang violence

- **Leadership, team-building and school-to-work programs mentioned above:** many are specifically targeted for "at-risk" youth. YouthBuild, for example, has many former gang members now empowered as team leaders, with skills and a commitment to service; similar track records exist for Urban Gardening programs, Outward Bound, and alternative classrooms.

Conflict resolution curricula

- **National Association of Mediation in Education (NAME),** c/o Mediation Project, Box 33635, University of Massachussetts, Amherst, MA 01003, 413-545-2462
- **National Association for Multicultural Education (NAME),** c/o Donna M. Gollnick, 2101A North Rolfe Street, Arlington, VA 22209-1007, 202-416-6157, fax 202-296-6620

For more information . . .

- **FYI Youth** promotes youth development by linking young people directly to other young people, adults, and their communities. Contact: Greg Taylor, Academy for Educational Development, 1875 Connecticut Avenue NW, 9th Floor, Washington, DC 20009, 202-884-8273, gtaylor@aed.org
- **Rethinking Schools,** 1001 Keefe Ave, Milwaukee, WI 53212, 414-964-9646, fax 414-964-7220, RSBusiness@aol.com

Epilogue

It's been almost three years since I wrote the introduction to this book. As I reflect upon my initial words, I realize that my sentiments and passions have not changed much. What has evolved, however, is my confidence and calm in the face of adversity. I now fear oppositional belief systems and attitudes less and trust my convictions more.

In the years since I started this book, youth violence has continued to escalate. Committees to address the issue of violence are forming at national, state, and local levels in communities and school systems. Individual involvement on a large scale, however, is non-existent in most communities. Most parents would rather go to a sporting event or a home decorating party than organize or attend a parenting workshop. Most teachers would rather go to a workshop in their specific subject area than to a workshop on character education or conflict resolution. These may be harsh generalizations. They are based, however, on my observations and those of others present at these functions. Presenters and their participants often ask, "Where are the others? Where are the men? Where are the people who need to be here? How can society change if they don't come to learn how to make a difference for our children and our country's future?"

Violence may have to reach epidemic proportions before individuals realize that they play an important role in forming a peaceful culture. Many still believe that police force and stricter laws and prison terms are the primary solution. On the contrary, the primary solution lies in educating youth, parents, teachers, and the community about the roots of conflict and its resolution. When we decide to use our tax dollars and our personal time to contribute to conflict education, we will see a cultural shift. It won't happen overnight, but it will happen.

So what can you do? Take one step at a time. Think about what you have read in this book. Follow up on some of the resources. Read more books. Attend parenting and educational seminars. Look in the mirror, face your own attitudes and beliefs. Become self-aware. Have an open mind. Believe you can make a difference. Talk to your friends, neighbors, school district staff, congressmen, clergy, and business associates about what you believe. Encourage people to take action. Take a bigger step: bring people together to implement strategies for change. Encourage others to do the same. Find creative ways to overcome obstacles in your path. If you choose an issue or cause that *you* are passionate about for the sake of *your* children, you will be able to move mountains. As I state in every one of my workshops, you may not agree with everything I say. At times, you may disagree strongly. My goal is *not* to convince you that I am right, that my way is the only way. My goal is to provoke thought, to heighten awareness, and to motivate people into action. If you can't use all of the ideas in this book, then take what you need and leave the rest. If nothing else, for the sake of our children, *take action* to nurture strong, peaceful minds.

APPENDICES

Appendix A
DEVELOPMENTAL STAGES AND STAGES OF MORAL DEVELOPMENT AND THEIR IMPACT ON THE CURRICULUM

PRESCHOOL 3-5 YRS OLD	LOWER ELEMENTARY 6-8 YRS OLD	UPPER ELEMENTARY 9-11 YRS OLD	JUNIOR HIGH 12-13 YRS OLD	HIGH SCHOOL 14-18 YRS OLD
Piaget: Pre-Operational • Young children demonstrate an inability to take another's viewpoint. • Emotions and conflicts weigh upon cognitive advances. Practice of rules is egocentric • The extent of the consequence is more significant than the intention. • Cannot distinguish between dreams, wishes, imaginings, and reality. • Justice = the law. • Conscious of rules, considers them sacred and untouchable	*Piaget:* 7+ Concrete Operations – Logical thinking limited to physical reality • Starts to play with others • Considers others' feelings • Searches to justify his/her own viewpoints and to coordinate the views of others • Actively seeks out new experiences • Has the ability to relate the concept of self to the concept of events in the outside world • Can think of the abstract fears around him/her • There is a profound shift towards responsibility at 7. Egocentric Stage and Heteronomy: Rules are external laws which are sacred because they have been laid down by adults. • Rules are considered essential for regulating social activities. • Intention more significant than the extent of the consequence • From 7 to 10, a lie is something that isn't true, including mistakes, exaggerations, etc. • Empathy, mutual respect and solidarity = the development of "character"		*Piaget:* Transition—Logical thinking abstract and unlimited • Sees his/her view as one of many possible views • Able to consider abstract models. Cooperation Stage and Autonomy: 10+ Rules are seen to be the outcome of a free decision and worthy of respect in the measure that they have enlisted mutual consent. • A lie is any statement that is intentionally false. • Justice = equality • Equality and fairness overrule obedience.	*Piaget:* 13+ Formal Operations – Thinking becomes more abstract and hypothetical. Teens can consider many alternative solutions to a problem, make deductions, contemplate the future, and formulate personal ideals and values. • Systematic approach to problem-solving. Codification Stage: 11+ Rules provide the structure for cooperation. • Closest correlation between consciousness of rules and practice of them. • Justice = "Stage of Equity" which consists of never defining equality without taking into account individual circumstances

DEVELOPMENTAL STAGES AND STAGES OF MORAL DEVELOPMENT AND THEIR IMPACT ON THE CURRICULUM (continued)

PRESCHOOL 3-5 YRS OLD	LOWER ELEMENTARY 6-8 YRS OLD	UPPER ELEMENTARY 9-11 YRS OLD	JUNIOR HIGH 12-13 YRS OLD	HIGH SCHOOL 14-18 YRS OLD
Erikson: Initiative vs. Guilt – When children begin to make their own decisions, constant discouragement or punishment could lead to guilt and a loss of initiative.	*Erikson:* Industry vs. Inferiority – Children take pride in their ability to master skills. •Too much criticism of their work at this stage can lead to long-term feelings of inferiority.		*Erikson:* Identity vs. Role Confusion – Teens are trying to develop their own separate identity while 'fitting in' with their peers. • Failure leads to confusion over their sense of who they really are.	
Kohlberg: Level I Preconventional: **Stage 1** — *Heteronomy Morality* — Children choose behavior to avoid punishment or because of the superior power of authorities. • **Stage 2:** *Individualism* — They make choices according to self-interest.	*Kohlberg:* (If not stuck at stage 1) Level II Conventional: **Stage 3** — *"Good Boy" - "Nice Girl" Orientation* Children make choices based on a need to be good in their own eyes as well as in those of others. • Want to be what "society" says is good • See point of view through the concrete Golden Rule		*Kohlberg:* (If not stuck at a previous stage) Level II Conventional: **Stage 4** — *Law and Authority Orientation* • Blindly accept social rules. • Emphasis falls on doing their duty • Laws are upheld except where extreme conflict occurs with some other social duty • What is right is what contributes to society or the group • Take the point of view of the system that makes the laws as opposed to any one person	*Kohlberg:* (If not stuck at a previous stage) Level III Postconventional or Principled : **Stage 5** — *Social Contract or Utility and Individual Rights* • Choose what is right because they are focused on posterity, humanity, justice, freedom, peace, equality, and the globe • Adhere to conscience • Would sacrifice self for Human Rights
Gilligan: Females construct the moral problem as a problem of care and responsibility in relationships rather than as one of rights and rules. The logic at the basis of an ethic of care is the logic of relationships as opposed to the logic of fairness and justice based on the good of society as a whole (Gilligan, 1993).				

Appendix B
Corporal Punishment – Facts and Alternatives

"In a violent society, violence is used to control violence."
— Murray Straus

Facts
According to studies on corporal punishment done by Murray Straus
(1994), children who were spanked frequently are
- four times as likely to hit their spouses later in life
- more likely to be aggressive with siblings, in school, and as adults
  with spouses and children
- more likely to have thoughts of suicide
- more likely to be aroused by sadomasochistic sex (The buttocks are an
  erogenous zone.)
- more likely to engage in violent crime
- more likely to develop a sense of powerlessness and depression, and
  a lack of internalized moral standards
- more likely to be labeled as discipline problems
- more likely to lie and cheat to avoid getting spanked
- less likely to internalize the difference between right and wrong or to
  develop a conscience
- less likely to obtain a high-level job with a high income

To parents who say, "I was spanked and I didn't turn out violent," Straus
responds: "Only one-third of the people who smoke die of lung cancer.
But anyone who smokes is at an increased risk. The same is true for spanking and violence."
Katharine C. Kersey, Early Childhood Educator from Old Dominion
University in Norfolk, Virginia, lists additional reasons for not spanking children. Spanking can and often does

- lower the child's self esteem
- breed hostility and anger
- lead to child abuse
- teach that 'might makes right'
- lead to a desire for revenge or retaliation
- lead to fear and avoidance
- weaken the relationship between the hitter and the one who is hit
- increase the risk of child abuse
- give the child a model for aggression and violence
- block the learning process

...more

Other reasons not to spank:

- Spanking can teach children to rely on others for control of their behavior. Children who learn to rely on external control are more apt to let circumstances, events, and other people influence their actions than to use their own resources.
- Spanking is not an effective means of changing behavior. The effects of spanking are immediate but usually short-term.
- Spanking tells a child what not to do. It does not teach them appropriate behavior. It teaches them that hitting is OK.
- Families in which parents frequently use corporal punishment often produce hyperaggressive and hyperactive children[1]
- Spanking can confuse the child. Spanking is usually followed by affection. This teaches children that love involves hitting and hurting, a belief that is held by victims and abusers in relationship and domestic violence.
- Spanking can lead to parent abuse in the future when the roles have reversed and the parent is dependent on the child.

A note on the old adage "Spare the Rod and Spoil the child". Shepherds did not beat their sheep with their rods and their staffs. Physical injury to their flock could jeopardize their livelihood. They used the rod and staff to guide them!

Alternatives to spanking

- Calm yourself. Take a deep breath. And another. Then remember you are the adult.
- Close your eyes and imagine you're hearing what your child is about to hear.
- Be kind but firm when correcting inappropriate behavior.
- Put your child in a time-out chair.
- Give choices
- Use logical consequences.
- Have the child do restitution as a consequence.
- Lock yourself in the bathroom. Think about why you are angry: Is it your child, or is your child the target of your stress, frustration, or anger?
- Leave the room. Tell the child you will deal with the situation when you are both calm and can communicate effectively.
- Read parenting books that provide alternatives (see Annotated Bibliography).
- Take a parenting course — not because you are not good enough — but because you want to be better!

[1] Gordon, T. (1989). Teaching Children Self-Control. New York: Times.

Appendix C

TV Violence

What you can do to protect your child from tv violence and verbal bullying portrayed in tv shows

- Limit the amount of TV your child watches. Try to keep it between 1 to 2 hours a day.

- Monitor the programs your child watches. Set firm rules about which stations and programs he/she is allowed to watch.

- Help your child choose positive, non-violent programs. Programs that find humor in name-calling, sarcasm, and disrespect are teaching your child that this form of bullying is funny and acceptable.

- Watch TV with your child. Talk to your child about the program:

  - Is it real or pretend?

  - Is the behavior of the characters respectful? Peaceful?

  - Are the characters acting like bullies?

  - Are the characters using their mind or their fists to solve problems?

  - Which is the better way? What other choices to the characters have?

- React with 'moral feeling' (Lickona) against violence and bullying. Let your child know that you feel angry and sad when people are hurt by violence and bullying.

                                                              ...more

TV Violence (continued)

Does tv really intensify violent behavior?

Having reviewed hundreds of research findings, the authors of three major national studies have concluded that heavy exposure to televised violence is one of the significant causes of violence in society:

- The Surgeon General's Commission Report (1972)

- The National Institute of Mental Health Ten-Year Follow-up (1982)

- The report of the American Psychological Association's Task Force on Television in Society (1992)

Viewing violence on the screen has the following negative effects:

- It increases the viewer's fear of becoming a victim of violence, with a resultant increase in self-protective behaviors and increased mistrust of others.

- It desensitizes the viewer to violence, resulting in a callused attitude toward violence directed at others and a decreased likelihood of taking action to help a victim of violence.

- It increases the viewer's appetite for becoming involved with violence.

- It often demonstrates how desirable commodities can be obtained through the use of aggression and violence.

- Sexual violence in X- and R-rated videotapes widely available to teenagers has also been shown to cause an increase in male aggression against females.

These effects are both short-term and long-lasting. A longitudinal study of boys found a significant relation between exposure to TV violence at 8 years of age and antisocial acts — including serious violent criminal offenses and spouse abuse — 22 years later.

Excerpted from American Psychological Association, APA Briefing Paper: Is Youth Violence Just Another Fact of Life? For a complete copy, contact the Office of Public Communications, 202-336-5700.

Appendix D
Bullying

IS YOUR CHILD BEING BULLIED?

Children who are being bullied may

- be frightened of walking to or from school

- beg you to drive them to school

- arrive home with unexplained bruises or torn clothes

- refuse to go to school or complain of stomach aches or headaches in the morning

- avoid going to certain areas in the school, such as the bathroom

- start doing poorly in school and/or lose interest in school work

- ask for extra money for lunch (because lunch money is being taken)

- begin stealing

- act moody, sullen, withdrawn

- become distressed

- not eat at mealtimes, claiming lack of hunger

- have trouble sleeping, or wake up with nightmares

- cry themselves to sleep

- demonstrate a lack of self-esteem

- begin to carry weapons for self-protection

- refuse to talk about what's wrong or give excuses that don't make sense

Appendix D
Bullying (continued)

WHAT CAN YOU DO TO HELP
VICTIMS OF BULLIES?

- Tell the child <u>not</u> to react to the bully, but rather to look as confident as possible. Bullies feed off of the reactions of their victims. If the victim appears afraid and reacts with crying, a weakly whined "Leave me alone," or flight, bullies feel powerful and in control. This reaction fuels and rewards their efforts.

- Have the child document the bullying. The child should keep a detailed journal of the bullying. This journal should list the names of the bullies, the time and place of the incidents, and a detailed description of what happened. An adult may help the younger child keep this journal.

- Encourage the child to stay with trusted friends. The child should try not to go anywhere alone.

- Encourage the child to tell an adult when the bullying occurs. Identify some adults who the child can turn to if and when he/she is bullied.

- Teach children verbal assertiveness skills. Teach the child to stand straight with head high, to look the bully right in the eyes, and to say in a loud, clear, firm voice: "Stop! If you_____again, I'm going to tell ." Or "Stop! I refuse to fight. I'll talk this over with you but I will not fight." A bully is looking for easy prey. A child who stands up to the bully may discourage the bully from continuing.

Appendix D
Bullying (continued)

MENTAL SELF-DEFENSE TECHNIQUES[1]

- Stay calm, focused, centered, and aware

- Offer kindness

- Use humor (not sarcasm) to diffuse the situation

- Trick the bully

- Ignore and walk away or refuse to fight

- Agree with the bully

- Watch your language — words and body

- Scream or yell, become "the lion"

- Tell authority — safety measure vs. tattling

- Reason with the bully

- Stand up to the bully

- Follow the rules for fighting fair

- Be courteous

- Avoid dangerous situations

A Note on Courtesy

Many times conflict arises because an accident happens, someone gets bumped, an innocent comment is taken as an insult, etc. If people choose to sincerely say "Excuse me," "Please," "Thank you," "Are you all right?" "I'm sorry, I didn't mean to hurt you," etc., much conflict can be diffused and avoided before it begins. One cannot place too much importance on the significance of common courtesy.

[1] Adapted from Atrium Society Publications, Middlebury, VT 05753.

Annotated Bibliography

Arnow, Jan. (1995). *Teaching Peace: How to Raise Children to Live in Harmony — Without Fear, Without Prejudice, Without Violence*. New York: The Berkley Publishing Group.
Jan Arnow offers excellent insight and practical tips for raising and teaching children to be peaceful. She addresses the subject from the point of view of the home, the classroom, and the community. The text is filled with resource information, checklists, and examples to help any parent and/or youth educator teach peace.

Borysenko, Joan. (1987). *Minding the Body, Mending the Mind*. Reading, MA: Addison-Wesley.
This book shows the reader how to use meditation and the power of the mind to treat illness, or simply to find inner peace. The reader is taken through exercises and skills practice to learn how to implement techniques Borysenko describes in this book. This is a doer book: you read, then do. It draws on both Western science and Eastern philosophy.

Canada, Geoffrey. (1995). *Fist Stick Knife Gun: A Personal History of Violence in America*. Boston: Beacon Press.
If you have never really understood inner city or gang violence, if you live in the inner city or must deal with gang violence, or if you are prone to pass judgment on inner city youth, read this book. *Fist Stick Knife Gun* will open your eyes about violence in America and factors contributing to that violence.

Carlsson-Paige, Nancy and Levin, Diane. (1990). *Who's Calling the Shots?: How to Respond Effectively to Children's Fascination with War Play and War Toys*. Gabriola Island, BC: New Society Publishers.
Through interviews with parents and teachers and observations of children at play, the authors explore why war play is different today than it was 20 years ago. What role do the media and toy industry play in shaping children's attitudes about war play? If you have concerns about children's war-play and want to know what is normal, healthy behavior, and what is not, read this book.

Cecil, Nancy Lee. (1995). *Raising Peaceful Children in a Violent World*. San Diego: LuraMedia.
The author divided the broad topic of this book into three manageable sections: peaceful communication, peaceful entertainment, and peaceful relationships. In each section, she presents sound theory and common sense on the subject matter. She includes wonderful, practical suggestions including family activities, family reading, and reading for children. There are also seven family posters that can be strategically placed throughout the home to serve as daily reminders of a commitment to live peacefully.

Charney, Ruth Sidney. (1991).*Teaching Children to Care: Management in the Responsive Classroom*. Greenfield: Northeast Foundation For Children.
This is a thorough and practical resource for helping teachers establish an ongoing curriculum in self-control, social participation, and human development. Realistic, do-able techniques are offered for using logical consequences, problem-solving class meetings, and clear positives. The Responsive Classroom approach includes most of the five components necessary for educating strong, peaceful minds.

Edelman, Marian Wright. (1993). *The Measure of Our Success: A letter to my children and yours.* New York: Harper Collins.
I love this book. It moves me. T. Berry Brazelton sums it up best: "*The Measure of Our Success* is a book to turn lives around: a compassionate message for parents trying to raise moral children, a tough and searching book that ought to be required reading for every young American."

Elium, Don and Jeanne (1992). *Raising a Son: Parents and the Making of a Healthy Man.* Hillsboro: Beyond Words Publishing.
This text provides wonderful insight into the male psyche and the development of a healthy male personality. I found the authors' wisdom on disciplining the male child through stages of development enlightening. I especially appreciated the description of the mother/son relationship and the ramifications of maternal behavior in that relationship.

— (1994). *Raising a Daughter: Parents and the Awakening of a Healthy Woman.* Berkely, CA: Celestial Arts.
Raising a Daughter is an excellent resource for parents. It has the developmental wisdom of Carol Gilligan's work and the environmental awareness of Mary Pipher's *Reviving Ophelia*. It is practical, down-to-earth, and meaningful.

Facing History and Ourselves National Foundation. *Facing History and Ourselves,* 25 Kennard Road, Brookline 02146.
Facing History and Ourselves is an award winning program that engages students of diverse backgrounds in an examination of racism, prejudice, and anti-Semitism in order to promote the development of a more humane and informed citizenry.
(Description adapted from Survivors of the Holocaust web page: http://www.turner.com/survivors/index.html)

Faithquest. (1994). *Just Family Nights: 60 Activities to Keep Your Family Together In a World Falling Apart.* Elgin: Brethren Press.
Just Family Nights provides sixty activities for families to do together — activities that build family unity and foster healthy values. This book sorts activities according to the yearly calendar and themes. Family meetings can become the forum to celebrate holidays, holy days, and seasonal events. They can also be a time to reinforce the themes of peacemaking and family unity. The activities require prep time, but the results are well worth it.

Fishel, Elizabeth. (1991). *I Swore I'd Never Do That!: Recognizing Family Patterns and Making Wise Parenting Choices.* Berkeley: Conari Press.
Fishel based her book on interviews with nearly 200 parents. She explores the ways in which unresolved issues from our childhood regarding discipline, intimacy, and self-esteem prevent us from being the parents we want to be. The author writes with humor and compassion.

Fountain, Susan. (1995). *Education for Development: A Teacher's Resource for Global Learning.* Portsmouth: Heinemann.
My first experience with this book was at Norwich University at the Parents, Teachers, and Students for Social Responsibility International Peace Conference where I participated in an activity taken from the book. I was so impressed by the effectiveness of the activity that I bought the book. I was not disappointed. Activities are geared for ages 7

through adult. The breakdown of activities per age is developmentally appropriate. I highly recommend this book.

Healy, Jane M. (1990). *Endangered Minds: Why Children Don't Think and What we Can Do About it*. New York: Touchstone Books.

I highly recommend this book for anyone who works with, lives with, or is involved with children in any way. This work provides an understanding and substantiation of a problem plaguing our children and supplies solutions to deal with it. Jane Healy has systematically analyzed what she considers to be the roots of the educational crisis here in America and increasingly also in European countries. She builds a strong case for the fact that our children's brains are different physically from those of children 50 years ago. This physical difference manifests itself in distinct strengths and weaknesses unlike those of previous generations of children. She examines the relationship between the brain and language learning, attention, and passivity. Her work is backed with hard research. If there was ever a solid proof for the impact the media are having on our children, this is it!

Kaufman, Gershen and Raphael, Lev. (1990). *Stick Up For Yourself: Every Kid's Guide to Personal Power and Positive Self-Esteem*. Minneapolis: Free Spirit Publishing.

I found this book an exceptional resource for working with teens on personal power and self-esteem. The authors emphasize a sense of ownership in the reader for his/her own happiness. I used it with students aged 15 through 18. I had to reword some of the stories because the book appears to be written for the pre-teen and young teen and can seem hokey to older teens. There is a teacher's guide to go with the book.

Kreidler, William J. (1984). *Creative Conflict Resolution*. Glenview: Educators for Social Responsibility.

— (1990). *Elementary Perspectives 1*. Cambridge: Educators for Social Responsibility.

These are activity-based resource books for teachers to teach their students how to solve problems peacefully.

Lerner, Harriet Goldhor. (1985). *The Dance of Anger: A Woman's Guide To Changing Patterns of Intimate Relationships*. New York: Harper & Row.

The author challenges women's typical actions and reactions when angry. In very readable text, she helps readers to understand anger, patterns of behavior when angry, and ways to change those patterns to become healthier, happier adults. This is a preferred resource.

Levin, Diane E. (1994). *Teaching Young Children in Violent Times: Building a Peaceable Classroom*. Gabriola Island, BC: New Society Publishers.

The background and developmental information provided in this book enhances its effectiveness as a source. The basic concepts can be adapted to older children. This is a useful resource for creating a peaceful learning environment in your classroom. It is not an activity book; it is a practical 'how to' book.

Levy, Barrie and Giggans, Patricia Occhiuzzo. (1995). *What Parents Need to Know About Dating Violence*. Seattle: Seal Press.

This book is essential reading for parents of pre-teens about to enter dating relationships. It provides parents with information regarding what dating violence is, how it develops, how it entraps its victims, and how to get help. Levy and Giggans draw on real-life experiences of parents and teens as well as on their professional experience.

Ideally, parents have this information before their daughters get involved in a violent dating relationship.

Lickona, Thomas. (1992). *Educating for Character: How Our Schools Can Teach Respect and Responsibility*. New York: Bantam Books.
I hold this book up as a must read at every one of my workshops. It is filled with dozens of useful and practical ideas. It shows teachers how to promote and teach the values necessary for our children's moral development. His twelve-point program offers practical strategies designed to help parents, teachers, and communities work together to form a decent and humane society. The book received a 1992 Christopher Award "for affirming the highest values of the human spirit."[2]

Lickona, Thomas. (1983). *Raising Good Children: How to help your child develop a lifelong sense of honesty, decency, and respect for others*. New York: Bantam Books.
Thomas Lickona's work is reality-based! *Raising Good Children* provides parents with information regarding the moral development of children . This knowledge helps parents to understand why children do what they do and, more importantly, that their child is normal. Lickona also has a common sense approach to discipline. Parents can relate to his techniques. The book deals with ways of helping your child through the stages of moral reasoning (from preschool to adulthood) and concerns that cut across ages and stages.

Miedzian, Myriam. (1991). *Boys Will Be Boys: Breaking the Link Between Masculinity and Violence*. New York: Doubleday.
This book addresses our society's attitudes towards violence and males. It questions the acceptance of violence as a way of life. It addresses fatherhood and its effect on sons. Miedzian looks at school programs that work and discusses the impact our media and commercial market have on our children. She lists countless examples, including words to songs our teens are listening to. *Boys Will Be Boys* is a profound work pursuing a priority issue.

Olweus, Dan. (1993). *Bullying At School: What We Know and What We Can Do*. Oxford: Blackwell Publishers.
Olweus' studies are some of the most significant research studies on school bullying. This book is the result of his work.

Paley, Vivian Gussin. (1992). *You Can't Say You Can't Play*. Cambridge: Harvard University Press.
Vivian Gussin Paley deals with a difficult, age-old problem in a practical, realistic, and sensitive way. Bullying in schools most often takes the form of exclusion. Exclusion of children by other children leaves the rejected feeling like outsiders, hopelessly alone. Paley attacks this problem with her students in a sensitive, yet straightforward way.

Pincus, Debbie. (1994). *Feeling Good About Others: Activities to Encourage Positive Interaction*. Good Apple.

— (1994). *Manners Matter: Activities to Teach Young People Social Skills*: Good Apple.
These two worksheet/activity books are useful addenda to a conflict education and social skills curriculum. The worksheets and activities get right to the point. The author and publisher give permission for the purchaser of the book to copy student activity pages for use in the classroom.

Pipher, Mary. (1994). *Reviving Ophelia: Saving the Selves of Adolescent Girls.* New York: Ballatine Books.

If there is one book that parents of daughters should read, it's this one! As the parent of a girl, I was brought to the edge of tears several times while reading this book. The reality of what my daughter will be subjected to in pre-adolescence and adolescence is heartbreaking. The thought of my daughter stifling her free-spirited, confident personality to conform to society's expectations is frightening. The awareness of what she will encounter is, however, indispensable. Only with that forewarning can I prepare her for what is to come and guide her through her teen years.

Price, Alvin and Parry, Jay A. (1983). *Discipline: 101 Alternatives to Nagging, Yelling, and Spanking.* Salt Lake City: Brite Music.

Price and Parry's alternatives promote children and parents working together to solve problems. Suggestions include role-playing, reflective listening, helping the child to own the problem. The book is handy and interesting. The authors suggest some novel approaches to handling discipline problems.

Prothrow-Stith, Deborah. (1987). *Violence Prevention Curriculum for Adolescents*: Education Development Center.

This curriculum is an attempt to address the issues of violence and homicide among young people by helping students to become more aware of
- homicide and the factors associated with it
- positive ways to deal with anger and arguments, the leading precipitants of homicide
- the ways fights begin and escalate
- the choices, other than fighting, that are available to young people in conflict situations.

Prutzman, P., Stern, L., Burger, M. and Bodenhamer, G. (1988). *The Friendly Classroom for a Small Planet: A Handbook on Creative Approaches to Living and Problem Solving for Children.* Gabriola Island, BC: New Society Publishers.

This is not a simple activity book. It is a practical, reality-based handbook for teachers that considers the child's learning environment as a whole: the physical, emotional, and academic aspects of the classroom. Affirmation, cooperation, communication, and conflict resolution are key components of the friendly classroom. Another important difference between this and similar books is the authors' approach to understanding the roots of violence, and not merely the symptoms. These roots lie in our culture. I highly recommend this book for teachers.

Schmidt, Fran, Friedman, Alice and Marvel, Jean. (1992). *Mediation for Kids: Kids in Dispute Settlement. Miami:* Grace Contrino Abrams Peace Foundation.

This book is a clearly written handbook for how to set up a mediation program in your classroom. Included are worksheets and mini-posters to assist the teacher and kids in successfully using a mediation program.

Smith, Charles A. (1993). *The Peaceful Classroom: 162 Easy Activities to Teach Preschoolers Compassion and Cooperation*: Gryphon House.

This book, a winner of the Benjamin Franklin Award, is a well written and organized collection of activities for children ages 3 through 5. My day care providers called it "wonderful". Sample letters to parents are included so that they can be kept informed as to what their child is learning in school. There are many activities for belonging and friendship, compassion, cooperation, and kindness.

Staley, Betty K. (1988). *Between Form and Freedom: A Practical Guide to the Teenage Years*. Bath: Hawthorn Press.

There is an incredible developmental difference between a fourteen-year-old and an eighteen-year-old. Betty Staley understands this developmental difference. She presents a view of the adolescent more accurate than any other I have read. Everything that I have experienced in working with teenagers over the years is written and clarified in the pages of her book.

Stein, Nan and Sjostrom, Lisa. (1994). *Flirting or Hurting?: A Teacher's Guide on Student-to-Student Sexual Harassment in Schools*. Washington: NEA Professional Library.

This teacher's guide is geared towards grades 6 through 12. The first two chapters offer helpful information regarding teaching styles and their impact on lessons, suggested teaching formats, and activities (these are topically cross-referenced). The text addresses flirting vs. sexual harassment, myths about what is or isn't sexual harassment, and students rights. The book presents case-studies for discussion. It also provides a sample letter from a victim to an offender. Much other useful and empowering information is included in this text. It is an outstanding resource.

Strauss, Susan. (1992). *Sexual Harassment and Teens*. Minneapolis: Free Spirit Publishing.

This is an outstanding, practical, teen-friendly 3-unit course. It provides the structure to successfully address the following questions:

- What is sexual harassment?
- What are the causes of sexual harassment?
- How can we prevent and stop sexual harassment?

It gives teens a safe, supervised way to learn the facts, to discover their feelings, and to examine their attitudes and behaviors.

Webster- Doyle, Terrence. (1991). *Why is Everybody Always Picking On Me?* Middlebury: Atrium Society Publications.

This book is for middle-school aged children concerned about being bullied. It is filled with creative stories and activities on resolving conflicts peacefully. The book is also for adults looking for a way to help their children deal with the 'bullies' in life, whether those bullies are other children, other adults, obvious bullies, or deceptive bullies. There are curricula based on this book available to teachers and martial arts instructors. The curricula are beautifully organized, sequential, consistent, and complete. I have seen little available that is as well done as this curriculum.

— (1989). *Brave New Child: Education for the 21st Century*. Middlebury: Atrium Society Publications.

This book presents a solution to the problem of psychological conditioning. Its purpose is to examine the inward and outward nature and structure of conflict. This book explores a perspective in education that lays the foundation for a completely original way of learning and living.

— *War: What is it Good For?* Middlebury: Atrium Society Publications.

This text is designed for classroom use. It contains daily lesson plans with stories, activities, and role-playing ideas to teach students about relationships, the roots of conflict, and the basic factors that can condition them to be warlike. Grades 9-12.

Wichert, Susanne. (1989). *Keeping the Peace: Practicing Cooperation and Conflict Resolution with Preschoolers*. Gabriola Island, BC: New Society Publishers.
I got more excited reading this book than any other pre-school activity book I have found in print. This author is living in reality. She is not writing for an idealistic, non-violent world. She approaches the topic with the understanding that violence exists and that sometimes a child may need to fight to preserve his/her own safety, but that all efforts must be made to teach children at a young age to resolve conflict peacefully whenever possible. It is more than an activity book. It is a philosophy book, a psychology book, and a 'how to' book. I herald the author for a job well done.

Wolf, Anthony E. (1991). *Get Out Of My Life but first could you drive me and Cheryl to the mall?: A Parents' Guide to the New Teenager*. New York: The Noonday Press.
Wolf humorously portrays adolescent behavior, offering insight and helpful suggestions for parents. He describes adolescents, explains what they do and why, and addresses what it means to be the parent of a teenager.

Wyckoff and Unell, Barbara C. (1984). *Discipline Without Shouting or Spanking: Practical Solutions to the Most Common Preschool Behavior Problems*. New York: Meadowbrook Press.
This book is a 134-page resource for disciplining preschool children. The authors identify the ABC's of disciplined parenting, explain why shouting and spanking are counterproductive, and provide an alphabetical guide to problem behaviors and possible discipline techniques. They describe the problem, suggest how to prevent it and advise what to do and what not to do. The book is easy and quick to use.

Zerafa, Judy. (1994). *The Relationship Workbook for Teens: What You Can Do To Attract That Special Someone*: Confidence Building Publishers.
Despite its subtitle, this book and many of its activities can be used for teens in any relationship. It explains the subconscious mind and its impact on behavior. Simple, concrete activities are given for changing negative thinking into positive thinking. It is a worthwhile addendum to a current program.

Bibliography by Subject Area

CONFLICT RESOLUTION/CONDITIONED MIND

Arnow, Jan. (1995). *Teaching Peace: How to Raise Children to Live in Harmony — Without Fear, Without Prejudice, Without Violence.*

Borysenko, Joan. (1987). *Minding the Body, Mending the Mind.* Reading, MA: Addison-Wesley

Carlsson-Paige, Nancy and Levin, Diane. (1990). *Who's Calling the Shots?: How to Respond Effectively to Children's Fascination with War Play and War Toys.*

Cecil, Nancy Lee. (1995). *Raising Peaceful Children in a Violent World.*

Charney, Ruth Sidney. (1991).*Teaching Children to Care: Management in the Responsive Classroom.*

Cohen, Herb. (1993). *Negotiating The Game: New Perspectives on Negotiating.* New York, NY: Harper Collins.

Covey, Stephen R. (1989).*The Seven Habits of Highly Effective People.* New York: Simon & Schuster

Drew, Naomi. (1987). *Learning The Skills Of Peacemaking.* Rolling Hills Estates, CA: Jalmar Press

Fisher, Roger and Stone, Douglas. (1991). *Working it Out: A Handbook on Negotiation For High School Students.* Cambridge, MA: Harvard University Press

Fisher, Roger and Uri, William. (1983). *Getting to Yes: Negotiating Agreement Without Giving In.* NY: Penguin Books

Fountain, Susan. (1995). *Education for Development: A Teacher's Resource for Global Learning.*

Kaufman, Gershen and Raphael, Lev. (1990). *Stick Up For Yourself: Every Kid's Guide to Personal Power and Positive Self-Esteem.*

Kreidler, William J. (1984). *Creative Conflict Resolution.*

Lerner, Harriet Goldhor. (1985). *The Dance of Anger: A Woman's Guide To Changing Patterns of Intimate Relationships.*

Levin, Diane E. (1994). *Teaching Young Children in Violent Times: Building a Peaceable Classroom.*

Lickona, Thomas. (1992). *Educating for Character: How Our Schools Can Teach Respect and Responsibility.*[2]

Miedzian, Myriam. (1991). *Boys Will Be Boys: Breaking the Link Between Masculinity and Violence*

Olweus, Dan. (1993). *Bullying At School: What We Know and What We Can Do.*

Paley, Vivian Gussin. (1992). *You Can't Say You Can't Play.*

Pincus, Debbie. (1994). *Feeling Good About Others: Activities to Encourage Positive Interaction.*

Prutzman, P., Stern, L., Burger, M. and Bodenhamer, G. (1988). *The Friendly Classroom for a Small Planet: A Handbook on Creative Approaches to Living and Problem Solving for Children.*

Schmidt, Fran, Friedman, Alice and Marvel, Jean. (1992). *Mediation for Kids: Kids in Dispute Settlement*

Shapiro, Lawrence E. (1995). *How I Learned To Be Considerate Of Others*. PA: The Center for Applied Psychology Inc.

— (1995). *How I Learned To Be Considerate Of Others: A Workbook of Activities To Teach Consideration Towards Others*. PA: The Center for Applied Psychology Inc.

Smith, Charles A. (1993). *The Peaceful Classroom: 162 Easy Activities to Teach Preschoolers Compassion and Cooperation*.

Webster- Doyle, Terrence. (1991). *Why is Everybody Always Picking On Me?*

— (1991). *Brave New Child: Education for the 21st Century*.

Wichert, Susanne. (1989). *Keeping the Peace: Practicing Cooperation and Conflict Resolution with Preschoolers*.

Zerafa, Judy. (1994). *The Relationship Workbook for Teens: What You Can Do To Attract That Special Someone*

HUMAN DEVELOPMENT/RELATIONSHIP BUILDING

Ames, Louise Bates, and Ilg, Francis L. (1979). *Your Six-Year-Old: Loving and Defiant*.

— (1988). *Your Ten-To Fourteen Year-Old*. NY: Dell Publishing

Canada, Geoffrey. (1995). *Fist Stick Knife Gun: A Personal History of Violence in America*.

Duska, Ronald and Whelan, Mariellen. (1975). *Moral Development: A Guide to Piaget and Kohlberg*. NY: Paulist Press

Edelman, Marian Wright. (1993). *The Measure of Our Success: A letter to my children and yours*.

Glasser, William. (1984). *Control Theory: A New Explanation of How We Control Our Lives*.

— (1975). *Reality Therapy: A New Approach To Psychiatry*. NY: Harper & Row

Hancock, Emily. (1989). *The Girl Within*. NY: Ballantine Books

Healy, Jane M. (1990). *Endangered Minds: Why Children Don't Think and What we Can Do About it*.

Miller, Karen. (1985). *Ages and Stages: Developmental Descriptions & Activities Birth Through Eight Years*. MA: Telshare Publishing

Staley, Betty K. (1988). *Between Form and Freedom: A Practical Guide to the Teenage Years*. BATH: Hawthorn Press

Wood, Chip. (1994) *Yardsticks: Children in the Classroom Ages 4 - 12*. Greenfield: Northeast Foundation for Children

CURRICULA

Facing History and Ourselves National Foundation, *Facing History and Ourselves*.

Lindsey, M., McBride, W. and Platt, C. (1993). *AMEND: Breaking the Cycle: A Workbook for Ending Violent Behavior*. Littleton: Gylantre Publishing Co.

NICEL/NCPC. (1992). *Teens, Crime, and the Community*. MN: West Publishing

Prothrow-Stith, Deborah. (1987). *Violence Prevention Curriculum for Adolescents*.

Stein, Nan and Sjostrom, Lisa. (1994). *Flirting or Hurting?: A Teacher's Guide on Student-to-Student Sexual Harassment in Schools*.

Strauss, Susan. (1992). *Sexual Harassment and Teens.*

Webster- Doyle, Terrence. (1991). *War: What is it Good For?*

Levy, Barrie and Giggans, Patricia Occhiuzzo. (1995). *What Parents Need to Know About Dating Violence.*

PARENT RESOURCES

Elium, Don and Jeanne. (1992). *Raising a Son: Parents and the Making of a Healthy Man.*

— (1994). *Raising a Daughter: Parents and the Awakening of a Healthy Woman.*

Faithquest. (1994). *Just Family Nights: 60 Activities to Keep Your Family Together In a World Falling Apart.*

Fishel, Elizabeth. (1991). *I Swore I'd Never Do That!: Recognizing Family Patterns and Making Wise Parenting Choices.*

Lickona, Thomas. (1983). *Raising Good Children: How to help your child develop a lifelong sense of honesty, decency, and respect for others.*

Pipher, Mary. (1994). *Reviving Ophelia: Saving the Selves of Adolescent Girls.*

Price, Alvin and Parry, Jay A. (1983). *Discipline: 101 Alternatives to Nagging, Yelling, and Spanking.*

Wolf, Anthony E. (1991). *Get Out Of My Life but first could you drive me and Cheryl to the mall?: A Parents' Guide to the New Teenager.*

Wyckoff and Unell, Barbara C. (1984). *Discipline Without Shouting or Spanking: Practical Solutions to the Most Common Preschool Behavior Problems.*

Additional Resources

CHILDREN'S BOOKS ON PEACE, FEELINGS, AND RELATIONSHIP

Aborn, Allyson, (1994). *Everything I Do, You Blame on Me!* :The Center for Applied Psychology.

Asch, Frank and Vagin, Vladimir. (1989). *Here Comes The Cat!*. New York: Scholastic.

Berenstain, Stan and Jan. (1993). *The Berenstain Bears and the Bully*. New York: Random House.

Bosch, Carl W. (1988). *Bully on the Bus*: Parenting Press.

Bourgeois, Paulette and Clark, Brenda. (1993). *Franklin is Bossy*. New York: Scholastic.

Carlson, Nancy. (1994). *How to Lose All Your Friends*. New York: Penguin.

CityKids. (1994). *CityKids Speak on Predjudice*. New York: Random House.

Cosgrove, Stephen. (1978). *Serendipity Books Series*: Price Stern Sloan.

Doleski, Teddi. (1983). *The Hurt*: Paulist Press.

Goffe, Toni. (1991). *Bully for You*. New York: Child's Play.

Goffe, Toni. (1991). *War and Peace*. New York: Child's Play.

Jampolsky, Gerald G. and Cirincione, Diane. (1991). *Me First and the Gimme Gimmes*. FL: Health Communications.

Karnes, Frances A. and Bean, Suzanne M. (1995). *Girls and Young Women Inventing: 20 True stories about inventors plus how you can be one yourself*. Minneapolis: Free Spirit Publishing.

Klamath County YMCA Family Preschool. (1993). *The Land of Many Colors*. New York: Scholastic.

Loupos, Sifu John C. (1994). *Tales and Strategies from the Jade Forest and Beyond.*: Jade Forest Press.

Millman, Dan. (1991). *Secret of the Peaceful Warrior*: H. J. Kramer.

Moser, Adolph. (1991). *Don't Feed the Monster on Tuesday*: Landmark Editions.

Page, Haven, and Abrams. (1988). *Getting Along: A Fun-Filled Set of Stories, Songs and Activities to Help Kids Work and Play Together*. The Children's Television Resource and Education Center.

Petty, Kate and Firmin, Charlotte. (1991). *Being Bullied*. New York: Aladdin Books.

Ross, Tom and Barron, Rex. (1994). *Eggbert The Slightly Cracked Egg*. New York: G. P. Putnam's Sons.

Scholes, Katherine. (1989). *Peace Begins with You*. Little, Brown and Company.

Shapiro, Lawrence E. (1995). *Sometimes I Like To Fight, But I Don't Do It Much Anymore*. PA: The Center for Applied Psychology.

— (1994). *The Very Angry Day That Amy Didn't Have*: Childswork/Childsplay.

Simon, Norma. (1974). *I Was So Mad*. IL: Albert Whitman and Co.

UNICEF. (1994). *I Dream of Peace*. New York: Harper Collins.

Webster- Doyle, Terrence. (1991). Middlebury.: Atrium Society Publications.

- *Fighting the Invisible Enemy: Understanding the Effects of Conditioning.*
- *Operation Warhawks: How Young People Become Warriors.*
- *Tug of War: Peace Through Understanding Conflict.*
- *Why is Everybody Always Picking On Me?: A Guide to Handling Bullies.*

Zolotow, Charlotte. (1969). *The Hating Book.* New York: Harper Collins.

PRODUCTS

Atrium Society Publications, PO Box 816, Middlebury, VT 05753, 1-800-848-6021

*, Inc. PO Box 65688, Salt Lake City, UT 84165-0688, (801) 263-9191

Childswork/Childsplay, Center for Applied Psychology, Inc., PO Box 1586, King of Prussia, PA 19406 1-800-962-1141

Cognitive Therapeutics, 3420 S. Dixie, Suite 104, Dayton, OH 45439

Educators for Social Responsibility, 23 Garden St., Cambridge, MA 02138

Free Spirit Publishing, Inc. , 400 First Avenue North, Suite 616, Minneapolis, MN 55401, (612) 338-2068

Grace Contrino Abrams Peace Education Foundation, Inc., 3550 Biscayne Blvd., Suite 400, Miami, Florida 33137-3854

Sunburst Communications, Room A, 920 Mercer St., Windsor, ON, N9A 7C2

Teaching Tolerance, 400 Washington Avenue, Montgomery, AL 36104

ORGANIZATIONS WITH PEACEFUL GOALS

American Friends Service Committee, 1501 Cherry St., Philadelphia, PA 19102-1403

Amnesty USA, 322 Eighth Ave., New York, New York 10001, (212) 807-8400

Center to Prevent Handgun Violence, 1255 I Street, NW Suite 1100, Washington, DC 20005, (202) 289-7319

Children's Defense Fund, 122 C Street, Washington, DC 20001, (202) 628-8787

Children of the Earth Coalition, PO Box 217, Newfane, VT 05345, (802) 365-7616 Fax (802) 365-7798

Cumberland Center for Justice and Peace, PO Box 857, Sewanee, TN 37375, (615) 598-5369

D.A.R.E. America, PO Box 2090, Los Angeles, CA 90051, (800) 223-DARE

Educational Development Center, 55 Chapel Street, Newton, MA 02158, (617) 969-7100

Educators for Social Responsibility, 23 Garden St., Cambridge, MA 02138, (617) 492-1764

Fellowship of Reconciliation, PO Box 271, Nyack, New York 10960

Kids Against Crime, PO Box 22004, San Bernardino, CA 92406, (714) 882-1344

National Crime Prevention Council, 1700 K Street, NW Second Floor, Washington, DC 20006-3817, (202) 466-6272

National Institute Against Prejudice and Violence, 31 South Greene St, Baltimore, MD 21201, (301) 358-5170

National School Safety Center, 4165 Thousand Oaks Blvd. Suite 290, Westlake Village, CA 91362, (805) 373-9977

Parents For Peace and Justice Network, 4144 Lindell, #124, St. Louis, MO 63108

Peace At Home, Inc., 95 Berkeley Street, Suite 107, Boston, MA 02116, (617) 482-1851
Fax (617) 482-6504

Peace Development Fund, PO Box 270, Amherst, MA 01007, (413) 256-8306

Project P.A.V.E. (Promoting Alternative to Violence through Education), The Conflict
Center, 2626 Osceola Street, Denver CO 80212, (303) 433-4983

The Consortium on Peace Research, Education and Development, c/o Institute for Conflict
Analysis and Resolution, George Mason University, Fairfax, VA 22030

The Prejudice Institute Center for the Applied Study of Ethnoviolence, Towson State
University, Stephens Hall Annex, Room 132, Towson MD 21204, (410) 328-2435

War Resisters League, 339 Lafayette St. New York, NY 10012, (212) 228-0450

Young and Teen Peacemakers, 37 Lebanon St., Hamilton, New York 13346, (315) 824-
4332

Youth Crime Watch of America, Dadeland Towers, North Suite 320, 9200 South Dadeland
Blvd., Miami, FL 96284, (305) 670-2409

Internet web sites

I have spent hours scouring the Internet to find sources for information on the topics
of peace, conflict resolution, and empowerment. Sometimes I found what I was looking for on the first try, sometimes it took hours — depending on how many different
search engines I used, which keywords I typed in, and so on. Sometimes, I found great
links by accident. As I found links, I bookmarked them. I am including several links
here to aid you in your Internet search for materials. Please understand that by the
time this book is printed and resting in your hands, some of the web page addresses
will likely have changed. Sometimes a link's server is temporarily down, so if you try
later, you will achieve a successful connection. If a link has moved, try a keyword
search on a multi-search engine such as MetaCrawler. Or use AltaVista, Lycos, or
another search engine to find your link. Good luck in your search!

PEACE/CONFLICT/EMPOWERMENT RESOLUTION LINKS

* Celebrating Cultural Diversity, Unlearning Prejudice:
  http://www.hooked.net/~prejudice
* Central Committee for Conscientious Objectors Home:
  http://www.libertynet.org/~ccco">
* Conflict Research Consortium:
  http://www.Colorado.EDU/conflict
* Conflict Resolution Lesson Plans:
  http://www.stark.k12.oh.us./Docs/units/conflict/lessons">
* Empowering People Books, Tapes and Videos home of Positive Discipline by Jane
  Nelsen and Developing Capable People by H. Stephen Glenn:
  http://www.empoweringpeople.com/index.html
* ESR Teaching About Diversity:
  http://www.benjerry.com/esr/resources/elementary.html

- Heinemann:
  http://www.heinemann.com/index.html
- Institute for Global Communications: Peacenet/conflictnet, etc:
  http://www.igc.org/igc
- *New Society Publishers:*
  http://www.newsociety.com
- PAVENET:
  gopher://pavnet.esusda.gov:70/11/violence
- Peace Ideas:
  http://www.sequel.net/peace/peace_op.htm
- Peace Works:
  http://www.igc.apc.org/peaceworks/
- Personal Empowerment Programs:
  http://www.empowerme.com/index.html
- Physicians for Social Responsibility:
  http://prometheus.nucmed.buffalo.edu/psr
- Positive Discipline/ Empowering People:
  http://www.empoweringpeople.com
- Quest International: skills for living — adolescent prevention program:
  http://www.quest.edu:80/aboutquest.htm
- *Susan Gingras Fitzell:*
  http://reg.seresc.k12.nh.us/~sfitzell/index.html
- Teaching Peace — No-Bully Program:
  http://www.fortnet.org:80/~dtitle/bully.htm
- The Nonviolence Web:
  http://www.nonviolence.org/~nvweb
- UNESCO Education WWW Server:
  http://www.education.unesco.org/unesco/index.html
- UNICEF Home Page:
  http://www.unicef.org
- Violence prevention: Home Alive:
  The Arts in the Act: http://www.homealive.org/
- Voices of Youth Home Page:
  http://www.unicef.org/voy
- War Resisters League:
  http://www.nonviolence.org/~nvweb/wrl
- White Dispute Resolution Institute:
  http://www.cba.uh.edu:80/center/aawdri.html
- Woodring Educational Resources:
  http://www.wce.wwu.edu/edsites/pubs.html

Endnotes

Introduction

1. The Education for Peace Series is available from Atrium Society Publications, Middlebury, VT 05753, 1- 800-848-6021.

Chapter 2

1. Bland, Karina. 'Power Rangers' Too Violent? Outcry in Europe Doesn't Keep Fox, Kids From Morphin'. *The Phoenix Gazette*, Oct. 20, 1994.

2. Chafetz, Michael D. (1992). *Smart for Life: How to Improve Your Brain Power at Any Age*. New York: Penguin.

Chapter 3

1. Labinowicz, Ed. *The Piaget Primer*.

2. Ekman, Paul (1989). *Why Kids Lie: How Parents Can Encourage Truthfulness*. New York: Penguin Books.

Chapter 4

1. The classroom teacher identified this boy as the class bully during my first session. I don't believe in name-calling; however, in a less than ideal world, children with many bullying behaviors are often referred to as bullies. For the purpose of this narrative, I will refer to him as the 'bully.'

2. Marano, Hara Elstroff. (Sept/Oct. 1995). Big. Bad. Bully. *Psychology Today*, Vol. 28, No. 5, 50-82.

3. The Development Studies Center, *At Home in Our Schools*.

4. Spring, Joel. (1994). *The American School*. New York: McGraw Hill.

5. For more practical information on dealing with cliques and building community, see Lickona (1992), Chapter Six: "Creating a Moral Community in the Classroom."

Chapter 5

1. Education for Peace techniques, or the Twelve Ways to Walk Away With Confidence, are described in Webster-Doyle (1992).

2. *The American Heritage® Dictionary of the English Language, Third Edition*, 1992, Houghton Mifflin, Electronic version licensed from InfoSoft International, Inc.

3. Irving Spergel et al. "Gang Suppression and Intervention: An Assessment." National Youth Gang Suppression and Intervention Program. School of Social Service Administration. University of Chicago. Prepared under grant numbers 87-JS-CX-K100 and 90-JD-CX-K001 from the Office of Juvenile Justice and Delinquency Prevention. Office of Justice Programs, US Department of Justice, 1993: 3.

4. Adapted from Dan, Korem (1995) *Suburban Gangs - The Affluent Rebels*. Richardson: International Focus Press.

5. For more practical information on setting up class meetings, see Lickona (1992), Chapter Eight: "Creating a Democratic Classroom Environment: The Class Meeting."

6. Gilligan, Lyons, and Hanmer. (1990). *Making Connections*. Cambridge: Harvard University Press.

7. Gilligan, Ward, Taylor, and Bardige, (1988). *Mapping the Moral Domain.* Cambridge: Harvard University Press.

8. Gilligan, Carol (1993). *In a Different Voice.* Cambridge: Harvard University Press.

9. Sadker, (1995). *Failing at Fairness: How Our Schools Cheat Girls.* New York: Touchstone.

10. Belenky, Clinchy, Goldberger and Tarule. (1986) *Women's Ways of Knowing: The Development of Self, Voice and Mind.* New York: Basic Books.

11. Rivers, Barnet and Baruch, *Beyond Sugar and Spice: How Women Grow, Learn & Thrive.*

12. Johnson, Kaufman and Raphael, *Stick Up for Yourself: A Ten-Part Course in Self-Esteem and Assertiveness for Kids.*

Chapter 6

1. Erikson, (1968). *Identity: Youth and Crisis.* New York: Norton.

2. David Elkind, (1984). *All Grown Up and No Place To Go.* Reading, MA: Addison-Wesley.

3. Lauton and Freese, (1981). *The Healthy Adolescent: A Parent's Manual.* New York, New York: Charles Scribner's Sons.

4. Mead, (1928). *Coming of Age In Samoa.* New York: Morrow, and Mead, Margaret. (1935). *Sex and Temperament In Three Primitive Societies.* New York: Morrow.

5. Gilligan, (1982). *In a Different Voice: Psychological theory and Women's Development.* Cambridge, MA: Harvard University Press.

6. Lickona, (1992) defines Universal Values as "values that bind all persons everywhere because they affirm our fundamental human worth or dignity." Example: Treating all people justly and respecting their lives, liberty, and equality.

7. Task Force on Youth Development and Community Programs, (1992).

8. Harris, Lynn. "The Hidden World of Dating Violence," *Parade Magazine* (1996).

9. Wilson, H. (1974). Parenting in Poverty. *Journal of Social Work,* Vol. 4, 241-54.

10. Levy, Barrie. (1993). *In Love and In Danger.* Seattle: Seal Press.

11. The American Heritage® Dictionary of the English Language, Third Edition. (1992). NY: Houghton Mifflin. Electronic version licensed from InfoSoft International.

12. Sabo, Donald. (1994). *Sex, Violence and Power in Sports: Rethinking Masculinity.*

13. Shen, Fern. (1993). Welts betray a dark side of teen dating. *Washington Post.* (July 18).

14. Harris, (1996).

15. Levy, Barrie. (1991). *Dating Violence: Young Women in Danger.* Seattle: Seal Press.

16. National Woman Abuse Prevention Project.

17. Ibid.

18. Burke, P.I., Stets, J.E. and Pirog-Good, M.A. (1989). Gender Identity, Self-esteem, and Physical and Sexual Abuse in Dating Relationships. In M.A. Pirog-Good and J.E.Stets (Eds.), *Violence in Dating Relationships.* New York: Praeger 72-93.

19. Halpern, Howard M. (1982). *How to Break Your Addiction to a Person.* New York: Bantam.

20. Strauss, Murray. (1994). *Beating the Devil Out of Them*. New York: Lexington.

21. Riak, Jordan. (1996). *Plain Talk about Spanking*. Alamo: Parents and Teachers Against Violence Education.

22. Sources for the cycle of violence: Levy and Giggans, Kirschenbaum, *The Menninger Letter*; and Peace at Home.

23. Lindgren, H. (1995). *Couple Violence: Stop It, Treat It, or Leave It*. Lincoln: University of Nebraska.

24. These quotations were originally researched by Project YANO, 619-753-7518. For more such quotations, please contact either YANO or CCCO.

25. Adapted from information provided by CCCO, 655 Sutter St., #514, San Francisco, CA 94102, Tel: 415-474-3002, Fax: 415-474-2311.

Index

OTHER CONFLICT EDUCATION AND CONFLICT RESOLUTION RESOURCES FROM NSP

If you have enjoyed *Free The Children!*, then you may want to check out our other resources in the same subject area including:

KEEPING THE PEACE: Practicing Cooperation and Conflict Resolution with Preschoolers, by Susanne Wichert

8.5" x 11" 112 pages Exercises Photographs Bibliiography

Pb US$12.95 / CAN$15.95

TEACHING YOUNG CHILDREN IN VIOLENT TIMES: Building a Peaceable Classroom, by Diane E. Levin

8.5" x 11" 176 pages Illustrations Dialogs Bibliography Index

Pb US$16.95 / CAN$21.95

PLAYING WITH FIRE: Creative Conflict Resolution for Young Adults, by Fiona Macbeth and Nic Fine

8.5" x 11" 192 pages Exercises Handouts Reading list Index

PB US$19.95 / CAN$24.95

For a full catalog of NSP's educational and parenting resources, please call
1-800-567-6772

NSP